the **SOUND ON SOUND** book of

MIDI
for the
technophobe

Printed in the UK by MPG Books, Bodmin

Published by: Sanctuary Publishing Limited, 45-53 Sinclair Road, London
W14 0NS, United Kingdom

www.sanctuarypublishing.com

Sound On Sound web site: www.sospubs.co.uk

ISBN: 1-86074-444-3

the **SOUND ON SOUND** book of

MIDI
for the
technophobe

paul white

Sanctuary

Also available by Paul White from Sanctuary Publishing

Creative Recording I - Effects & Processors
Creative Recording II - Microphones, Acoustics, Soundproofing & Monitoring
Home Recording Made Easy
Live Sound For The Performing Musician
Recording & Production Techniques
Music Technology - A Survivor's Guide
Desktop Digital Studio

The BASIC series

basic DIGITAL RECORDING
basic EFFECTS & PROCESSORS
basic HOME STUDIO DESIGN
basic LIVE SOUND
basic MASTERING
basic MICROPHONES
basic MIDI
basic MIXERS
basic MIXING TECHNIQUES
basic MULTITRACKING
basic VST EFFECTS
basic VST INSTRUMENTS

contents

CHAPTER 4

CHAPTER 5

CHAPTER 6

CHAPTER 11

INTERFACES

CHAPTER 12

SOFTWARE INSTRUMENTS

CHAPTER 13

MIXERS, MONITORS AND EFFECTS

introduction

I t's probably no exaggeration to say that the introduction of MIDI has had a greater effect on the way in which we create and record music than almost any other event since the development of written musical notation. Prior to MIDI, virtually the only way of hearing a new musical composition was to have it performed by live musicians, but nowadays musical compositions can be created, recorded and replayed by a single musician using MIDI, sequencers and synthesisers.

The affordability of MIDI equipment has also empowered a vast number of musicians to be able to create and record their own music without the need to use traditional recording studios. Symphonies, pop songs, TV commercials, soundtracks and experimental music may be created by anyone prepared to turn their imagination to music. Indeed, a whole cottage industry has been built up of providing music for TV, film, CDs, tapes, computer games and multimedia presentations.

Traditional keyboard-playing skills are still immensely valuable, of course, but because of the flexibility offered by MIDI sequencing, even musicians with very limited technique and no knowledge of traditional musical notation can still bring their ideas to fruition. Some music traditionalists see this as cheating, but this is to overlook the fact that a composer is primarily selling his or her musical ideas, not their musical virtuosity.

Musicians who work with MIDI on a daily basis must occasionally wonder how they ever managed without it, but a far greater number of musicians who could reap the benefits of this new technology are frightened off by the jargon, the apparent complexity and the change in working methods required to use it effectively. They're also unsure of what MIDI can actually help them achieve.

My own first experiences with MIDI were far from comfortable, and ironically the main problem seemed to be the books that purported to explain the subject! They'd invariably dive in with explanations of bits, bytes, data structure and so on, whereas all I wanted to know was how to use MIDI. You don't have to be able to understand the workings of the internal combustion engine to be able to drive a car, so why should you need to become a computer expert to use MIDI?

After buying my first MIDI system and playing about with it for a few days, I was surprised at how straightforward and logical everything was, but I was even more surprised by the fact that I hadn't needed to know more than a tiny fraction of what current books on MIDI implied that I needed to know. The purpose of this book, therefore, is to explore the applications of MIDI in as straightforward and practical a manner as possible, by using analogies with familiar everyday processes. In a very short time, you'll have a sound grasp of what goes on in a MIDI system, you'll know what you can expect to achieve and you'll know how to go about achieving it. This revised version also includes information on MIDI automation, virtual effects and processor plug-ins, as well as software instruments.

chapter 1

introducing MIDI

I n the mid '80s, MIDI was regarded as a technology for keyboard players and computer nerds, and in those situations where it was used in serious recording it ran in parallel with conventional recording techniques. Today, the majority of home studios are based around the computer rather than traditional recording hardware, the main benefit being that both MIDI and conventionally recorded audio parts are handled within the same graphic editing environment. Nevertheless, even though MIDI is approaching its 20th birthday, newcomers to the subject often find it confusing, which is why I wrote this book. The obvious questions are: What is MIDI? What can it help me achieve? And what do I need to buy to get started? While it's very tempting to jump straight in and start talking about MIDI synthesisers, soundcards, keyboards and interfaces, the first thing to do is to try to create an overview of what MIDI is all about, and for that we have to wind back the clock to the early '80s, when, in a rare moment of international co-operation, the major manufacturers of synthesisers got together and agreed on a standard system by which electronic instruments from different manufacturers could be connected together as part of the same system. Their initial aims were relatively modest, and they can hardly have known what an impact MIDI was going to have on music making in the future.

Rather than deluge you with information and then leave you to dig your way out, I'm going to try to explain the general concept of MIDI in terms with which you're already familiar and then, as soon as possible, get you trying things out for yourself. It's one thing reading about a process, but until you see it happen for yourself, it somehow isn't real!

During the many years in which I've been a technical writer, I've encountered hundreds of handbooks for musical instruments, studio equipment, computers, software and so on, and it still astounds me how badly some of them are put together. All too often they jump straight in by throwing facts at you before they've even given you an overview of the equipment in question. The information is all there, but you're often given no indication as to why you might need this information or how best to apply it. I find this approach as difficult to deal with as anyone else, which is why I've always been in favour of explaining the question properly before trying to provide an answer.

I must also confess, at this stage, that I intend to over-generalise, where appropriate, and if there's anything technical that can be safely omitted, then I'm not going to put it in. We all create our own personal models of the world that allow us to get on with life without actually understanding more than the tiniest fraction of what really makes the universe tick, and it's my intention to do the same on the subject of MIDI. There are many definitive works on MIDI, but this isn't one of them; my aim is to help you become a MIDI user, not a computer expert!

why?

Before even attempting to explain MIDI, let's take a look at what sort of things you might want to be able to do with it. Indeed, why do we need it at all?

If you are an accomplished piano player who has no interest in recording or multipart composition, it's probably fairly safe to say that MIDI is unlikely to play a major part in your life, but even so, don't hang up just yet, because some MIDI sequencers have very advanced score-writing facilities that you might find useful. On the other hand, if you play an electric keyboard and would like to put together multipart compositions featuring the sounds of other instruments, complete with drums and percussion, all without having to hire or coerce other musicians, then MIDI sequencing was made for you.

MIDI isn't applicable only to keyboard players, but as the keyboard is the best suited means of generating MIDI information, the majority of MIDI music is made using keyboards. However, there are practical alternatives for musicians who prefer to pluck, bow, blow or hit things, and these will be covered in Chapter 8, "Alternative MIDI Instruments".

a virtual orchestra

Imagine being able to record all of the different musical parts of a score from your keyboard, one at a time, and then hear them playing together in perfect synchronism, each part played back with the instrument sound of your choice. Furthermore, consider the benefits of being able to pick different sounds to play back the various parts, even after all of the recording is complete. Even the simplest MIDI sequencing system will allow you to do this, providing you with your own virtual orchestra or band at your fingertips. It will also enable you to change the tempo of your finished recording without affecting the pitch, transpose the piece without affecting the tempo and allow you experiment with the musical arrangement by providing the facility to copy verses and choruses to new locations within a song.

The information that's communicated from a sequencer to a synthesiser via MIDI is exactly the same as that communicated between a composer and a performer, except that the medium is computer memory and magnetic disks instead of a written score and the instruments are electronic rather than traditional.

the meaning of MIDI

To see how this is possible, we need to know a little about MIDI. The acronym MIDI stand for Musical Instrument Digital Interface, and the term defines a standard system by means of which products from different manufacturers may be connected together as part of the same system. Prior to MIDI, there were some attempts at providing ways of connecting instruments, but none were entirely standard and all were very limited. At its simplest, MIDI will allow a keyboard player to play several instruments from a single keyboard rather than having to dash around the stage whenever a change of instrument is required.

Shortly after the introduction of MIDI came the MIDI sequencer, a special type of multitrack recorder capable of recording not sound but MIDI information. Before I elaborate on this statement further, you'll have to take on board a few basic facts about what MIDI does and doesn't do. I'd also like to assure you that, contrary to what some people would have you believe, MIDI isn't something that "takes over" your music or makes your work sound mechanical; it's simply a tool to do a job and, like any tool, it can be used well or it can be used poorly.

the keyboard

Whatever type of MIDI system you decide to use, you'll need a MIDI keyboard, but it needn't be expensive. Even if you decide to use an alternative controller, such as a MIDI guitar system, you'll probably still find a keyboard useful. If possible, choose a keyboard that has something called *velocity sensitivity*, because this will respond like a "real" instrument in that, the harder you hit the keys, the louder the notes will be. If you don't have velocity sensitivity, all of the notes will be the same level, like on an organ.

You can choose a "dumb" master keyboard, with no built-in sounds or you can choose to use a conventional keyboard synthesiser with built-in sounds as your master. Either will work perfectly well, so the choice is entirely yours. However, if you choose a keyboard synth for use with a sequencer, it's important that it has a MIDI Local Off facility. The reason for this will be explained later, but for now don't rush out and buy a synth until you can be sure that you can switch it to Local Off mode.

what is MIDI?

On the outside, MIDI is simply a neat cable connecting two pieces of MIDI equipment, but inside it's a complicated digital-data-transmission system that requires quite a lot of specialised computer knowledge to understand fully. Thankfully, the inner workings of MIDI can be largely ignored by the musician using the system, in the same way that the workings of an international telephone exchange can be safely ignored by someone trying to phone their grandmother in Australia. In other words, the knowledge required to make use of MIDI bears little relationship to the complexity of the underlying technology. Indeed, most of the confusion surrounding MIDI seems to have been engendered by books that try to explain its inner workings in far too much depth.

the MIDI link

Linking MIDI instruments is accomplished by means of standard MIDI cables – twin-cored, screened cables with five-pin DIN plugs on either end. And again, if you don't know what a DIN plug is, or if you have no desire to further explore the inner world of twin-cored screened cable, it doesn't matter; you just go to the music shop and ask for a MIDI cable. The only technical parameter you'll need to know is how long you'd like it!

So MIDI is a standard communication system that enables MIDI-equipped electronic instruments to be linked together in a musically useful way, regardless of the model or manufacturer. Like computers, the data is in a digital form – a sort of ultra-fast Morse code for machines. The method of MIDI connection, as we shall see shortly, is quite straightforward, but what is more important at this early stage is to appreciate precisely what "musically useful" information can be passed from one MIDI instrument or device to another.

The following description covers the most important and basic aspects of MIDI but is by no means comprehensive. New concepts will be introduced only when they are needed, and for now information will be handed out on a strictly need-to-know basis. There are many excellent books that delve into the more frightening complexities of MIDI, and if, having read this book, you feel better prepared to tackle them, I will have done what I set out to do.

anatomy of a note

Electronic keyboard instruments are not like acoustic pianos, which use a physical hammer to hit a string, causing it to vibrate at the pitch at which it is tuned. Inside an electronic keyboard, the action of pressing a key simply generates electronic messages telling the internal circuitry what note to play and how loud to play it. When a key is depressed on a MIDI keyboard, a signal known as a Note On message is sent, along with a note number identifying the key, and when the key is released a Note Off message is sent. This is how the MIDI instrument knows what note to play, when to play it and when to stop playing it. Up to 128 different notes can be handled by MIDI, and each key on the keyboard has its own number.

The loudness of the note played depends on how hard the key is hit, which is really the same thing as saying how fast the key is pushed down. This speed, or velocity, is read by circuitry within the keyboard and this information is used to control the volume of the sound being played. (The term *velocity* should be committed to memory, as it is one piece of MIDI jargon that will crop up time and time again in reference to how loud a note is played or how hard a key is struck.) The pitch of the note is determined by which key is pressed, although it's quite possible to transpose MIDI data before it reaches its destination, so that pressing a middle C doesn't have to result in a C being played by the instrument at the receiving end, if that isn't what you want. However, to keep things simple, let's assume that, unless otherwise stated, pressing a key results in the corresponding musical note being played.

MIDI note data

If information concerning pitch and velocity as well as Note On and Note Off messages all exist in the form of electronic signals, it should be possible to send all of this data along wires to control a MIDI instrument some distance away from the keyboard, and at its most basic this is exactly what MIDI allows us to do. A small computer inside the keyboard monitors the physical motions of the keys and converts these to MIDI messages, which appear at the MIDI Out socket of the keyboard. If the MIDI Out of the keyboard currently being played (which is called the *master keyboard*) is plugged into the MIDI In socket of a second MIDI instrument (known as the *slave*), the slave is able to play the notes as performed on the master keyboard. This simple MIDI connection is shown in Figure 1.1, but don't try it out just yet as there are a few more terms you need to learn first:

- **MIDI Out** sends information from a controlling MIDI device (master) to other MIDI devices that it is controlling (slaves).

- **MIDI In** receives MIDI information, which is then passed on to the MIDI Thru socket unchanged, although if any of the incoming information is "addressed" to the instrument in question, it will act on that MIDI data exactly as if it were being controlled directly from a keyboard.

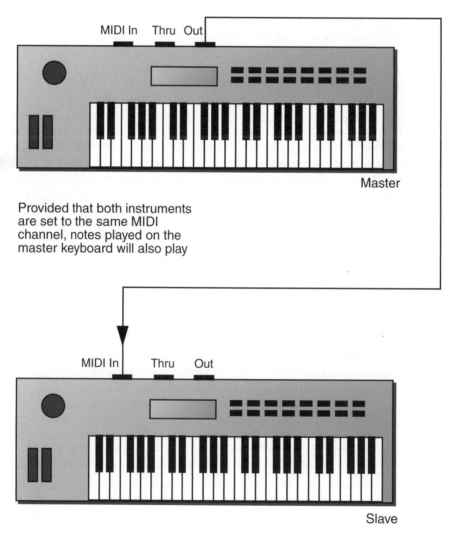

Figure 1.1: Basic MIDI master/slave connection

- **MIDI Thru** sends a copy of the MIDI In signal, allowing several MIDI instruments to be linked together.

instructions, not sounds

Before moving on, it's important to understand that MIDI isn't about transmitting sounds; it's about transmitting information that tells the instrument what your fingers were doing on the keyboard. Think of it as operating like one of those paper-roll player pianos, where the paper roll is the recorded sequence and the piano itself is the sound module. It's surprising how many people listen patiently to a description of MIDI sequencing and then ask if they can record their voice over MIDI as well! There are ways of recording conventional audio into certain computer-based MIDI sequencers, but that part of their operation has nothing at all to do with MIDI and would serve only to confuse the subject if introduced at this time.

the keyboardless synthesiser

The ability to link a second instrument via MIDI means that the sounds of both instruments can be played from just one keyboard – convenient, maybe, but hardly likely to revolutionise music as we know it! However, a little further thought reveals that the second instrument doesn't actually need a keyboard at all, because everything is done from the master keyboard.

This leads nicely onto the so-called *MIDI module*, which is simply the sound-generating and MIDI-interfacing electronics component of a keyboard instrument packaged in a rather more compact and generally less expensive box. This reduction in design brings about two very real advantages: we save money, because modules are much cheaper to build than full-sized keyboard instruments, and we save a lot of space, as the electronics for a typical synthesiser module can be made to fit into a box little larger than a box of chocolates. There's also no reason not to control multiple modules from a single master keyboard. However, to appreciate the full implications of this, the concept of MIDI channels must first be introduced.

MIDI channels

MIDI channels are the means by which certain messages are "addressed" to be acted upon by specific instruments. In a typical master/slave MIDI system, the daisy-chain way in which the instruments are linked means that they all receive the same MIDI information, so the MIDI channel system was devised in order to allow the master instrument to communicate with just one specific slave without all the others trying to play along. The principal idea is that MIDI note messages are tagged with an invisible address label carrying their MIDI channel number, so that the messages are only acted upon when they are received by a MIDI instrument or device set to the same MIDI channel number – all other MIDI devices will politely ignore the message. The following explanation may make this clearer.

There are 16 MIDI channels which are, logically enough, numbered 1 to 16, and the concept of their operation isn't that different to that of television channels. After all, many different TV broadcasts arrive at the same aerial and reach the TV set down the same piece of wire, but we can only ever see one channel at a time. The channel that we actually watch depends on the one that we select on the TV set. The key point here is that all of the programmes are fed into the TV set simultaneously, but the channel system allows us to tune into them one at a time.

It's exactly the same with MIDI, where the information sent down the MIDI lead can be sent on any one of 16 channels, as selected on the master keyboard. Likewise, the connected instruments may be set to receive on any of the 16 channels. So, if we set the master keyboard to MIDI channel 1, for example, and connect three different MIDI instruments set to receive on channels 1, 2 and 3, only the instrument set to channel 1 will respond. (Figure 1.2 shows this arrangement.) The other channels still receive the information, but the MIDI data tells it that the information is not on their channel, so they simply ignore it. By switching channels on the master keyboard, up to 16 different MIDI instruments set to 16 different channels can be addressed individually, even though they are all wired into the same system. The concept of MIDI channels will become vitally important when we move onto MIDI sequencers, but if you feel like trying the example in Figure 1.1 now, go ahead. Just make sure that both devices are set to the same MIDI channel.

Omni mode warning!

Although this next piece of information shouldn't really appear until much later, I'm introducing it now because, if a MIDI instrument is inadvertently set to Omni mode (an option usually buried in the MIDI Set-up menu), the system won't behave as you'd expect. As I said, most MIDI instruments can be set to receive on any of the 16 MIDI channels, but there is also a setting called Omni mode that allows a MIDI instrument to respond to all incoming data, regardless of the channel to which it's set. In other words, everything that comes along the MIDI cable is played rather like having one member of an orchestra trying to play all parts of a score at the same time.

Some MIDI devices – especially older models – tend to default to Omni

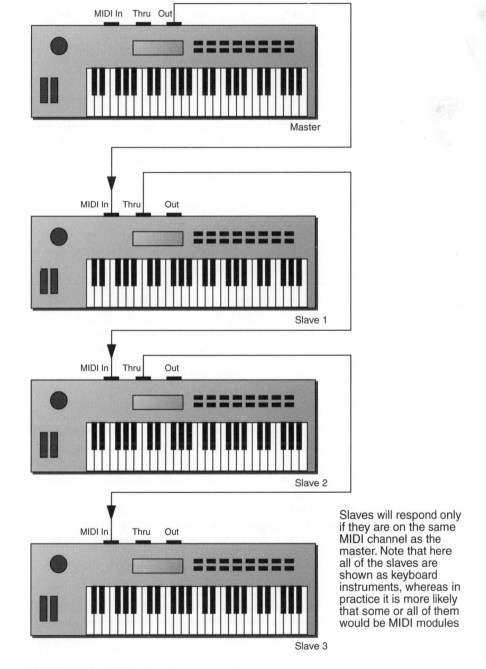

Slaves will respond only if they are on the same MIDI channel as the master. Note that here all of the slaves are shown as keyboard instruments, whereas in practice it is more likely that some or all of them would be MIDI modules

Figure 1.2: Multiple slaves on different MIDI channels

mode whenever they're switched on, which means you have to set up the correct channel before you can do any work. Fortunately, the vast majority of instruments remember what mode they're in, even if they've been switched off. For normal 16-channel operation, instruments should be set to Poly mode. That's enough for now – more about modes later.

more about modules

This book contains chapters that separately describe the basic workings of MIDI synthesisers and other MIDI instruments, but there are some aspects of MIDI synthesiser modules that need to be dealt with now in order for everything else to make sense. So far, I've described modules as being MIDI synthesisers in boxes but without keyboards, and this definition is true enough, as far as it goes. However, a great many modern modules actually contain several independent sound-generating sections, each of which can be addressed on a different MIDI channel. These sound-generating sections are often known as *parts* because, in a typical system, each section can be made to play a separate musical part. For example, a 16-part multitimbral module can play back up to 16 different musical sounds at the same time, each controlled via a different MIDI channel. For most purposes, you can visualise a multipart module as being analogous to several synthesisers sharing the same box. (See also Chapter 11, "Interfaces".)

multitimbrality

Multipart modules like those described above are said to be *multitimbral*, although the individual synthesiser sections that they contain are rarely entirely independent of each other – for example, they all share the same set of front-panel controls and some parameters may affect all of the voices globally. What's more, on low-cost modules (and soundcards), the outputs from the various parts are usually mixed to stereo and then emerge via a single stereo pair of sockets. However, you'll invariably find that you have independent control over which of the available sounds (or *patches*, as they call them in synth-speak) are selected, the relative levels of the different voices, the left/right pan positions and the amount of effects – such as reverberation – added to each part.

Samplers also tend to be multitimbral, but at this point in the discussion they can be considered as being just a specialised type of synthesiser. (Refer to Chapter 7, "Samplers And Sampling" for more detail on this subject.)

Drum machines may also be considered as being MIDI modules, although they have their own built-in sequencers that allow them to store and replay rhythm patterns and complex arrangements comprising numerous different rhythm patterns. Most drum machines are not multitimbral – that is, they can only play one part at a time. If you want to control their sounds from a keyboard or via an external MIDI sequencer, however, it's possible to access their sounds externally over MIDI.

The main difference between the ways in which standard synth patches and drum machines organise their sounds is that a synthesiser tends to interpret incoming MIDI note data as different pitches of the same basic sound, whereas a drum machine produces a different drum, cymbal or percussion sound for each MIDI note. Most multitimbral synthesiser modules and computer soundcards tend to have one part dedicated to drum sounds, so it's no longer essential to buy a separate drum machine. (See the Chapter 2, "General MIDI" for more details.)

MIDI sockets

On the back of a typical MIDI keyboard, instrument or sound module are three MIDI sockets labelled "MIDI In", "MIDI Thru" and "MIDI Out" (although some models may not have all three). It's now time to find out what these are for.

The master instrument in a simple MIDI chain sends information from its MIDI Out socket, which must be connected to the MIDI In socket of the first slave. The MIDI Thru of the first slave is then connected to the MIDI In of the second slave and its Thru connected to the MIDI In of the next one, and so on. The result is a *daisy chain*, and while in theory this can be indefinitely long, this turns out not to be the case in practice. What actually happens is that the MIDI signal deteriorates slightly as is passes through each instrument, and after it has gone through three or four instruments it starts to become unreliable and notes start getting stuck on or refuse to play at all. It's rather like the old game of Chinese whispers, where you try to pass a message along a line of people to see how much it has changed when it arrives at the other end!

A solution is to use a MIDI thru box, which takes the Out signal from the master keyboard and then splits it into several Thru connections, which feed the individual modules directly. (Figure 1.2 shows the standard method of daisy-chaining and Figure 1.3 shows the same system wired up via a MIDI thru box.) A MIDI thru box is a relatively simple and inexpensive device that takes one MIDI input and provides two or more outputs carrying identical signals to the MIDI input data. In effect, it splits a single MIDI signal several ways. Thru boxes may also be used in combination with daisy-chaining – for

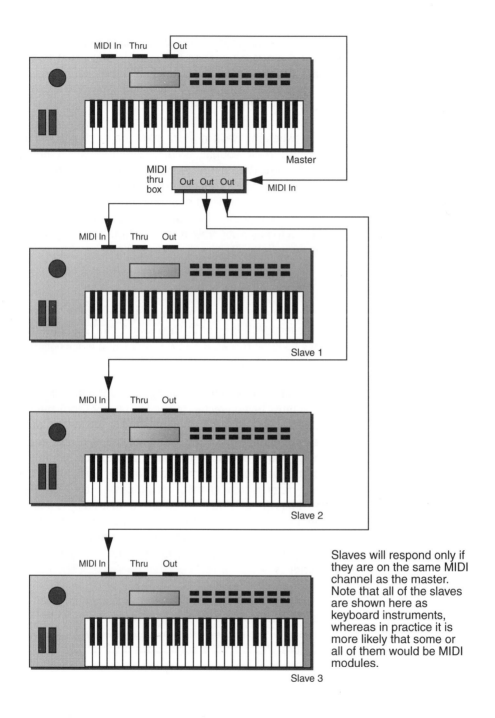

Slaves will respond only if they are on the same MIDI channel as the master. Note that all of the slaves are shown here as keyboard instruments, whereas in practice it is more likely that some or all of them would be MIDI modules.

Figure 1.3: Using a MIDI thru box

instance, if an instrument is fed from a thru box, its Thru socket may be linked to another module to form a short daisy chain, the only proviso being that these individual chains are no more than one or two devices long.

Some people believe that daisy-chaining MIDI Thru connectors causes timing delays, but this is simply not true. Most MIDI delays can be attributed to either too much data being sent at the same time or delays within the instruments themselves. For example, some synthesisers take several milliseconds to respond once a MIDI Note message has been received. (For more on MIDI delays, see Chapter 9, "Practical Sequencing".)

programs and patches

We've established that MIDI operates on 16 channels and can be used to send information concerning note number, timing and velocity from a MIDI-compatible master instrument to a MIDI-compatible slave, but what I haven't mentioned yet is that there's a lot more useful information that goes down the wire, too!

Modern synthesisers are, in the main, programmable, which means that they have the ability to "remember" many different sounds, each identified by its patch or program number. (The terms *program* and *patch* in this instance tend to be interchangeable.) New instruments inevitably come with some preset factory patches (which can't be changed), plus room for users to store their own patches. These user patches may be filled with sounds that you can edit at will, or they may be empty, depending on the model of instrument. (The term *patch* is a throwback to very early electronic synthesisers, which used patch cables to connect the various sound-generating building blocks, rather like in an old-fashioned telephone exchange.)

MIDI can directly access up to 128 patches, sometimes numbered from 0 to 127 and sometimes from 1 to 128 – even standards aren't always all that standard! The buttons that are used to select the patches on the master keyboard also enable patch information to be transmitted to the slave synthesiser modules, so that now, not only is it possible to play the modules remotely, you can also select the sound or patch to which they are set. These patch-changing commands are known as Program Change messages, and their use isn't limited to MIDI instruments; they may also be used to call up effects patches on MIDI-compatible effects units. If you have two MIDI instruments linked up so that you can play the slave from the master, try pressing the Program Change buttons on the master. You should find that the slave also changes to the new patch number.

Instruments containing more than 128 patches must have these organised into two or more banks containing a maximum of 128 patches per bank, because Program Change messages can access only 128 patches directly. Bank Change commands, meanwhile, comprising specific controller data, are used to switch from one bank to the next.

Some studio effects units are MIDI controllable - ie MIDI Program Change commands can be used to call up specific effects from within a library of different effects patches - but MIDI Program Change messages are just the start. There's an awful lot more useful information that can travel down that deceptively simple MIDI cable. MIDI also serves a secondary purpose in allowing synchronisation signals to be sent between devices such as drum machines and sequencers, and Chapter 4 is devoted to this subject.

control and controllers

Real musical instruments aren't just about note pitches and loudness, they're also about expression. A violin player, for example, may add vibrato to a note or slide from one note to another. To help the keyboard player imitate the expression of a real instrument, a typical MIDI synthesiser or master keyboard has two or more performance wheels mounted to the left of the keyboard, at least one of which is invariably dedicated to pitch bend. The other wheel (or wheels) is sometimes reassignable to allow it to control various different effects, although the most common application is to control depth of vibrato. Like the keys themselves, these controllers work by generating electronic signals, which in turn control the circuitry that creates the sound. And, like note information, control information may also be sent over MIDI - simply move the control wheel on the master and the slave will respond. Further control may be provided by means of foot-pedal inputs, which allow a conventional volume pedal to be used as a means of varying MIDI control functions.

Because pedals and wheels can be set to any position, rather than simply being on or off, they are known as *continuous controllers*. In everyday terms, the position of a car's steering wheel or accelerator could be thought of as being a continuous controller, whereas the direction indicators are simple switched controllers that are either on or off. Continuous controllers aren't as continuous as they might seem, however; MIDI deals with numbers, and because of the data structure used the available range is from 0 to 127. This means that all continuous controllers really operate over a series of tiny steps, but these steps are so small that the impression is one of continuous change.

There are a number of different means by which a musical instrument may be controlled, and these include performance wheels, joysticks, levers, pedals, footswitches, breath controllers, ribbon controllers and other less obvious but equally ingenious devices. All can be employed to exert their influence via MIDI controllers, which is why MIDI provides for so many different controllers to be used at the same time. You don't have to worry about MIDI channels or other technicalities when using controllers, as the data goes automatically to the same destination (ie MIDI channel) as the notes played on the keyboard.

Even though you have only two hands and two feet, MIDI provides the means to operate up to 128 controllers, although not all are used for expression control. The reason why there are so many is so that you can pick which aspect of the sound being played that you control with your wheels, pedals or switches.

If more precision is required than can be afforded by 128 steps, two controllers must be used together, and the MIDI spec reserves a number of controllers for this purpose in a way this is perfectly transparent to the user. However, this degree of precision is rarely necessary or desirable, as the more MIDI data is generated, the more chance there is of creating a MIDI-data overload.

pitch-bend scaling

By changing parameters in the MIDI Set-up menu, MIDI instruments can often be "scaled" so that, for example, the maximum travel of the pitch-bend wheel might cause a pitch shift of as little as one semitone or as much as a whole octave. As you can imagine, it's important to ensure that any instruments likely to play at the same time are set with the same scaling values, especially for pitch bend. Otherwise, when you try to bend a note on the master keyboard, the sound coming from the master instrument might go up by a third and the sound from the slave by a fourth – clearly not desirable, unless you're inventing a new strain of modern jazz. For general use, most people set up a pitch-bend range of two semitones so that a range of plus or minus one whole tone is available from the centre position of the wheel. Pitch-bend wheels are of course spring loaded, so that they automatically return to their neutral position when released. Interestingly, however, although the pitch-bend wheel is involved in expression control, it doesn't form a part of the MIDI controllers group but instead exists in a category of its own. This is almost certainly because of historic reasons.

more controllers

One other controller not mentioned so far is master volume – some instruments send and respond to it while others don't. On an instrument that does, turning up the master-volume slider will send the appropriate control information (controller 7) over MIDI and the receiving synth will respond to it. A multitimbral module receiving a master-volume control message will alter the volume of whichever part is being addressed in accordance with the MIDI channel of the message. Be warned, though, that some older instruments don't respond to controller 7, so any attempts to control the volume of these via MIDI will be fruitless.

Other commonly implemented MIDI controllers include the sustain pedal, which prevents the note envelopes from entering their release phase until the pedal is released. This operates rather like the sustain pedal on a piano.

The MIDI specification is constantly evolving, and not all 128 possible controller numbers are used – yet! Controllers 0 to 63 are used for continuous controllers, while 64 to 95 are used for switches. 96 to 121 are as yet undefined and 122 to 127 are reserved for Channel Mode messages. A full listing of controller numbers and their functions follows, but don't panic if some of them don't make any sense at the moment.

controller listing

0	Bank Select	66	Sostenuto
1	Modulation Wheel	67	Soft Pedal
2	Breath Controller	68	Legato Footswitch
3	Undefined	69	Hold 2
4	Foot Controller	70	Sound Variation/Exciter
5	Portamento Time	71	Harmonic Content/ Compressor
6	Data Entry	72	Release Time/Distortion
7	Main Volume	73	Attack Time/Equaliser
8	Balance	74	Brightness/Expander-Gate
9	Undefined	75	Undefined/Reverb
10	Pan	76	Undefined/Delay
11	Expression	77	Undefined/Pitch Transpose
12	Effect Control 1	78	Undefined/Flange-Chorus
13	Effect Control 2	79	Undefined/Special Effect
14	Undefined	80-3	General Purpose 5-8
15	Undefined	84	Portamento Control
16-19	General Purpose 1-4	85-90	Undefined
20-31	Undefined	91	Effect Depth (Effect 1)
32-63	LSB (Least Significant Byte) for Control Changes 0-31 (where greater resolution is required)	92	Tremolo Depth (Effect 2)
		93	Chorus Depth (Effect 3)
		94	Celeste Depth (Effect 4)
64	Damper/Sustain Pedal	95	Phaser Depth (Effect 5)
65	Portamento	96	Data Increment

97	Data Decrement	120	All Sound Off
98	Non-Registered Parameter Number LSB (Least Significant Byte)	121	Reset All Controllers
		122	Local Control
99	Non-Registered Parameter Number MSB (Most Significant Byte)	123	All Notes Off
		124	Omni Mode Off
100	Registered Parameter Number LSB	125	Omni Mode On
101	Registered Parameter Number MSB	126	Mono Mode On
102-19	Undefined	127	Poly Mode On

Note that not all controllers deal with performance control. In addition to the last four controller numbers, which change MIDI modes, there are also Bank Change messages, an All Notes Off message (to cut off all notes that may still be playing), Local On/Off and a Reset All Controllers message, which ensures that all controller values are reset to their default values. Most of these will have little impact on your day-to-day use of MIDI, but where they are important, they will be discussed further. Most of the time – while you're first getting to know MIDI, at least – you'll be concerned mainly with selecting and playing sounds, using the performance wheels on the master keyboard and possibly using a sustain pedal (also plugged into the master keyboard).

The initials MSB and LSB stand for Most Significant Byte and Least Significant Byte, which roughly translated from computerspeak means coarse and fine adjustments. Both MSBs and LSBs have a possible numerical range of 0-127, so no surprises there! In fact, all variable controllers have values of between 0 and 127, while switched controllers are usually set at 0 for off and 127 for on. Most modern instruments will also accept any value of 64 and above as on and any below 64 as off, although some older instruments are more pedantic.

Pitch bend can provide control in two directions, so its default position is at 64, midway between the two extremes. Again, you don't need to get involved at this stage – your sequencer will take care of most of the obscure MIDI dialogue to and from your keyboard and modules for you – but when you come to edit MIDI sequence data, it is helpful to know the more common controllers and what their values mean.

non-registered parameters

Because not all synthesisers use the same type of synthesis, it would be impossible to provide a standard range of controllers able to access every parameter that had an influence over the sound being produced. Of course, a few parameters are common to all instruments, and these are known as *registered parameters*, but to allow manufacturers to provide access to all of the relevant parameters of different instruments the NRPN (Non-Registered Parameter Number) system was added to the MIDI specification.

The registered parameters are Pitch-Bend Sensitivity, Fine Tuning, Coarse Tuning, Change Tuning Program and Change Tuning Bank. Of course, the vast majority of controls are non-registered, but for precisely that reason it's usually necessary to use some form of customised hardware interface or editing software to access them. Because they are non-defined, the typical user has no means of knowing what they are unless they are detailed in the MIDI spec at the back of the instrument manual. However, NRPNs provide a convenient back door for designers and software writers, allowing them to access the invisible sound-control elements inside synthesisers without having to get involved with the complexities of system-exclusive messages.

channel voice messages

Most MIDI messages are channel specific, in that they are only accepted by the receiving device if it is on the same channel as the data that is being sent. MIDI Note On and Off messages are channel messages, as are all other types of performance data relating to velocity, pitch bend, controller data, program changes and so on.

A single musical note can be represented by a fairly concise MIDI message comprising only a channel number, a Note On event followed by a Note-Off event, plus a velocity value. Controller information, on the other hand, is rather more data intensive, because as long as you're moving a controller it is sending out a continuous stream of MIDI data.

aftertouch

Another source of musical performance control information is *channel aftertouch*, produced by some keyboards when you press hard on the keys. This works via a pressure sensor under the keyboard and sends out lots of MIDI data, whether the receiving device responds to aftertouch or not, so if you're not using the Aftertouch option on your master keyboard, turn it off to prevent clogging up the system with unnecessary data. I tend to leave it off as a matter of course unless I specifically need it because, when you're working with a computer sequencer, unnecessary controller data takes up a lot of memory, as well as hogging MIDI bandwidth.

Aftertouch can be assigned to various functions, such as brightness, loudness, depth of vibrato and so on, and it's a useful way of adding expression to a performance, but you should keep in mind that channel aftertouch affects all of the notes that are currently playing, not just the one you're pressing down.

A few exotic instruments also feature *polyphonic aftertouch*, which means that, when you press down on a key, the data sent applies to only that note, not to all of the notes that are currently playing. Polyphonic aftertouch can generate a vast amount of MIDI data and so must be used sparingly, but very few instruments support this facility.

Another very rare feature is *release velocity*. All velocity-sensitive instruments generate MIDI velocity data, the level of which depends on how quickly you push down the keys, but on an instrument with release velocity additional information is generated depending on how quickly you release the keys.

sound banks

As discussed earlier, the maximum range of a conventional MIDI message is from 0 to 127, meaning that MIDI can address a maximum of 128 different notes or send controller information with a maximum of 128 discrete values. Similarly, you can directly address only 128 different patches, but to get around this limitation some synths organise their sounds into multiple banks, with a maximum of 128 patches per bank. MIDI Bank Change messages (which are also forms of controller message, usually involving controller numbers 0 and 32) are then used to access the different banks. Not all Bank Change messages are standard, but the relevant controller values are supplied in MIDI implementation tables in instrument handbooks. Some of the more modern sequencers include a library of Bank Change commands for the more common instruments in circulation so that, once you've told your sequencer what instrument is connected to it, it'll automatically send the right Bank Change command.

assignable controls

Often, instruments allow you to assign which physical control device relates to a specific MIDI controller, so the modulation wheel on your synth could be redirected to control something quite different, such as reverb amount or the brightness of the sound being played.

How much you want to get involved with the various controllers is up to you. At first, you'll probably be happy to use the pitch-bend and modulation wheels and the sustain pedal, but as you get more familiar with MIDI you may be attracted by the possibilities of using a sequencer to automate your performance by controlling levels, creating automated panning, changing effects and patches and so on. The great thing about MIDI is that you can start off very simply, making music right from the outset, and then, as you get more comfortable with the concept, you can try out more ambitious things.

MIDI Clock

Unlike channel-specific messages, MIDI messages related to synchronisation and sequencer control have no channel address and so are received by all of the instruments in a MIDI system. Perhaps the most important of all these messages is MIDI Clock.

MIDI Clock is a tempo-related timing code and comprises 96 electronic "clocks" or ticks for each four-beat bar of music. Think of it as the invisible conductor that keeps your drum machine and sequencer, or sequencer and tape recorder, playing together rather than going their own separate ways. You can't hear these ticks, but they are picked up by any drum machine or sequencer set to External MIDI Sync mode, enabling the slave machine to stay in sync with the master. A practical use of MIDI Clock is to sync up a drum machine to a sequencer, either one of which can be the master. Using a suitable interface box, it's also possible to use MIDI Clock to keep a sequencer running in time with a recording on tape. The slave machine must be set to External MIDI Sync, which means that it will follow exactly the tempo generated by the master device.

Start, Stop and Continue

The slave device also needs to know when to start and stop, so MIDI also includes Start, Stop and Continue messages. Even so, these are of use only if you start your master playing from the beginning of the song; otherwise, the slave won't know where it's supposed to start from. To get around this, the MIDI Song Position Pointer message was added to the MIDI specification. This is quite transparent to the user, but on starting the sequence a message is sent which tells the receiving device where to start from. As a result, the slave device can lock up almost instantaneously. So-called Smart FSK (Frequency Shift Keying) tape-to-MIDI sync boxes using MIDI SPPs are often used to make a MIDI sequencer sync to a tape machine. (Chapter 4, "MIDI And Synchronisation", contains much more information on this subject.)

serial killer

While I've promised to try to keep this book as non-technical as possible, it helps in understanding the limitations of MIDI to know that it is a serial system – in other words, information moves in single file. At this point, many books on MIDI present you with an in-depth description of the bits and bytes that make up a MIDI message, and if you're technically minded, this can be quite interesting. However, as this doesn't really help the typical user to make better use of MIDI, I make no apology for omitting it entirely.

The main point here is that, because MIDI is relatively fast, things may seem to happen all at once, but in reality, when you play a chord, the notes start to sound one after the other, not simultaneously. The times in question are far too short to be perceptible when only a few events are concerned, but if you were to try to play, say, 64 notes at once, you might just hear a delay between the first and the last.

In reality, the speed of MIDI is seldom a limitation when you're dealing with only notes, but if you're trying to replay a multipart MIDI sequence that also contains lots of controller information you could end up with the MIDI equivalent of a traffic jam, resulting in obvious timing errors. In practice, it's wise to use controllers only when necessary and to switch off your master keyboard's aftertouch facility whenever you don't need it. The better sequencers give priority to MIDI note timing when traffic gets heavy so that problems here are less likely to be audible.

MIDI modes

Instruments are generally set to Poly mode for conventional operation, although some older instruments default to Omni mode every time they are switched on. Because the vast majority of work is done using Poly mode, most users rarely give MIDI modes a second thought, but there are actually four different MIDI modes, their functions defined as follows:

- **Mode 1: Omni On/Poly** – The instrument will play polyphonically but MIDI channel data is ignored. Whatever you send to it, on whatever channel, it will play.

- **Mode 2: Omni On/Mono** – The monophonic equivalent of mode 1 and hardly ever used.

- **Mode 3: Omni Off/Poly** – The "normal" MIDI mode, especially for sequencing or multitimbral operation. In mode 3, the instrument responds to messages sent only on its own MIDI channel and plays polyphonically.

- **Mode 4: Omni Off/Mono** – The monophonic equivalent of mode 3. Mode 4 is mainly for MIDI guitar players who need to have each string working on a separate MIDI channel in order to be able to bend notes or apply vibrato on independent strings. Because each string of a guitar is monophonic (ie, it can play only one note at a time), it makes sense to use the receiving synth in Mono mode to mimic the way in which a real guitar plays.

active sensing

MIDI also includes something called *active sensing* (rare on modern instruments), which is MIDI's way of checking that a connection exists between devices. In reality, it's the MIDI equivalent of the receiving device shouting, "Are you still there?" and, a short while later, the transmitting device shouting back, "Yes!" If a yes is not forthcoming, the receiving device assumes that the transmitting device has gone off in a sulk and, metaphorically speaking, takes its ball home!

What actually happens is that, if the receiving device doesn't get back an "all's well" message, it shuts off all notes that are playing. If it didn't do this and the MIDI cable was accidentally unplugged between a Note On and a Note Off message being sent, the receiving instrument would continue to play that note until it eventually rusted away! Happily, this operation is also completely hidden from the user, but it's nice to know it is there. Having said that, most modern instruments have dispensed with active sensing.

song select and tune request

Because MIDI sequencers can hold more than one song in memory, the MIDI spec also includes a Song Select message. As you might expect, this allows tune to be requested by number, in the range of 0-127.

We're very used to MIDI instruments being perfectly in tune, but it's still possible for MIDI-controlled analogue synths to drift out of pitch over a period of time, unless they have intelligent auto-retuning systems. However, many of them do have an internal tuning routine which can be initiated manually or over MIDI using a Tune Request command. If a Tune Request command is sent, all of the MIDI instruments in the system that have a tuning routine will give themselves a quick check over and retune to their own internal references.

system-exclusive messages

System exclusive is a term that strikes terror into the hearts of those who know just enough about MIDI to know where the tricky bits are, but I mention it here mainly so that, if you decide to ignore it, at least you'll know what you're ignoring!

System-exclusive (or sysex for short) messages are part of the MIDI system message portfolio, but whereas the rest of MIDI is pretty precisely defined, sysex is provided so that manufacturers can build instruments with different facilities yet which still conform to the MIDI specification. Rather than use the MIDI channel system for locating their targets, sysex messages contain ID codes unique to the types of instrument for which they are intended. Where two or more identical instruments are being used in the same system, it's often possible to assign an additional ID number of between 1 and 16 to each one so that no two have exactly the same ID. If they did, they'd all respond to the same sysex data.

In the main, sysex allows those clever people who write sound-editing software to gain access to all of the sound-generating parameters that might need adjusting. The programming parameters of analogue and digital synths tend to be quite different, so if you want access to these parameters via MIDI, manufacturers have got to be allowed to specify "exclusive" codes, just as they provide NRPNs to allow you to access certain unique parameters using MIDI controllers. This obviously couldn't be done using standardised codes, as every different make and type of synth has different parameters, so a system such as sysex is the only viable means of doing it.

Because sysex messages are recognised only by the instrument type for which they are designed, there's no worry that your drum machine might try to interpret a message intended for one of your synths and blow a fuse. If the manufacturer's ID heading up the sysex message code isn't recognised by the receiving instrument, the message is ignored.

patch dumping

Only very experienced MIDI users tend to have more than a passing association with MIDI sysex data, but anyone can use it at a basic level for copying patches or banks of patches from a synth into a MIDI storage device such as a sequencer or MIDI data filter.

You'll find that most modern MIDI instruments have a sysex dump facility tucked away in their MIDI configuration pages somewhere – all you have to do is connect the MIDI Out of the instrument to your sequencer's input, put the sequencer into Record and start the dump procedure. The sysex data will be recorded in exactly the same as MIDI notes, except that, if you look in the Edit list to see what's there, it will look like nonsense. But don't worry – the synth knows what it means, and that's all that matters.

Sysex dump data usually takes a few seconds to record, after which it can be played back into the instrument at any time to restore the patches you saved. If you're in the habit of using lots of different patches in your songs and you don't have enough user memory to hold them all, you can store a sysex dump right at the start of each song to set up the required patches. Depending on how long the dump takes, you may have to leave a few bars of count-in to allow it to finish loading before the music starts, and once you've loaded your new sounds it might be a good idea to mute the sysex track or the patches will get reloaded every time you start the song from the top. Also, don't quantise the sysex dump after recording or it may not play back properly. (If this last section doesn't make sense, read it again after you've read Chapter 3, "Introducing Sequencers". That's the trouble with MIDI – because of the way it evolved, it isn't always possible to keep everything in a perfectly logical order!)

compatibility

If you expect every MIDI instrument to support every feature implemented in the MIDI specifications, you're destined to lead a sad and disappointed life. Most new instruments support most of the features, but few are actually compulsory and about the only thing that you can take for granted is that a MIDI synth will send and receive MIDI note data, although virtually all will accept MIDI Program Change messages and velocity information. If a MIDI message is received by an instrument incapable of responding to that message, the message is simply ignored, in much the same way as you might ignore junk mail written in a foreign language.

However, you should be aware that different instruments can legitimately respond to the same MIDI message in different ways. To take an example mentioned earlier, the pitch-bend range of an instrument is not tied to the data received but is set up in the MIDI menu of the instrument itself. Here, full movement of the pitch-bend wheel (the full range of which is 128 steps, with 64 denoting the middle position) can be made to shift the pitch by as little as one semitone or by as much as an octave. Unless all of your instruments are set to the same pitch-bend range (two semitones is popular), you could end up with an horrendous discord.

Also mentioned earlier is the fact that very few instruments incorporate polyphonic key pressure (aftertouch) or release velocity, but just about everything you can buy now (other than some really basic home keyboards) is velocity sensitive, and even relatively inexpensive keyboards have channel aftertouch. Some older instruments don't respond to MIDI Bank Change messages, even if they have banks of sounds accessible from the front panel, which can be rather frustrating, and you may also

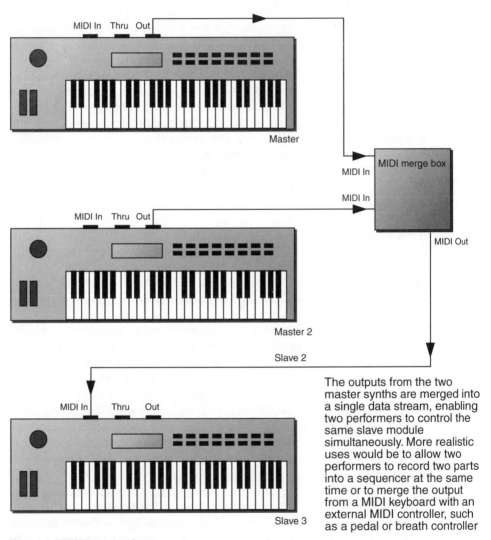

The outputs from the two master synths are merged into a single data stream, enabling two performers to control the same slave module simultaneously. More realistic uses would be to allow two performers to record two parts into a sequencer at the same time or to merge the output from a MIDI keyboard with an external MIDI controller, such as a pedal or breath controller

Figure 1.4: A MIDI merge box in use

find some instruments that refuse to respond to controller 7 (master volume) commands. If in doubt, the back of the relevant equipment manual should show a table of the MIDI facilities that are supported by your instrument, with "O" showing the facility is present and "X" showing that it isn't supported. This is known as the *MIDI implementation table*, and once you know how to use it, it can tell you a lot about the capabilities of your instrument in a very short space of time.

introducing General MIDI

Soundcards and general-purpose synths and modules frequently include a set of General MIDI preset sounds that at least ensure you of nominal compatibility, sound-wise, between cards of different makes. Some GM synths sound noticeably better than others, but if you've created a composition for piano and play this back over a GM-compatible synth, at least you know it's going to play back with a piano sound, not a violin or a helicopter! General MIDI was a relatively late addition to the MIDI spec and is discussed more fully in the next chapter. Its main use is in allowing MIDI sequencer files to be played back via a wide variety of different instruments so that all the parts will be played by the correct type of instrument.

MIDI merge

If there's a need to split the same MIDI signal to two or more destinations, you can use either the Thru connectors fitted to the various MIDI instruments or a MIDI thru box, but merging two streams of MIDI data isn't quite so simple. MIDI data is quite complicated, so if you were try to join two MIDI cables with a Y-lead, the result would be a jumble of meaningless data.

To merge two or more MIDI data streams, a specialised merge box is needed, inside which is a small computer designed to interleave the data in a coherent way. Merge facilities are needed when a sequencer needs to be controlled by a master keyboard at the same time as receiving MIDI sync signals, or when you want to play two keyboard into your sequencer at the same time, although there are other requirements for MIDI merge facilities which will be explained as they come up. Figure 1.4 shows how a MIDI merge box might be used to merge the MIDI output from a keyboard and from a dedicated sound-editing device, enabling both to be fed into a sequencer at the same time.

Although stand-alone MIDI merge boxes are available, many of the more sophisticated multiport MIDI interfaces also include two or more mergeable inputs. A merge facility can also enable two or more MIDI keyboards to be routed to the system at once – for example, when there are two players wishing to record different parts of a musical sequence at the same time.

a crash course in MIDI

- MIDI is used mainly to send note and performance/controller information between instruments, although it can also carry Patch Change commands, tempo-related timing information and Start, Stop and Continue commands for the remote control of sequencers and drum machines. There is also a protocol for controlling compatible tape machines and hard-disk recorders, known as MMC (MIDI Machine Control). This allows remote access to the main transport controls and Record Status buttons of a multitrack recorder, which can be useful if your multitrack recorder is on the opposite side of the room to your sequencer.

- MIDI data describes keyboard (and expression controller) actions, not sounds.

- In any MIDI system, there is one device designated as master; the other devices function as slaves. In a basic system, the keyboard is usually the master. However, when a sequence is played back from a sequencer, the sequencer is master.

- MIDI operates on 16 channels, thus allowing up to 16 different devices to be controlled independently at one time. If more than 16 channels are required, a multiport MIDI interface is needed to provide two or more groups of 16 channels each. (This topic will be covered in later chapters.)

- MIDI is a standard system, but not all MIDI instruments and devices support all of the functions described in the MIDI specification. However, the functions that they do provide must conform to the MIDI specification.

chapter 2

General MIDI

G eneral MIDI was given a brief mention in the preceding chapter, but it is a very important concept and deserves further explanation. General MIDI is simply another stage of standardisation that has been added to the existing MIDI specification, but it doesn't have to be adopted by all MIDI instruments, only by those bearing the GM logo. Furthermore, a GM machine may also be able to function as a non-GM machine, in which case it will have a dedicated GM mode for those times when General MIDI operation is required. Some serious musicians talk disparagingly of General MIDI, as it provides only a restricted and, some might say, unimaginative sound set, but its benefits are significant, as you're about to discover.

The idea behind GM is to enable manufacturers to build synthesisers and synth modules that exhibit a specified degree of compatibility in terms of which sounds are located in which patches, which keys the various drum sounds are mapped to and the minimum performance capability of the machine, in terms of multitimbrality and polyphony. Essentially, the aim was to allow a MIDI sequence recorded using one GM module to be played back on any other GM module without the need to remap patches, move drum-note allocations or worry about running out of parts or polyphony. This doesn't mean that all GM synths have to sound exactly the same, but it does mean that, for example, a piano preset on one machine must be in the same patch location as a similar-sounding piano preset on any other GM machine. If you buy a computer with a soundcard that has sound-synthesis capabilities, it's almost certain to offer at least the basic set of GM sounds, enabling it to play back with reasonable accuracy songs created on other GM systems.

MIDI compatibility

Normally, whenever you record a piece of music using a sequencer, you insert the appropriate Program Change command at the start of each track so that, whenever you play back the sequence through the same instruments and modules, the correct sounds will automatically be called up. However, if you play the sequence back on a friend's MIDI system, you may well find that all of the sounds are completely wrong because not only are the patches completely different in sound but also any that are suitable are probably stored in different patch locations. In the case of programmable instruments, this kind of chaos is difficult to avoid, because most users have their own systems for storing their edited sounds. Furthermore, the factory presets provided with non-GM instruments tend to be arranged fairly arbitrarily. By standardising the locations and types of a core set of sounds, General MIDI ensures that a song recorded on one GM system will play back correctly on another.

drum mapping

Another potential stumbling block is the percussion part. Even if your friend's drum sounds are on the same MIDI channel as you've used, the chances are that some or all of the drum sounds will be assigned to different keys. Synth manufacturers Roland have had their own more or less standard drum mapping system for some time now, but some other manufacturers haven't been as well organised, so when playing back a song on a friend's system, where you programmed a bass drum, your friend's set-up might play a cowbell. Furthermore, you may have written the piece using drum sounds that don't have a close equivalent on your friend's drum machine. With General MIDI, all drum sounds are mapped to the same keys.

MIDI too versatile?

Let's say that you strike lucky and you manage to get all of your sounds mapped out. There's still a good chance that you'll come unstuck when it comes to interpreting controller information. Perhaps one of your friend's modules doesn't respond to controller 7 (master volume), or maybe his pitch-bend ranges are all set to three semitones and you do all of your work with the range set to two. MIDI is a wonderful system, but its flexibility means that no two people's MIDI systems behave in exactly the same way.

General MIDI was devised to provide a solution for situations where a high degree of compatibility is essential - for example, when replaying pre-recorded MIDI song files. Now, musicians working with GM synths can play each other's GM song files and be confident that they will sound more or less the way that they should, even though there are subtle subjective differences between one manufacturer's GM machine and another. This has opened up the market for commercially available MIDI song files.

polyphony and multitimbrality

The problem with polyphony and multitimbrality is that you can never have enough of it! GM MIDI instruments provide the ability to play back 16 parts on 16 MIDI channels, with a total polyphony of at least 24 notes. In other words, there may be 16 different sounds running on 16 different MIDI channels, but the total number of notes playing at once can never exceed the maximum polyphony of the instrument.

If you try to play more notes than the instrument can handle, note-robbing takes place and previously played notes start to drop out. What's more, where a synth layers two voices to make up a sound, the actual polyphony may be further reduced depending on how the manufacturer chooses to interpret the GM MIDI spec on polyphony. The whole idea of specifying a minimum level of polyphony is so that you don't run out of polyphony when trying to play a MIDI song file conforming to the GM format.

Roland's enhanced GS format

Much of the present GM format owes its existence to Roland's own protocols, so it's hardly surprising that Roland have gone one step further and devised an enhanced version of General MIDI that they call GS. Realising that many users wouldn't be satisfied with 128 preset sounds, Roland have designed their GS machines to offer several alternative banks of sounds, with the basic GM set – described as *capital tones* – being the first bank (bank 0). There are then up to seven *variation tones*, based on each of the capital tones, and these are arranged so as to have the same Program Change numbers as the tones from which they are derived. In other words, all of the variation tones of a piano capital tone will still be pianos, although they will all sound subtly different. Further banks are provided for sounds known as sub-capital tones, which are less obviously related to the capital tones. A Bank Change command allows the user to switch between the various banks and conventional Program Change commands are then used to select the sounds within each bank – a neat way to get around MIDI's limitation of being able to address directly only 128 patches.

Yamaha also introduced their own expanded General MIDI format which they call XG. Like Roland's GS mode, this enhances the basic General MIDI sound set with several banks of alternative sounds, but unfortunately a different Bank Change command is required to access these. Most Yamaha XG instruments also support Roland's GS format, though, so it looks as though GS will become the *de facto* standard for enhanced-GM instruments.

editing

Because General MIDI is based on the concept of the same sounds being always in the same place, it stands to reason that any attempt to edit the sounds will risk negating any advantages accorded by the system. Different instruments handle this dilemma in different ways, but as a rule, where editing is permitted, you can switch between a GM mode based on preset sounds or a non-GM mode.

commercial MIDI song files

Commercial GM song files are now available that cover all musical styles, from pop to classical, and they have many applications, from general interest to song analysis. They are also used by solo performers to provide musical backings, within the conditions imposed by music copyright law.

A huge advantage of MIDI song files over pre-recorded backing tapes is that the key of a piece can be changed at the touch of a button, making life much easier for the solo entertainer. The overall sound quality is generally better, too, as with pre-recorded tapes you have to either play the original night after night and risk wearing it out or copy it onto another cassette and contend with the consequent loss of quality. Virtually all of the MIDI songs files available over the internet are in GM format, again to ensure that the user hears the music as the composer intended.

the rules of General MIDI

In 1991, General MIDI was ratified with the aim of defining a minimum set of MIDI capabilities to which all GM devices must adhere. The main points are as follows:

*   A GM instrument must support all 16 MIDI channels simultaneously to provide 16-part multitimbrality.

*   Percussion parts must be on MIDI channel 10, a minimum set of 47 standard sound types (including the most common drum and Latin percussion sounds) must be provided and these must all be mapped in accordance with the GM standard. This mapping owes a lot to Roland's original mapping system.

*   GM instruments must be capable of 24-note polyphony and notes must be allocated dynamically. However, the specification allows eight notes to be reserved for percussion, leaving 16 for the other instruments.

*   All 128 preset sounds are defined in accordance with their type and

patch location, as shown in the GM voice table below. Although there is some variation in sound between one module and another, the instrument type and even its playing style – in the case of basses, for example – for each patch location is quite rigidly defined, right down to the dog barks, helicopters and gunshots in the special-effects section. Some of the more abstract pad sounds are a little more flexible, but they must still be of a roughly similar tone and character.

- All GM instruments must respond to the same set of MIDI controllers, and the default ranges set for these controller must be standard. The MIDI controller implementation function includes the ability to change master tuning and the range of the pitch-bend wheel via MIDI, as well as commands such as Reset All Controllers and All Notes Off, the latter of which silences any notes currently playing. All GM machines must also respond to pitch-bend, velocity and aftertouch information.

General MIDI voice table

Program Number	Instrument	Program Number	Instrument
1	Acoustic Grand Piano	24	Tango Accordion
2	Bright Acoustic Piano	25	Acoustic Guitar (Nylon)
3	Electric Grand Piano	26	Acoustic Guitar (Steel)
4	Honky-Tonk Piano	27	Electric Guitar (Jazz)
5	Electric Piano 1	28	Electric Guitar (Clean)
6	Electric Piano 2	29	Electric Guitar (Muted)
7	Harpsichord	30	Overdriven Guitar
8	Clavichord	31	Distortion Guitar
9	Celesta	32	Guitar Harmonics
10	Glockenspiel	33	Acoustic Bass
11	Music Box	34	Electric Bass (Finger)
12	Vibraphone	35	Electric Bass (Pick)
13	Marimba	36	Fretless Bass
14	Xylophone	37	Slap Bass 1
15	Tubular Bells	38	Slap Bass 2
16	Dulcimer	39	Synth Bass 1
17	Drawbar Organ	40	Synth Bass 2
18	Percussive Organ	41	Violin
19	Rock Organ	42	Viola
20	Church Organ	43	Cello
21	Reed Organ	44	Contrabass
22	Accordion	45	Tremolo Strings
23	Harmonica	46	Pizzicato Strings

Program Number	Instrument	Program Number	Instrument
47	Orchestral Harp	88	Lead 8 (Bass And Lead)
48	Timpani	89	Pad 1 (New Age)
49	String Ensemble 1	90	Pad 2 (Warm)
50	String Ensemble 2	91	Pad 3 (Polysynth)
51	SynthStrings 1	92	Pad 4 (Choir)
52	SynthStrings 2	93	Pad 5 (Bowed)
53	Choir Aahs	94	Pad 6 (Metallic)
54	Voice Oohs	95	Pad 7 (Halo)
55	Synth Voice	96	Pad 8 (Sweep)
56	Orchestra Hit	97	FX 1 (Rain)
57	Trumpet	98	FX 2 (Soundtrack)
58	Trombone	99	FX 3 (Crystal)
59	Tuba	100	FX 4 (Atmosphere)
60	Muted Trumpet	101	FX 5 (Brightness)
61	French Horn	102	FX 6 (Goblins)
62	Brass Section	103	FX 7 (Echos)
63	SynthBrass 1	104	FX 8 (Sci-Fi)
64	SynthBrass 2	105	Sitar
65	Soprano Sax	106	Banjo
66	Alto Sax	107	Shamisen
67	Tenor Sax	108	Koto
68	Baritone Sax	109	Kalimba
69	Oboe	110	Bagpipe
70	English Horn	111	Fiddle
71	Bassoon	112	Shanai
72	Clarinet	113	Tinkle Bell
73	Piccolo	114	Agogo
74	Flute	115	Steel Drums
75	Recorder	116	Woodblock
76	Pan Flute	117	Taiko Drum
77	Blown Bottle	118	Melodic Tom
78	Shakuhachi	119	Synth Drum
79	Whistle	120	Reverse Cymbal
80	Ocarina	121	Guitar Fret Noise
81	Lead 1 (Square)	122	Breath Noise
82	Lead 2 (Sawtooth)	123	Seashore
83	Lead 3 (Calliope)	124	Bird Tweet
84	Lead 4 (Chiff)	125	Telephone Ring
85	Lead 5 (Charang)	126	Helicopter
86	Lead 6 (Voice)	127	Applause
87	Lead 7 (Fifths)	128	Gunshot

(Note: Some manufacturers number their patches 0-127 rather than 1-128.)

General MIDI drum map

Note Number	Drum Sound	Note Number	Drum Sound
35	Acoustic Bass Drum	59	Ride Cymbal 2
36	Bass Drum 1	60	High Bongo
37	Side Stick	61	Low Bongo
38	Acoustic Snare	62	Mute Hi Conga
39	Hand Clap	63	Open Hi Conga
40	Electric Snare	64	Low Conga
41	Low Floor Tom	65	High Timbale
42	Closed Hi-Hat	66	Low Timbale
43	High Floor Tom	67	High Agogo
44	Pedal Hi-Hat	68	Low Agogo
45	Low Tom	69	Cabasa
46	Open Hi-Hat	70	Maracas
47	Low Mid Tom	71	Short Whistle
48	High Mid Tom	72	Long Whistle
49	Crash Cymbal	73	Short Guiro
50	High Tom	74	Long Guiro
51	Ride Cymbal 1	75	Claves
52	Chinese Cymbal	76	High Woodblock
53	Ride Bell	77	Low Woodblock
54	Tambourine	78	Mute Cuica
55	Splash Cymbal	79	Open Cuica
56	Cowbell	80	Mute Triangle
57	Crash Cymbal 2	81	Open Triangle
58	Vibraslap		

introducing sequencers

At its simplest, MIDI can be used to "remote control" one or more instruments from a single master keyboard, but MIDI sequencing is where things get really interesting, as this makes it possible to use a multitimbral synthesiser to record and play multipart MIDI compositions, ranging from classical symphonies to rock and pop music. The word *sequencer* dates back to pre-MIDI days, when synthesisers could be controlled only via a sequencing device comprising a number of faders, each fader being used to tune one note in the sequence. When set to run, the sequence would run around the sequence – typically of up to 16 notes – and then it would repeat, with the tempo set by the user. While the effects that could be achieved by this method were limited, a new genre of synthesiser bands and artists emerged on the back of this technology. Of course, the modern sequencer is a very different thing altogether.

the MIDI sequencer

A modern MIDI sequencer is really a multitrack MIDI recorder (although the term *sequencer* is still with us) and today's sequencers can record "real" audio – such as vocals and guitar – alongside MIDI tracks, which can control synths.

In the context of recording, the term *track* refers to a means of recording a musical part in such a way that it may be edited, erased or re-recorded independently of the other parts. If you're familiar with the concept of multitrack tape, MIDI sequencing draws a close analogy with that way of working. Traditional musicians might prefer to visualise a sequencer track as being roughly equivalent to one stave of music in a multipart score. A modern MIDI sequencer will provide a bare minimum of 16 tracks and often many more.

recording in layers

With a MIDI sequencer, numerous separate musical parts can be recorded at different times, either by the parts being played one at a time on a MIDI keyboard, by note and timing data being entered manually or by a combination of "live" playing and editing. The individual parts may be monophonic or they may comprise chords – how much you want to record on each track is up to you. In fact, a difficult part could be split over two or more tracks and then recorded in several takes. For example, a piano player with limited skills might first record the left-hand part on one track and then record the right-hand part later on a different track. Once recorded, these parts may be played back via any MIDI-compatible synthesiser or collection of synthesisers.

Unless you have a sequencer with a built-in synthesiser, it can't play back any sounds on its own; it has to be used to control one or more synthesisers, and the number of different musical parts you can play back at once depends on the number and types of synthesisers. Fortunately, most modern synthesisers and computer soundcards are capable of playing back up to 16 different sounds at once, each controlled by a different MIDI channel. More on this later...

ethics

To those used to playing and recording using traditional methods, the MIDI sequencer is sometimes viewed as little short of cheating, but to the sequencer user MIDI and sequencing are seen as practical tools that make complex multipart composition and performance a reality. Before MIDI, few people could compose a symphony or even a pop song, for that matter, and ever expect to hear it performed, but now almost anyone can turn their musical ideas into a performance using affordable technology. Before getting onto the mechanics of sequencing, however, I'd like to tackle the notion that sequencing is somehow cheating by looking at how things were done before the introduction of MIDI.

traditional composition

Having never written a symphony, I can't detail the exact stages, but I expect it goes something like this: The composer sits at his or her chosen instrument testing musical ideas, and the ones that are deemed viable are then written down on manuscript paper for the various sections of the orchestra to play. The composer imagines the parts already written down while adding new sections, harmonies and so on, and then, when the score is nominally finished, the score will be scrutinised and any required alterations made.

Once the score is complete, an orchestra will then be engaged to play the composition – they'll be given copies of the score and the music will be played back as written by the composer. Essentially, the composer - who may or may not be able to perform to an acceptable standard on a musical instrument - has conceived a piece of music and then written a list of instructions in the form of a musical score so that a musically proficient orchestra can perform it. The composer himself is not required to perform. Indeed, nobody has ever denounced the great classical composers for not being able to play all of the instruments for which they wrote scores, so why give the MIDI-sequencer user a hard time for doing exactly the same thing?

the MIDI composer

In contrast, how does the MIDI composer write? As with the orchestral composer, the work usually starts at the keyboard, but this time the keyboard is a MIDI instrument connected to a MIDI sequencer, not a piano. Instead of writing down a score on manuscript paper, the composer will record sections of the music into the sequencer against an electronic metronome set to the desired tempo, and instead of scanning a score to verify what's been done it's a simple matter to play back the recording via a suitable synthesiser to hear exactly what's been recorded. Those composers who can't play well enough to record the parts in real time can enter notes directly into the sequencer in much the same way as a composer would write notes onto paper - it's a tedious and time-consuming job, but it can be done.

Perhaps the best reason for using a MIDI sequencer is that you don't have to hire in an orchestra or a band of session musicians, because even a relatively inexpensive multitimbral synthesiser will provide all of the sounds you'll need. A multitimbral synthesiser is one that can play several musical parts at once, and when used in conjunction with a sequencer each "part" of the multitimbral synth can be used to play back one musical part. For example, you might have a couple of sequencer tracks dedicated to strings, one to horns, one to percussion and one to woodwind.

the sequenced score

In some ways, the sequencer is better than the written score, inasmuch as it can play back a part exactly as you played it in the first place. It doesn't have to "quantise" everything to equal subdivisions of a musical bar, as the written score does - although it can, if you want it to - and, just like the written score, if you're not happy with something you've done, you don't have to start from scratch; you can just erase the unwanted notes and "write" in new ones.

When examining the way in which a musician composes using a sequencer, it's easy to see that it's not that different from the way in which a traditional composer works. Both types of composer are likely to edit their compositions to some degree before they're entirely happy with them, and both will bring in performers to play the finished composition. It doesn't really matter whether the finished piece is played by a bank of synths or by a hired orchestra whose role is simply to reproduce the composer's original work as faithfully as possible.

I'm a firm believer that electronic composition is as legitimate as any other form of composition, and if you have the talent to write a major symphonic work using a sequencer and a rack of synthesisers, you can always have a real orchestra play it for you later. Indeed, if you have access to a computer-based sequencer with score-printing facilities, you can generate a written score directly from your recording.

Now, having covered the philosophical groundwork, it's time to look more closely at the MIDI sequencer.

MIDI and sequencing

It's often convenient to visualise a sequencer as being analogous to a multitrack tape recorder – as having transport controls and a record function – but it is vitally important to keep in mind that what is being recorded is not the sound itself but the electronic equivalent of a musical score. Just as a musical score is a series of instructions to the musicians, a MIDI sequence holds a series of instructions that tells your synths what to play and when to play it, more like the player-piano analogy described earlier. The essential difference is that, with MIDI, the punched paper roll is replaced by computer memory and computer disks capable of controlling numerous different instruments at the same time.

sequencer set-up

In a typical set-up, a master MIDI controller (usually but not invariably a keyboard) is connected to a sequencer via a MIDI cable, and when the sequencer is set to record, any notes played on the keyboard are recorded as MIDI data into whichever sequencer track has been selected for recording. In a simple system, you might have 16 MIDI tracks set up so that each is on a different MIDI channel, and if you feed the MIDI output of the sequencer to a 16-part multitimbral module you can play back all 16 tracks at once. If you only have an eight-part multitimbral module, you can play back only eight different sounds at once, in the same way as a real-life eight-piece ensemble can (generally speaking) play a maximum of only eight

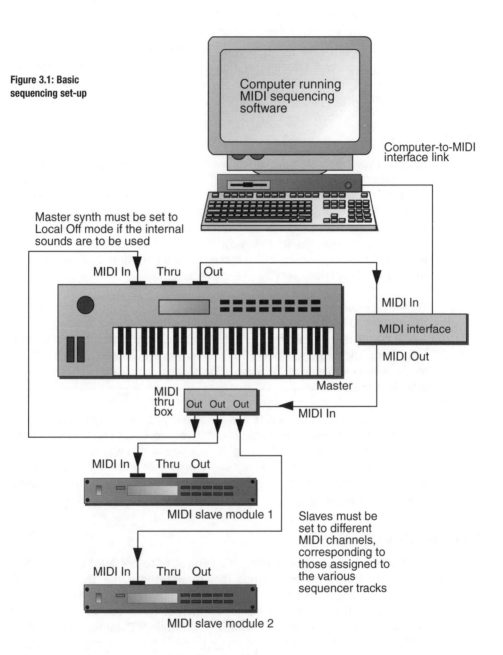

Figure 3.1: Basic sequencing set-up

Computer running MIDI sequencing software

Computer-to-MIDI interface link

Master synth must be set to Local Off mode if the internal sounds are to be used

MIDI In Thru Out

MIDI In

MIDI interface

MIDI Out

Master

MIDI thru box Out Out Out

MIDI In

MIDI In Thru Out

MIDI slave module 1

Slaves must be set to different MIDI channels, corresponding to those assigned to the various sequencer tracks

MIDI In Thru Out

MIDI slave module 2

different lines of music at the same time. If you have a keyboard that includes a synth, as shown in Figure 3.1, simply select Local Off mode and connect it up like any other synth module. Local Off isolates the synth's keyboard from its sound-generating circuitry so that, in effect, it behaves as if it were a separate dumb keyboard and MIDI synth module. This is necessary to prevent MIDI information from being fed around the system in a continuous loop, which usually causes trouble, as is explained in the "Troubleshooting" section in Chapter 9.

metronome

Although you can treat a sequencer simply as a multitrack recorder for MIDI information, its real power lies in the way in which it can modify or edit recorded data. When a recording is made, the sequencer is set to the tempo of the desired recording and a metronome click is made available so that the musical performance may be synchronised with the internal tempo of the sequencer. By working in this way, the MIDI data can be arranged in musically meaningful bars, which makes editing note timing or copying and moving whole sections very easy and precise.

For music incorporating tempo changes, it's possible to enter a new tempo at any bar and beat location, although some budget sequencers may impose a limit on the number of times that the tempo can be changed in each song. More sophisticated sequencers may even have a graphic tempo-editing mode where you can draw curves or slopes to create smooth tempo increases or decreases.

If you don't want to be tied to tempo at all, you can simply turn off the metronome click and play as you would if you were just playing into a tape recorder. The practical disadvantage of working in this way is that you can't use the internal beat and bar structure to plan your edits, and you can't use the quantise function, so the timing of your performance will be quite independent of the sequencer's internal tempo clock.

tracks and channels

At this point in the proceedings, it's very easy to get MIDI channels and sequencer tracks mixed up, but they're not the same thing at all. A sequencer track is simply something on which to record one layer of your composition, but the MIDI information in that track can be on any MIDI channel you want it to be. A track can even contain MIDI information relating to two or more MIDI channels, although to avoid confusion most of the time a single track records data on a single channel.

It's also possible to have several different tracks, all recording MIDI data set to the same channel. For example, if you're recording a complicated drum part, you might want to put the bass and snare drum on one track, the cymbals and hi-hats on another and any tom fills on yet another. All of the drum sounds may be on the same MIDI channel, but because they're on different tracks they're effectively recorded as different layers. Not only does this make the parts easier to play, but it also makes them less confusing to edit. Figure 3.2 shows the Arrange page of a popular computer-based sequencing package, showing the layout of the tracks and the way in which recorded sequences are represented.

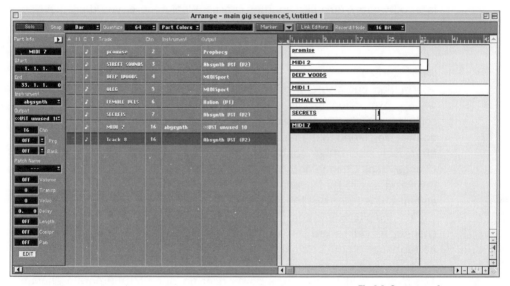

Fig 3.2: Sequencer Arrange page

rechannelling

On early sequencers, every time you wanted to record a part on a different MIDI channel, you had to select a new MIDI channel on your master keyboard. This was a tedious task when you were constantly wanting to hop from one music part to another, so to get around this problem modern sequencers convert the incoming MIDI data to the appropriate channel for the track on which you're recording. This is known as *rechannelling*. To use a postal analogy, the sequencer intercepts the MIDI messages as they come in, readdresses them by changing their MIDI channels and then sends them on to their new destinations. This is another feat that's accomplished without any intervention on behalf of the user, and it makes life very easy because, once you've finished recording one track, all you need to do is select the next one and play. It also ensures that you hear the right sound playing as you record each part.

cut, copy and paste

The remaining capabilities of a MIDI sequencer bear more resemblance to a word processor than anything else. Like a word processor, you can delete or replace wrong characters – musical notes, in this case – and if you want to use the same phrase more than once, you can copy it and paste exact copies into new locations so you don't have to key in the same information time and time again. For example, if a song has the same structure for each chorus, you need play the chorus only once and then copy it to any bar location where you'd like another chorus. What's more, you don't have to copy all the tracks; you could simply copy sections of the drum track, or perhaps the keyboard pad part.

We've already seen that MIDI information comprises not just note information but also controller data from modulation wheels, pitch-bend wheels, expression pedals and so on. Unless you deliberately filter out certain types of MIDI data (and indeed some sequencers have the facility to do this), you'll find that your sequencer captures velocity, pitch, modulation, aftertouch and other controller information, as well as MIDI Program Change, Bank Change and Note On and Off messages. A useful trick when recording a part that needs a lot of complicated pitch bending or vibrato added to it is to record the part straight on one track and then record the vibrato and pitch-bend controller data on another track set to the same MIDI channel. As you record the controller-data track, you'll hear it affecting the performance on the original track.

This may be a little early for a power-user tip, but a MIDI Program Change message recorded during the count-in period of a track will ensure that the synth being used for that track switches to the correct patch before playing commences. However, you can also insert a Program Change command partway through a track, if you want the sound to change for, say, a solo. This is the orchestral equivalent of writing a message on the score at a certain bar number to tell a violin player to put down his violin and play the next part on a flute! This isn't something you'd usually do in real life, of course, but a MIDI module is equally proficient on all instruments, and as yet MIDI modules don't have a trade union!

A sequencer track must also be told which synthesiser sound it is expected to control, so in addition to the MIDI channel (which tells it which instrument or part of a multitimbral instrument it is controlling) it is also necessary to enter the program number of the patch you want to hear and, if the synthesiser supports MIDI Bank Change messages, to tell it in which bank the sound is located. For this reason, it helps to photocopy the relevant patch lists from your synthesiser manuals and pin them to the wall close to your sequencer.

playback

When your MIDI sequence is played back, the sequencer transmits the MIDI information to the receiving synth in exactly the same order and with the same timing as you originally played it, although you can change the tempo after recording without affecting the pitch (unlike recording into a tape recorder, where you're dealing with sound rather than MIDI data). If you're still not sure why the pitch doesn't increase as the tempo goes up, think back to the orchestra-and-score analogy – if the conductor asks for a piece to be played faster, the orchestral instruments don't change in pitch. Similarly, if you pedal a pianola faster, the paper roll will be moving faster but the piano's tuning will remain the same.

In reality, MIDI does has a finite timing resolution, because the computer has to work to an internal timing routine based on an electronic clock, but in practice MIDI is far more accurate than a typical human performer and is capable of resolving a bar of music into at least 960 time divisions and frequently more.

editing

On the Edit page of a typical sequencer, you can change the value, start time, length and velocity of any of the notes you've played, or you can build up compositions by entering the notes manually, placing new notes onto the quantise grid in non-real time (ie not against the metronome), rather like writing out manuscript. If you have a package with a score-writing facility, it's also possible to enter notes directly onto the stave itself, almost as though you were jotting notes onto manuscript paper. The non-real-time entry of note information is sometimes referred to as *step-time entry*.

quantisation

One important feature common to both hardware and software sequencers is the ability to quantise data after recording, and this is a useful feature for those users not possessed of a perfect sense of timing. Essentially, when you opt to quantise something, the timing is changed so that each note you've recorded is pushed to the nearest exact subdivision of a bar. For example, if you're working in 4/4 time and you select 16 as your quantise value, every note moves to the nearest point on an invisible grid dividing the bar into 16 equal time slots.

The quantise function must be used carefully, however, as it can strip all of the feel from some types of music, but on the other hand, if you're writing dance music, where precise timing is essential, it is indispensable. Keep in mind that the quantise function will only produce meaningful results if your original recording was laid down in time with the metronome click of the sequencer. Furthermore, if your timing is really out, you may find that, when you click on the Quantise option, the occasional note snaps to a position one step away from where you originally intended it to go. Quantising pushes notes to the nearest step, and if your poorly timed note was more than half a step out, it will be quantised to the wrong step! Of course, you can move it back to the correct position manually.

The more recent computer-based packages allow you to unquantise data as well as quantise it, but some less advanced software sequencers and a number of hardware sequencers perform what is known as *destructive quantising* (a variety of destructive editing – see below), so it's vital that you keep a copy of the original version if you think that you might need to go back to it.

On more sophisticated sequencers, you'll find a percentage-quantise option that allows the notes you've played to be shifted towards the exact quantise division by a percentage. For example, if you set a 50% quantise value, the note will move to a position halfway between where you actually played it and the position of the nearest quantise division. This is great for tightening up your playing without losing all of the "feel".

Yet another quantise-related function is *swing*, where the quantise grid is moved away from regularly spaced slots to alternating longer and shorter slots. This can be used subtly to add feel or used more aggressively to turn a 4/4 track into a 2/4 track.

destructive and non-destructive

Although quantising is irreversible on some budget sequencers and sequencing packages, all serious systems will allow you to unquantise something at a later time, if required. In fact, many reversible procedures are made possible because the original recorded data isn't actually changed – you only hear changes because the data is processed in real time, as the sequence plays back. Such features are said to be *non-destructive*, because the original performance data is left intact. Although this makes the computer behind your sequencer work harder, it means that you don't burn your bridges behind you when you make changes.

A number of other related non-destructive editing options are often available, including the ability to transpose your music, either as you play or after recording; the ability to make the music louder or softer by adjusting the overall velocity; and the ability to use the same piece of data at different points within the same song. On some systems, you can even compress the dynamic range of your MIDI data to even out the differences between the louder notes and the softer ones.

It may also be possible to delay or advance tracks in relation to each other to change the feel of a piece of music. For example, using a negative delay to pull a snare drum beat forward will help make the track "drive along", whereas delaying the snare will make the beat "lay back". Such operations are frequently achieved by recalculating the note data during playback, but the real data isn't changed, which means that you can always revert to your original performance data if the edits don't work out as expected.

Of course, some edits are *destructive*, inasmuch as the changes are permanent - for example, moving a note to a new time or pitch and erasing or adding a note are destructive edits. However, even in these cases there's usually an Undo function that will allow you to reverse the last procedure carried out, and nothing is truly permanent until you hit Save.

MIDI drums

You can sequence the sounds from your drum machine just as you can the sounds from any other type of MIDI sound module, but you'll have to turn off the drum machine's External MIDI Sync mode first or, every time you turn on your sequencer, the drum machine's internal patterns will start to play. Unlike a conventional instrument, where each note on the keyboard plays a different pitch of the same sound, drum machines place different sounds on different keys, allowing access to many different drum sounds.

Because it's difficult to play a complete drum part in one go via a keyboard, it's common practice to spread the drum part over several sequencer tracks so that you can record, say, your bass and snare first, your hi-hats next and finally your fills. This way of working makes it easy to edit your drum tracks without having to work out which note plays which drum sound. Of course, once the drum part is completed, you can always merge the tracks into one, for convenience. (There's more on drum machines in Chapter 5, "The Basics Of Synthesis".)

types of sequencer

All MIDI sequencers are based on computer technology, but you have a choice of buying a sequencer system that runs on an existing computer (such as an

Atari ST, Apple Mac/PowerMac, IBM PC or Commodore Amiga) or opting for a piece of dedicated hardware that has everything you need built into one box. The two types work in a similar manner; what tends to vary is the way in which the recorded information is displayed and how easily it can be edited. Hardware sequencers also come built into workstation-type keyboard synthesisers and some hardware sequencers have built-in synthesiser modules.

For those who are relatively accomplished players, hardware sequencers offer the benefits of simplicity and convenience, but because they don't have the ability to display as much information as a full-sized computer screen, and because there's no mouse with which to manipulate data, editing is generally less comprehensive and more time consuming that it is on a computer-based system. However, the recording process is simpler, usually requiring you to simply select a track, hit Record and start playing. Another significant benefit of hardware sequencers is that they are more practical in live performance situations, as they are more compact and more rugged than a computer-plus-monitor outfit and you don't have so many things to plug in.

MIDI data storage

It's one thing to record a MIDI sequence, but what do you do with it once it's finished? There's no manuscript paper on which to store your work – instead, your song data is stored as a MIDI song file on a floppy disk or hard drive. Some MIDI sequencers – including all of the computer-based ones – lose their stored information when they're switched off, so it is vital to save your work to disk at regular intervals. Also, computers occasionally crash when you're least expecting them to, so don't wait until you've finished a day's work to save it; save your work every few minutes.

A single floppy disk will hold several songs of average complexity, and most hardware sequencers have a built-in disk drive for this purpose. However, some low-cost models use battery-backed-up memory instead of disks. On these models, once the memory is full, you have to either save your work to a MIDI data filer (which has a built-in disk drive) or erase your old project before you can start a new one. Usually, this kind of sequencer can store only a few songs at a time, so a model with a built-in disk drive is preferable.

computer complexity

Computer-based sequencers are capable of more sophistication than most hardware models, which means that there may be a steeper learning curve. You must also familiarise yourself with the general operation of the computer before trying to tackle a sequencer package. However, this drawback is more than made up for, in my opinion, by the amount of visual feedback available, especially when it comes to creating new song arrangements or editing what you've recorded.

the MIDI interface

With a hardware sequencer, you simply plug your master keyboard into the MIDI In socket, plug a synthesiser into the MIDI Out socket and you're ready to go. Computers, on the other hand, don't usually have MIDI sockets (the obvious exception being the popular but ageing Atari ST), which means that you'll need to buy an external MIDI interface or use one of the synth modules that comes with a MIDI interface built in. Therefore, to use a computer for MIDI purposes, you'll need a MIDI interface and suitable sequencing software. Typical systems will be covered later on.

MIDI interfaces for the older beige Apple Macintosh machines plug into the modem or printer ports on the back of the computer, while PC users need either an interface card that goes inside the computer or an external, plug-in interface. Most PC soundcards include a MIDI interface facility, although it may be necessary to buy a special adapter cable to make use of this.

Most modern computers and all modern Apple Mac models use USB (Universal Serial Buss) to connect MIDI interfaces, which has the advantage that many USB devices can be connected at the same time. These interfaces come with their own driver software, although Mac users who choose a MIDI interface that isn't directly supported by their music-software manufacturer may have to use a copy of Opcode's OMS (Open MIDI System) software to get the interface talking to the sequencer. Hopefully, this system will change to something simpler when Mac OS X support becomes more universal. Modern PCs, meanwhile, may also use USB interfaces.

Note that using generic USB interfaces can sometimes cause MIDI timing inaccuracies, so it's best to buy an interface designed specifically for your music software. For example, the Emagic AMT-8 and Unitor 8 Mk II interfaces (which were current at the time of this revision) use a specially developed system that sends MIDI data to the interface before it's needed and then clocks it out exactly when required, thus avoiding timing problems caused by data bottlenecks. Steinberg utilise a similar system for their Cubase-compatible interfaces.

Note that some controller keyboards have a built-in MIDI interface so that they can connect directly to the computer via USB or a serial port, and the same is true of some sound modules that also double as MIDI interfaces. These are useful in small systems but may be limiting for more sophisticated applications.

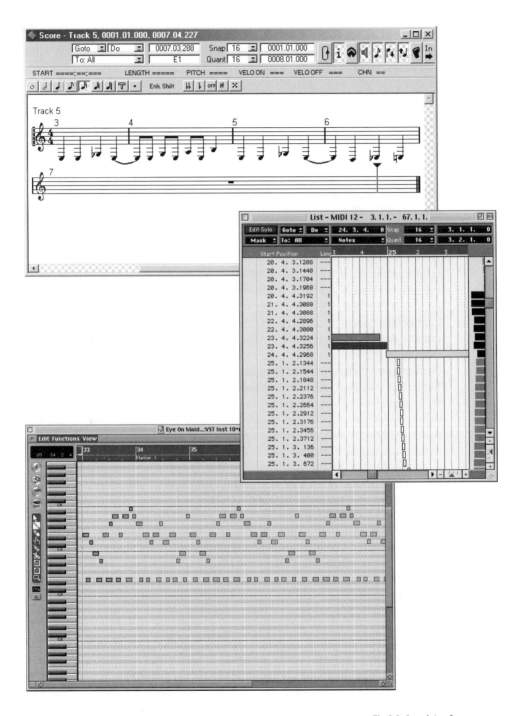

**Fig 3.3: A variety of sequencer
Edit pages**

the user interface

The majority of leading software-sequencing packages have adopted the style of interface pioneered by Steinberg in their Cubase software. This interface is based around a multitrack tape analogy, where the sequencer tracks are depicted as individual strips, one above the other, with bars of music running from left to right. Once a section of a track has been recorded, it shows up as a long brick running from the Record Start locater to the Record End locater. This sequence may then be dragged (with the computer mouse) to a new position in the same track, or it may even be moved to a completely different track so that it plays back with a different sound. Sequence building blocks may also be copied, split into shorter sections or deleted as required.

Most software sequencers comprise a main Arrange page to handle basic recording and track manipulation plus a number of further pages addressing various aspects of editing and, where applicable, scoring. The Record and Playback controls are invariably designed to look something like a tape recorder's transport-control buttons, and the edit pages usually allow you to examine (and change) the recorded data as a list of MIDI events, graphically as a "piano-roll" display or as a conventional music score. Most sequencers also have graphic editing capabilities to manipulate controller information. Figure 3.3 shows some of the edit pages from the Cubase VST and Logic Audio sequencers.

Some software sequencing packages also include sophisticated score-writing facilities that enable you to print out sheet music for your compositions, in which case you'll need a printer that is compatible with both your computer and the software package. However, some musical literacy is useful, because the computer doesn't always interpret what you play in the same way that a trained score writer would.

overview

MIDI sequencers are very powerful tools when it comes to both recording and composing music, and because they have now become so sophisticated there are still a great many things that I haven't discussed here. For example, MIDI allows you to remotely control the volume of your synths - by recording MIDI volume information, you can create automated mixes.

Wonderful though sequencers are, however, they are still far from being perfect. Aside from the inevitable software bugs that creep in, they tend to force you to work in a way that you probably wouldn't if you were playing and composing conventionally. Most insidious is the metronome click to which you have to play along, and although you can turn this off and record freestyle, heedless of bar positions, playing like this means that you won't be able to quantise your data and so won't be able to print out a meaningful score. This means that tempo changes have to be planned rather than intuited, and although software designers are now putting in features to help you in this area – such introducing as rebarring functions – it takes a lot of determination to move away from the fixed-tempo, four-to-the-bar music to which we've all become so accustomed.

Despite the pitfalls mentioned above, however, MIDI sequencing still offers many more advantages than disadvantages, and used creatively it makes many things possible that would have been far too impractical or expensive in the pre-MIDI era. And finally, don't think that sequencing is difficult; once you've made a start and seen how easy it is to handle the basics, you'll wonder why the manuals ever needed to be so thick!

hardware versus software

Software sequencers have several obvious advantages over hardware sequencers, but that doesn't mean that they're better; it all depends on what facilities you need and whether you want your sequencer to be portable. The main pros of software sequencers are as follows:

- They have a good visual interface.

- They have more comprehensive editing facilities.

- You can still use the computer for other purposes.

- You're not tied to one manufacturer for software upgrades – if somebody comes out with a better program, you can always move over to it.

- Most computer sequencers support multiple MIDI output ports via a special multiport MIDI interface (see the section on "MIDI Ports" later in this chapter). This means that you're not restricted to 16 MIDI channels. A typical system will provide six output ports, giving you up to 96 MIDI channels to work with. In contrast, the majority of hardware sequencers support only one or two MIDI output ports.

- The most popular sequencer software packages now allow you to transfer song data from one computer platform to another and, in some case, even from one manufacturer's software sequencer to another's.

- Professional-standard score printing is available on many sequencing packages, requiring either an inexpensive inkjet printer or a laser printer.

Hardware sequencers have their advantages, too, the main ones being listed below:

- They represent a one-box solution to sequencing.

- They're generally more reliable than computers in live situations or when being moved from studio to studio.

- Although they may have fewer editing options than a software sequencer, they also tend to be easier to learn to use.

- You don't have to learn to use a computer before you can begin to learn to operate your sequencing software.

- They involve no installation difficulties or hardware incompatibility problems.

MIDI ports

A basic MIDI interface provides a single MIDI output socket, which means that there are a maximum of 16 MIDI channels available. However, you may want to use two or more multitimbral synthesisers to create a composition with more than 16 parts, or – as is more often the case – you may have several synthesiser modules and want to change from one to the other without having to reconnect MIDI leads. The solution here is to use a MIDI interface with multiple output ports.

You can never have more than 16 MIDI channels, but if you use a multiport MIDI interface in conjunction with compatible sequencing software you can have several different sets of 16 MIDI channels. Within the sequencer, the ports may be designated by number or letter, so that you have 16 channels on port A, another 16 on port B and a further 16 on port C. If a different 16-part multitimbral synth module is connected to each of these ports, you have 48 different sound sources, each of which can be addressed individually by specifying a MIDI channel number plus a port letter – A, B or C. Figure 3.4 overleaf shows how a multiport system might be configured. It is important to realise that you must buy a multiport interface that is supported by the sequencing software you've chosen, and a list of suitable interfaces should be listed in the sequencer manual. If in any doubt at all, consult your dealer.

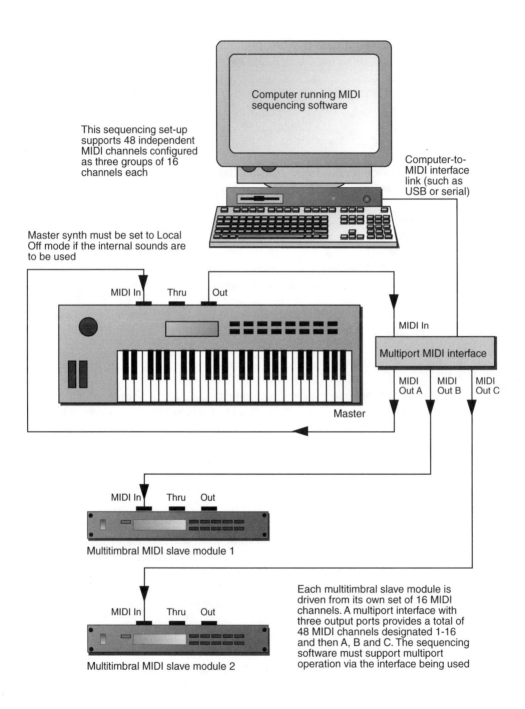

Computer running MIDI sequencing software

This sequencing set-up supports 48 independent MIDI channels configured as three groups of 16 channels each

Computer-to-MIDI interface link (such as USB or serial)

Master synth must be set to Local Off mode if the internal sounds are to be used

MIDI In   Thru   Out

MIDI In

Multiport MIDI interface

MIDI Out A   MIDI Out B   MIDI Out C

Master

MIDI In   Thru   Out

Multitimbral MIDI slave module 1

MIDI In   Thru   Out

Multitimbral MIDI slave module 2

Each multitimbral slave module is driven from its own set of 16 MIDI channels. A multiport interface with three output ports provides a total of 48 MIDI channels designated 1-16 and then A, B and C. The sequencing software must support multiport operation via the interface being used

Fig 3.4: Typical multiport system configuration

Hardware-based sequencers tend to have only one or two output ports, and with no means for expansion this constitutes one of their greatest limitations in a complex MIDI set-up. Hopefully, future designers will realise this problem and build in the opportunity for port expansion or, at the very least, support for external MIDI multiport interfaces.

main sequencer features

So what basic features can you expect from a MIDI sequencer? Obviously, every sequencer is different, but all should be capable of the following core functions.

* **Real-Time Recording** – This is the ability to key in a MIDI performance in real-time from keyboard and record it in much the same way as a tape recorder would. Unlike a tape recorder, though, you can transpose, change tempo, pick a different synth sound and quantise your data after recording. (If you want to use the quantise feature, you have to play to the internal metronome track.)

* **Step-Time Recording** – This means that notes are played in one at a time, rather like typing a letter with one finger! You decide where the notes go and how long they're going to be, after which you can play back your work at any tempo. Most people use mainly real-time recording with occasional recourse to step time when the going gets tough. With a piano-roll type of editing screen, you can also draw your notes directly onto the quantise grid and then use the cursor to stretch them to length. A package with scoring facilities will allow you to place conventional music symbols onto a stave.

* **Synchronisation Facilities** – Although you can make music entirely by sequencer, it's sometimes useful to be able to use a drum machine or tape recorder at the same time. In order to make the tempo of a sequencer synchronise to that of another MIDI device or tape machine (equipped with suitable sync interface), it must be equipped with sync facilities, and these are sometimes omitted on very cheap sequencing software. There are several sync options available, and these are described in Chapter 4, "MIDI And Synchronisation".

* **Multiport Interface Support** – In a complex MIDI system, one set of 16 MIDI channels may not be enough. A multiport MIDI interface, compatible with the sequencing software used, will provide up to eight separate MIDI outputs, each with its own set of 16 MIDI channels. This should not be confused with a simple multi-output interface, where multiple output sockets carry duplicates of the same

MIDI data. These are really just a combination of a single-port interface and a MIDI thru box.

- **File Import** – MIDI sequencers tend to save song data in a proprietary format that other sequencers may not be able to read. Some of the more advanced software systems include the ability to load and import song files from other sequencers, but a more common method of file transfer is to use the SMF (Standard MIDI File) format.

  SMFs were devised to allow complete interchangeability between MIDI song files, and they also make it possible for third-party companies to provide commercial sequencer files that can be read by any machine. However, SMFs can handle only 16 MIDI channels, not multiport data.

  Note: Although the file format may be standard, the floppy-disk formats used by different computers aren't always interchangeable. For example, Atari STs and PCs can read disks of the same format (although the ST can't handle HD [High Density] disks). Older Apple Macs can read PC disks only if they are running either System 7.5 software or upwards or are running a PC-to-Mac file-exchange program such as AccessPC. Today's Mac computers can read PC-formatted disks, but because the internal floppy drive has been discontinued an external USB floppy drive is required.

  Problems may also arise due to the Atari using only DD (Double Density) floppy disks, whereas modern machines use only HD disks. Unless the computer can read DD as well as HD floppies, the data will be unreadable.

  Hardware sequencers may have their own disk formats, in which case MIDI song files can only be loaded if they are stored on disks that have been formatted for the same type of machine.

- **Editing** – A typical sequencer will put a number of editing tools at your disposal to enable you to change your composition after recording, from shifting individual notes to altering entire arrangements and swapping instruments. The main editing operations are listed below:

  Quantisation: This is the ability to move your notes to the nearest accurate subdivision of a bar – for example, 16ths of a bar. The user can set the number of quantise subdivisions in a bar prior to quantising.

  Transposition: Notes can be transposed by any amount without altering their lengths while entire compositions or sections of compositions can easily be shifted to a different key.

Cut, Copy And Paste: Any section of music can be copied to different tracks or to different locations within a song. This is useful for duplicating repeated sections, such as choruses, or for doubling up a line of music on two tracks by copying a part and then assigning the copy to a different instrument sound to that of the original. The Cut command allows you to remove unwanted material.

Mute: Most sequencers allow you to mute tracks so that you can record a number of alternative tracks and then listen only to the ones you want. This is useful if you've just played three solos but you don't know which one was best.

Solo: This command mutes all of the other tracks so that you can hear the solo'd track in isolation.

Cycle: This function simply allows you to loop continually around a specific section of music while you record or edit. This mode is also useful for rehearsing parts prior to recording.

Undo: If provided, the Undo function lets you cancel the last operation. Usually, there is only one level of undo, although these days a few systems provide multiple levels.

MIDI problems

A basic MIDI sequencing set-up starts at your keyboard - it's here that the MIDI information originates. The master keyboard is connected via its MIDI Out to the MIDI In of your MIDI interface or directly to the MIDI In of your hardware sequencer or Atari ST. As mentioned earlier, if your keyboard includes a synth section (in other words, if it makes sounds), switch it to Local Off and patch a MIDI cable from the sequencer's MIDI Out to the keyboard's MIDI In. If you have other MIDI modules in the system, you can daisy-chain them together in any order by feeding the MIDI Thru of one piece of gear to the MIDI In of the next or by using a MIDI thru box.

If you have master keyboard that doesn't have a Local Off facility, consult your sequencer manual to see if you can disable MIDI Thru on the channel to which your master keyboard is set. Most sequencers provide for this eventuality.

Up to three modules can normally be daisy-chained in this way without problems, but longer chains may cause notes to become stuck or missed out altogether, due to corruption of the MIDI signal, in which case you should use a multiple-output MIDI thru box on the output of your sequencer and then feed each module (or short chain of two or three modules) from separate outputs on the thru box.

MIDI timing

As I said, MIDI has a finite timing resolution because the computer's internal timing routine is based on an electronic clock. It is also a serial data protocol, which means that all of the data moves in single file. Because the speed of data transfer is reasonably high, this isn't usually a problem, but if you try to send too much data at once, such as all 16 channels trying to play a large musical chord at exactly the same time, you get a musical traffic jam, causing the notes to be spread out slightly. Using lots of MIDI control data can also slow things up, but the better sequencing software packages give priority to note timing, which helps to reduce the problem.

In most normal musical compositions, MIDI timing shouldn't be an issue, but if problems do arise one tip is to put the most time-sensitive parts (such as drums) onto the first few tracks and less critical parts (such as slow-attack strings) onto the later tracks. This helps because the first track is usually dealt with first, in terms of timing priority.

Timing problems may also occur with older keyboards or instruments that take longer than they should to send out or respond to information. Some early MIDI keyboards took around 10ms to send a MIDI message after a key had been depressed, and a slow module or synthesiser could take the same time to respond to an incoming MIDI note message. Modern instruments are generally better, but some models are still noticeably faster than others.

checklist

If you've connected up your system as described but no sound comes out, here are a few things to check.

• Verify that everything is switched on and that your synth modules are set to Multi or Sequencer mode (assuming that you want to use them multitimbrally). Also, make sure that your synths are set to the same MIDI channels as those on which you're sending data.

• Check your MIDI cable connections and don't rule out the possibility of a faulty MIDI lead. Some modules have combined MIDI Out/Thru sockets, and if this is the case you should ensure that MIDI Thru is enabled. (See the handbook for that particular piece of equipment for details of how to do this.) To help isolate the problem, most sequencers have some form of indication that they're receiving MIDI data, and many modules have a LED or other indicator that blinks when data is being received.

* Check that Omni mode is switched off on all modules. (Poly mode is used most commonly.) If two or more instruments try to play the same part, the chances are that either you've got more than one module set to the same MIDI channel or something's been left set to Omni. If your master keyboard plays its own sounds whenever you try to record on any track or channel, check that Local Off is really set to Off. On some instruments, Local Off reverts to Local On every time you switch on the power.

* If playing a single note results in a burst of sound rather like machine-gun fire, or if you get stuck notes or apparently limited polyphony, the chances are that you have a MIDI loop. In a MIDI loop, MIDI data generated by the master keyboard passes through the sequencer and somehow gets back to the input of the master keyboard, where it starts its round trip all over again, rather like acoustic feedback. This usually happens when you have a keyboard synth as your master keyboard and you've forgotten to select Local Off.

  If you have one of those rare instruments with no Local Off facility, you'll probably find that your sequencer allows you to disable the sequencer MIDI Thru on the channel on which your master keyboard is sending (which most people leave set to channel 1).

  If you're unfortunate enough to have neither facility, all you can do is record with the MIDI In disconnected from your master keyboard and use the sounds from external modules. When you've finished recording, you can, if you wish, reconnect the master keyboard's MIDI In and use it to play back one of the recorded parts or layer it with an existing synth voice.

sequencing with audio

This chapter has concentrated on the MIDI aspect of sequencing, but modern sequencing software invariably integrates MIDI and audio within the same environment. This is clearly a huge advantage because, wonderful though MIDI is, you'll never get it to sing convincing lead vocals. By combining a carefully programmed MIDI arrangement with "real" vocals, guitars and so on, it's possible to create extremely professional-sounding, release-quality recordings. To that end, Chapter 10, "Sequencing With Audio", contains further information about recording in this way, while Chapter 12, "Software Instruments", deals with recording with VST-type plug-ins, a field of endeavour very relevant to the MIDI user.

chapter 4

MIDI and synchronisation

Sequencers with integral hard-disk audio-recording systems offer the most practical way of combining audio with MIDI, but many musicians feel that hardware is more reliable and certainly more controllable for recording audio, so they use hardware for audio and a sequencer for MIDI. In theory, you could simply record your finished MIDI composition onto two or more tracks of a multitrack tape/disk/holographic-ice-cube recorder then add your vocals, guitars and so on, but this isn't the most effective way of working. Multitrack recorders are limited by the number of tracks that they provide – and even though you can bounce (ie combine by mixing) recorded tracks, you lose the opportunity to rebalance, pan or add effects to those tracks that have been bounced.

In the early days of home recording, there was no alternative to recording everything on tape, but the introduction of MIDI sequencing changed all of that. Obviously, you can't use a MIDI-controlled instrument to replace every instrument or sound that you'd normally want to record, but in the context of pop music you can certainly use MIDI drums, bass and keyboard parts as well as samples of instruments such as piano, brass, flute, etc. If you're set on using separate audio-recording hardware, you'll have to find a way of making the sequencer and recorder run in perfect sync with each other. Working in this way, your multitrack recorder can be filled up with real voices and instruments, leaving the sequencer to look after the MIDI part of the performance. All of your sequenced sounds can then be fed into the final mix without them ever having been recorded on multitrack at all, meaning that you can change the sounds on your MIDI instruments right up to the moment before you mix, whereas if you mix your MIDI sequence and record it as audio, there's no way of changing it other than starting again.

When I wrote the first edition of this book, analogue tape recorders were still in common use, and even today they remain popular in some quarters because of their warm, musical sound. A surprising number of professional studios still run two-inch, 24-track analogue tape machines simply because they sound good and aren't subject to some of the catastrophes that beset digital systems (such as unexplained and total data loss!). Also, because they are old technology, analogue tape machines designed for the project studio can be picked up at bargain prices. Unfortunately, they are the least simple of recorders to synchronise with a MIDI set-up, but there is an answer, thanks to Hollywood.

In the movie industry, cine film and magnetic audio tape were originally kept in sync by means of sprocket holes cut into the edges of the film and tape. Both the tape and the film passed over toothed cogs fitted to the same shaft so that, once the two were lined up, they always stayed in sync. We may not rely on sprocketted audio tape in the music industry, but MIDI provides us with a number of ways of doing a similar thing electronically.

time codes

In addition to its ability to transmit note-related information, MIDI is also able to generate a sync code that can be recorded to analogue tape, digital tape or any other audio storage medium by using simple hardware. This basic MIDI timing code was touched on briefly in Chapter 1 and is called *MIDI Clock*. In effect, it constitutes a series of timing pulses that do the same job as the sprocket holes in cine film. One recorder track is used to record the necessary sync code, but in exchange for the sacrifice of one audio track you gain as many virtual tracks as your sequencer and collection of synth/sound modules can provide. For example, if you have an old four-track tape machine working on its own, the most you can get is four tracks, but if you sync a MIDI sequencer to run along with it, you have three tracks left on the tape after recording the time code, plus as many sequencer tracks as your sequencer and synth collection can give you. Figure 4.1 overleaf illustrates this in a set-up containing a cassette four-track recorder. The concept is simple, but to understand more about it, it's necessary to know a little more about MIDI Clock.

MIDI Clock

MIDI sequencers and drum machines have an internal tempo clock, a kind of invisible timing grid on which all notes are placed. Think of it as being like a metronome but one that, instead of giving you four ticks to each 4/4 bar, gives you 386. This MIDI Clock provides the electronic counterpart to the sprockets and gears used in the film industry, allowing two or more pieces of MIDI equipment to be run in perfect synchronisation where one device acts as master (and thus dictates the tempo) and the others function as

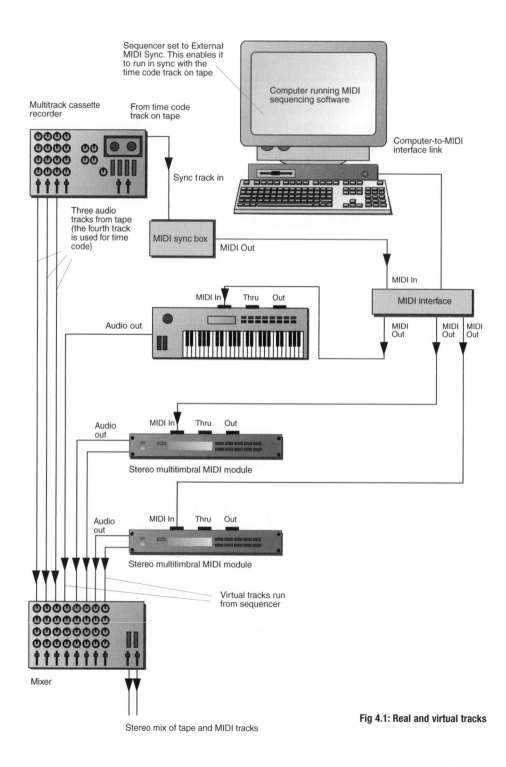

Sequencer set to External
MIDI Sync. This enables it
to run in sync with the
time code track on tape

Computer running MIDI
sequencing software

Multitrack cassette
recorder

From time code
track on tape

Computer-to-MIDI
interface link

Sync track in

Three audio
tracks from tape
(the fourth track
is used for time
code)

MIDI sync box

MIDI Out

MIDI In

MIDI In   Thru   Out

MIDI interface

Audio out

MIDI
Out

MIDI   MIDI
Out   Out

Audio
out

MIDI In   Thru   Out

Stereo multitimbral MIDI module

Audio
out

MIDI In   Thru   Out

Stereo multitimbral MIDI module

Virtual tracks run
from sequencer

Mixer

Stereo mix of tape and MIDI tracks

Fig 4.1: Real and virtual tracks

slaves. For example, by using just MIDI Clock, you can connect two drum machines so that they both run in sync, you can slave a sequencer to a drum machine or you can slave a drum machine to a sequencer, and with the aid of a suitable sync box sequencers may also be synchronised to tape machines. In this kind of set-up, however, because it's difficult to control the speed of a tape recorder precisely, the tape machine is nearly always the master and the sequencer the slave.

In physical terms, MIDI Clock is a part of the data stream coming out of the master device's MIDI Out socket. No additional cables or connections are needed, just a regular MIDI lead. The MIDI Clock data mingles invisibly with the MIDI note data. The MIDI Out of the master links to the MIDI In of the slave. The master machine constantly sends out MIDI Clock data at the tempo set by the user, regardless of whether it is playing or not, so that any slave devices plugged into it will know exactly the tempo at which to start running when they receive a MIDI Start command. (See "Start, Stop And Continue" in Chapter 1.)

external sync

When two MIDI devices are synchronised, the master unit is set to Internal Clock mode and the slave machine to External Clock mode so that, whenever the master machine is started, the slave starts with it, automatically, and runs in perfect sync with it. This is all very well if you simply want to run a drum machine and a sequencer together, but how does it work with a tape recorder?

What's needed is a device that makes a sequencer set to External Sync (Slave) mode think that it's hooked up to a MIDI master device when it's actually connected to a tape machine. Not surprisingly, such a device is called a MIDI-to-tape sync unit.

tape sync

Audio recorders can't record MIDI signals directly, so the job of a MIDI-to-tape sync unit is to convert MIDI Clock timing data into a form that can be recorded as an audio-frequency signal. In practice, there are several systems to choose from, although all convert the MIDI pulses into bursts of high-pitched sound that can be recorded onto tape, which is achieved by the unit switching between two different frequencies. Although this is quite transparent to the user and operating it requires no prior knowledge of its workings, it's interesting to note that this method is known as Frequency Shift Keying, or FSK for short.

A MIDI FSK sync box works something like this: After composing your sequence and deciding upon the final tempo of the piece, a MIDI-to-tape sync unit is connected between the sequencer and tape machine. The sequence is then played back while the time code is recorded onto tape, with the tempo of the song determining the speed of the MIDI Clock and hence the tempo embedded in the time code.

When playing back, the tape is run, the time-code track is played back through the MIDI-to-tape sync unit and its MIDI Out is patched to the sequencer's MIDI In, with the sequencer set to External MIDI Sync mode. As soon as the tape runs from the start of the song, the sequencer will start in sync with it.

On the whole, this system (shown in Figure 4.2) works fine, but with the simplest sync boxes it works only if you start at the beginning of the song each time, as otherwise the MIDI device has no way of finding out whereabouts in the song it's supposed to be. This is clearly unsatisfactory if you want to work on a section a long way from the start of your song, but that is easily solved by using a smarter form of MIDI sync box.

smart FSK

Smart FSK is a distinct improvement over dumb FSK systems, and it works in connection with a piece of hidden MIDI information known as the MIDI Song Position Pointer, or SPP. Again, SPPs are invisible to the user, and as most modern MIDI equipment recognises them you can forget all about them and let the computer or drum machine do the worrying. In effect, SPPs let MIDI devices know exactly where in a song they're supposed to be. Their great benefit is that you can start the tape anywhere and your slave sequencer will sync up at exactly the right place in the song.

A practical advantage of all MIDI Clock-based sync systems is that the tempo of the music is directly related to the clock rate of the sync code, and the sync code is created from the tempo of the original sequence. This means that any tempo changes in the original sequence will be followed automatically when the tape is run, and if the tape is sped up then the code speeds up with it, which in turn speeds up the sequencer. Unless you need anything more sophisticated, Smart FSK is the most worry-free and least costly way to achieve sequencer-to-tape sync. Of course, it may also be used to sync a drum machine to tape, if you don't have a sequencer.

Smart FSK MIDI-to-tape sync units are relatively inexpensive and they're made by a number of manufacturers, but if you can afford a unit with a built-

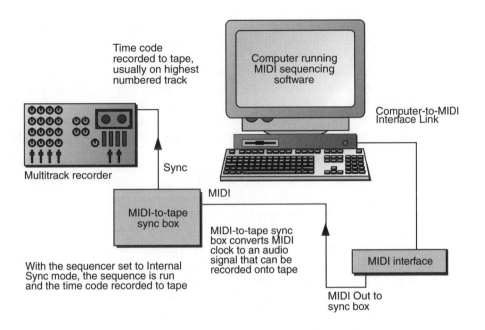

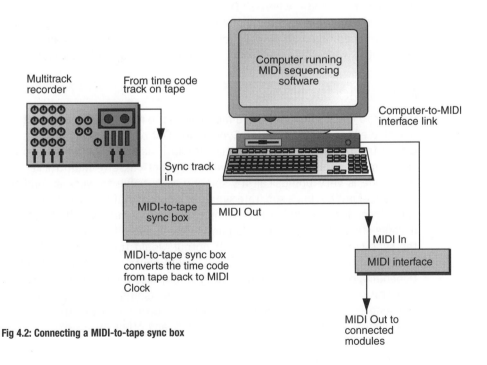

Fig 4.2: Connecting a MIDI-to-tape sync box

in MIDI merge function, it's worth paying the extra. The reason for this is that, if you don't have a MIDI merge facility, the MIDI In of your sequencer is occupied with reading time code, so you can't record any new MIDI sequencer parts while the sequencer and tape machine are sync'd up. However, if your sync box has a MIDI merge input, you can plug your master keyboard into it and record new MIDI parts while the tape and sequencer are running in sync. This can be important if you're playing a part that relies on you being able to hear recorded vocals or a guitar solo to get the right feel.

time code and noise reduction

Some types of tape-noise reduction can affect the reliability of time codes, so when using them it's best to switch off the noise reduction on your sync track, if at all possible. If the multitrack has a dedicated sync input and output, these will have been arranged to bypass the noise reduction and any EQ controls, thus allowing a reliable recording to be made. You may need to experiment with the code level, too, since, if it's recorded too high, it could bleed through to the adjacent tracks, making it audible in the final mix. Conversely, if recorded at too low a level, it might not be read reliably, causing the sequencer to hiccup or stop.

As a very general rule, DBX noise-reduction systems have the greatest effect on time code, whereas Dolby C doesn't seem to affect it at all. Unfortunately, some very early multitrackers only allow the noise reduction to be switched on or off globally for all four channels, which means that, if you want to work with a sync code, you'll have to put up with more tape hiss.

multitrack sync facilities

In order to use a sync unit with a multitrack tape machine, it's vital that the machine either has a dedicated Sync In and Out or that you can access the output from your sync track directly without it having to be added into the stereo mix (as might be the case with a budget cassette multitracker), as time code is very unmusical! It's sometimes possible to work around the problem of not having a separate sync-track output, but this usually involves some form of compromise. For example, with a tape machine that has only a single stereo output, you could pan the three audio tracks to the left and the sync code to the right. The left output would then contain all of the audio in mono while the right output would contain only the sync code. Depending on the machine you're using, it may also be possible to route the sync track to the outside world via one pre-fade (sometimes called *foldback*) aux send and turning the channel fader right down. Of course, this prevents that particular aux send from being used for any other purpose.

The MIDI Clock sync system described so far operates on the basis of the tempo of the song running in the controlling device (usually a sequencer or a drum machine), but there are alternative sync systems that work not on tempo but on absolute time.

SMPTE

SMPTE (pronounced "simptee") is an altogether more sophisticated synchronisation system, originally developed for the film industry but now also used in many musical applications. If you need to synchronise a sequencer to a video tape or film, some knowledge of SMPTE time code is essential and, as with MIDI Clock, a hardware interface box of some kind is required. Many of the more elaborate modern multiport MIDI interfaces have built-in support for both SMPTE and MIDI Time Code (which will be covered shortly).

SMPTE isn't directly related to MIDI in any way but is instead based on elapsed time rather than bars and beats, as is the case with MIDI Clock. SMPTE is unnecessarily sophisticated for syncing MIDI sequencers to tape machines, but if your model of sequencer has a dedicated, low-cost SMPTE sync unit available for it (SMPTE support is built into a number of MIDI interfaces), all of the complications will be taken care of for you.

So why is SMPTE more complicated than MIDI Clock? Well, because SMPTE time code is related to absolute time, not to tempo, it's rather like having an invisible ruler printed on your tape marking out hours, minutes, seconds and film frames. For example, the SMPTE readout for one hour, ten minutes, 30 seconds and eleven frames would look like this: 01:10:30:11. Because there's no tempo information embedded in the time code itself, a conversion has to take place somewhere along the line, either by the computer running the sequencing software or by the microprocessor inside the SMPTE-to-MIDI sync box. To convert the SMPTE frame rate to tempo requires a bit of basic maths, but any modern sequencer with SMPTE sync capability will handle this for you quite automatically. On earlier systems, you had to key in a tempo map telling the sync box or sequencer when the song started, its tempo and exactly where any tempo changes were. This was obviously tedious, especially if the music involved lots of tempo changes.

Fortunately, most modern software-based sequencers handle SMPTE sync without you having to decide anything other than when the song starts in relation to the SMPTE time code. However, it's important to note that some low-cost sequencer manufacturers leave out synchronisation facilities altogether to save on cost.

SMPTE frames

Because of the different film and TV frame rates used around the world, SMPTE is available in several frame formats, the most common being 30 frames per second (for US TV), 25fps (for European TV) and 24fps (for film). Strictly speaking, we should use the term SMPTE/EBU to cover all of the US and European formats, but most users abbreviate it to plain old SMPTE anyway. There's also a format called *drop frame*, which is used when converting one picture format to another, but this is rarely used for musical work and needn't be discussed further here. As a rule, you set your sync format to the local TV frame rate and leave it set that way, unless a video- or film-related project comes along that demands something different.

MTC

Unless you're planning to work with video and film, you're more likely to find yourself using MTC (MIDI Time Code). Most digital recorders generate MTC as standard and some remote control systems – such as the Alesis BRC (used to control ADAT tape and hard-disk recorders) – can output MIDI Clock, MTC and SMPTE. Because of its reliance on tempo, MIDI Clock isn't often used today in serious sync applications, although it still offers the most convenient means of locking sequencers to drum machines for those times when both devices need to follow the same tempo.

MTC follows the same format as SMPTE in that it is independent of musical tempo and expresses elapsed time in hours, minutes, seconds and frames, and all of the common SMPTE variants have an MTC equivalent. Standard MIDI Clock sync doesn't include any positional information – it's rather like the sprocket holes in cine film – so if a sync pulse gets lost, the sequencer will happily follow along one pulse late. SMPTE, on the other hand, comprises a continuous stream of positional data, so if a short section of code gets lost or corrupted, the system knows exactly where it's supposed to be the next time a piece of valid code is read. The better SMPTE and MTC sync systems incorporate what's know as *flywheel sync*, which enables them to run past short sections of damaged code, such as those that occur due to drop-out on analogue tapes (a loss of signal caused by damage to or flaws in the tape coating).

MTC also includes positional information, but because it has to share the MIDI data highway with other information, its data is sent in short bursts – four to each SMPTE frame. It takes eight of these "quarter-frame" messages to carry enough data to make up one complete set of location data, which means that the receiving MIDI device must read two frames of code before it knows where it's supposed to be. Technically, MTC can't pass on positional information as quickly or as accurately as SMPTE, but for practical tape-to-MIDI sync applications a little clever software writing from the sequencer designers ensures that there's no practical difference.

MTC and timing

If MTC has a weakness, it's that its position in the MIDI data stream can get jostled about when a lot of data is being sent, and if you have a multiport MIDI interface it's usually best to make sure that the port carrying the MTC signal isn't clogged with other MIDI data. If the MIDI data stream is running close to capacity, the MTC data may arrive a little behind schedule, which has the effect of introducing a small amount of timing jitter. In really adverse situations, this may be serious enough to be noticeable.

Fortunately, the major software sequencing packages support MTC very effectively and do all of the hard work for you, giving MTC timing priority. Furthermore, all of the current major sequencing packages handle MTC sync quite transparently, producing and storing a tempo map as part of the song file with nothing for the user to do but decide upon a start time in relation to the time code.

To make use of MTC sync with a traditional tape recorder, a hardware sync box is required to convert the MTC MIDI signal into an FSK signal that can be recorded onto tape. Such devices are available separately, but it's also possible to buy multiport MIDI interfaces with MTC sync capabilities built into them. However, as the use of analogue tape machines continues to decline, this becomes less relevant because, as mentioned earlier, most tapeless recording systems have the ability to generate MTC directly, in which case all that you need to sync up a sequencer is a MIDI cable.

striping tape

Before you can do any work with SMPTE or MTC, the code must be recorded onto tape – a process known as *striping* (and be sure that the correct frame rate is selected before you do this). Then, once the tape is striped, a start time must be entered into your sequencing software so that it knows where to start playing in relation to the code on tape. Many SMPTE and MTC systems don't work reliably when crossing the 00:00:00:00 "midnight hour", so it's quite common to enter a time offset when striping the tape (one hour is an easy amount to deal with) so that, when you start the tape a few seconds before the song begins, you don't go back across this threshold. Failure to observe this can result in a loss of sync or even a total freezing of the system. With most sequencer packages, once you've set up a SMPTE start time, the tempo map is created automatically and stored along with the song data when you save to disk. If the tempo is modified at any stage, the tempo map will be modified the next time you save your song.

Unlike MIDI Clock, when using MTC or SMPTE you don't have to create your sequence before recording the code onto tape. FSK, on the other hand, requires you to have programmed your sequence – as far as its length and tempo go, at least – before you start work. Furthermore, if you decide that a tempo change is in order, you'll have to re-stripe your tape with a new FSK code, whereas with SMPTE or MTC all you have to do is create a new tempo map.

MIDI Machine Control

MMC (MIDI Machine Control) is a means of sending "transport"-type commands via MIDI to start and stop machines recording and, in some cases, to arm tracks ready for recording and cause a remote machine to go into Record mode. Using MMC, you can control a remote recorder entirely from your sequencer, even though that recorder may actually be the master component of the system and the sequencer is the slave. When you send an MMC Play message on a sequencer, both the sequencer and the remote device start playing, but as soon as the sequencer detects time code from the remote recorder it locks to it and thereafter functions as a slave in the usual way.

key points

- The master machine in a sync system must be set to Internal Sync mode, while any slaves should be set to External Sync.

- When a MIDI Clock-based code is being recorded to tape, the sequencer is the master, but when it comes to playing back the code the sequencer becomes the slave and so should be set to External Sync.

- With any MIDI Clock-based synchronising system, it's not possible to alter the sequencer tempo once the code has been recorded to tape; once the sequencer is sync'd up, it will always play at the tempo of the code on tape, regardless of any new changes.

- With SMPTE and MTC, the time code is striped onto the tape before the session starts. You can even stripe the entire tape with code in one go and then enter the appropriate start time for each song into the sequencer software.

- Because SMPTE/MTC carries only real, absolute information, a tempo map must be created in order that the sequencer's tempo may be calculated. Most contemporary sequencing software packages manage this task automatically and save the tempo map as part of the song file.

- Analogue-tape noise-reduction systems can cause synchronisation codes to work unreliably. Many cassette multitrackers are equipped with a dedicated sync option that defeats the noise reduction on the track onto which the code is being recorded (which is usually the highest-numbered track). If no such facility is available, try setting the EQ to its flat position and experiment with different recording levels to determine which provides the most reliable operation. Most Dolby noise-reduction systems can be used with sync codes, although DBX often proves troublesome unless bypassed.

chapter 5

the basics of synthesis

I 've always been fascinated by synthesisers, even though it's true that the more you learn about them, the more obvious their limitations become. Certainly they still fall rather short of their original concept, which was to be able to imitate any conceivable sound. Having a keyboard instrument that could emulate any known instrument, produce an infinite range of new sounds and respond to the player's touch like a "real" musical instrument is an admirable goal, but the more you learn about the mechanics of sound, the further away this goal seems. Nevertheless, electronic designers have spawned a varied range of complex and fascinating instruments, all of which come under the generic heading of *synthesisers*.

The forerunner to the synthesiser was the electronic organ, which, unlike true acoustic instruments, can produce only fixed-level sounds that are tonally constant throughout their duration. What's more, the note produced by an organ starts abruptly when a key is pressed and stops abruptly when that key is released again. In contrast, real-life instruments are far more complex - their sound may start abruptly, or it may increase gradually, like that of a gently bowed violin or 'cello. Furthermore, the level of the note may decay, as is the case with a plucked string, and the harmonic structure may also change as the note evolves.

To approach synthesis in a meaningful way, it's important to know something about the fundamental principles of sound and how these principles apply to traditional musical instruments.

sound

Sound is produced by airborne vibrations, and these impinge on the human ear and are translated by the human brain into the sensation that we know as hearing. The textbook analogy of sound has us observing the ripples when a stone is thrown into a pond - the ripples spread outwards in a circular fashion and their level decreases as the distance from the source increases.

Indeed, sound is simply that – ripples in the air – and a human hearing system in good condition can register frequencies of between 50 ripples per second and 20,000 ripples per second. With sound, each ripple is known as a *cycle*, and the official SI measurement for cycles per second is *hertz*, or *Hz* for short. Multiples of 1,000 cycles are known as *kilohertz*, or *kHz*.

The higher the frequency of vibration that causes the sound, the higher the perceived musical pitch, and a doubling in pitch produces a rise of one octave. But there's a lot more to sound than mere pitch. For instance, what is it that gives each instrument its unique tonal character? And why does a flute playing middle C sound totally different to a piano playing the same note?

waves

The simplest sound is a pure tone, which means that only a single frequency is present. If the changes in air pressure caused by a pure tone were plotted onto a piece of graph paper, the result would be a sine wave, as shown in Figure 5.1. The electrical output of a microphone picking up this signal would also be a sine wave, but in this case the air vibrations would be represented by a sinusoidal modulation of voltage (ie one resembling a sine curve).

A continuous sine wave sounds like a whistle or test tone - every cycle of the waveform is identical, there's no variation in level and, as a sound, it's musically uninspiring. A continuous, pure tone possesses a fundamental pitch, a level and nothing else. In contrast, real-life sounds are infinitely

Fig 5.1: A pure-tone sine wave

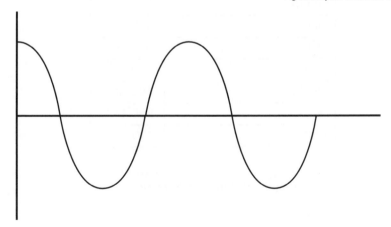

A sine wave generates a pure tone at a single frequency

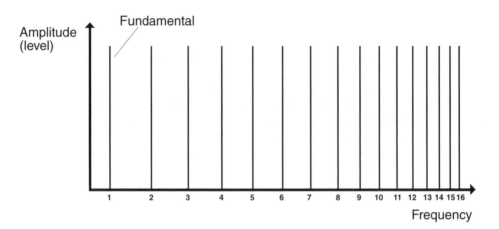

Harmonic series for the note A (110Hz) as
far as the tenth harmonic. Note that all of
the harmonics are shown as being of
equal amplitude. This would not be the
case for naturally generated sounds

Harmonic	Frequency
Fundamental (A)	110Hz
Second	220Hz
Third	330Hz
Fourth	440Hz
Fifth	550Hz
Sixth	660Hz
Seventh	770Hz
Eighth	880Hz
Ninth	990Hz
Tenth	1100Hz

Each harmonic in the series is a whole-
number multiple of the fundamental

Fig 5.2: The harmonic series (odd and even)

more complex – instead of being made up of single tones, they are comprised of a whole series of tones known as *harmonics* and *overtones*. Harmonics are simply other frequencies present in a sound that are exact multiples of the basic or *fundamental* pitch.

Most musically meaningful sounds generally exhibit a strong fundamental frequency, which determines the musical pitch or note, and this is accompanied by a series of harmonics that are higher in frequency (pitch) but generally lower in level than the fundamental. As stated, harmonics occur at exact multiples of the fundamental frequency; if they are even multiples, they are called even harmonics, whereas if they are odd multiples, they are called odd harmonics. Figure 5.2 shows how the harmonic series is constructed.

Sounds may also contain frequencies that aren't directly related to the fundamental frequency, and these are known as *non-harmonic overtones*. Sounds such as bells contain many such complex overtones, but even instruments that are perceived to have a single pitch often contain some overtones.

timbre

The character or timbre of a sound is determined by two key factors: the harmonics and non-harmonic overtones that make up that sound and the way in which these components change in both level and pitch as the sound evolves. In other words, most sounds can be viewed as dynamic events, not as continuous or constant. This is in direct contrast to the electric organ, which tends to produce notes with the same harmonic structure from start to finish.

The way in which the levels of the different harmonics and overtones change with time determines the so-called *envelope* of the sound, and this has a profound bearing on how we interpret what we hear. For example, a percussive sound starts very suddenly, but then the vibrational energy dies away because no new energy is being applied to sustain the sound. It follows, then, that a typical percussive sound will start suddenly and then decay, as shown in Figure 5.3a overleaf.

A bowed sound, on the other hand, may build up relatively slowly, as the energy driving the sound is being applied over a period of time, not in one hit. When the driving energy – the bow – is removed, the string vibrations will decay in much the same way as a percussive sound, as the energy emitted by the vibrating string is gradually absorbed by the instrument and the surrounding air. Figure 5.3b shows the envelope produced by a typical bowed string.

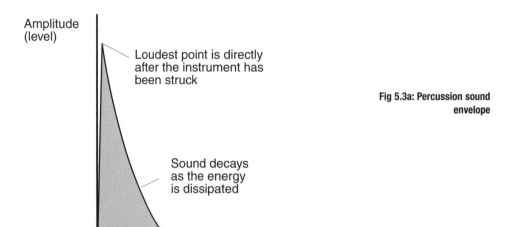

Amplitude
(level)

Loudest point is directly
after the instrument has
been struck

Fig 5.3a: Percussion sound
envelope

Sound decays
as the energy
is dissipated

Time

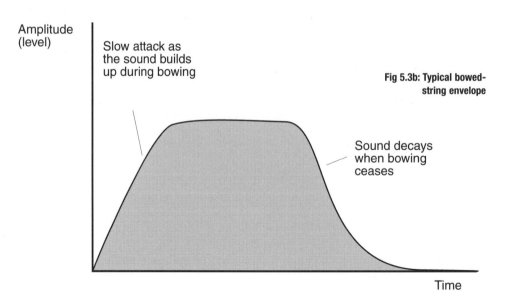

Amplitude
(level)

Slow attack as
the sound builds
up during bowing

Fig 5.3b: Typical bowed-
string envelope

Sound decays
when bowing
ceases

Time

When most natural sounds – including acoustic instrument sounds – decay, the higher-frequency harmonics decay faster than the low-frequency components because high-frequency energy is dissipated more rapidly than low-frequency energy. Knowing this can be useful when it comes to synthesising natural sounds.

additive synthesis

To synthesise accurately a "real" sound, it would be necessary to recreate all of the harmonics and overtones present in the sound in question, set their relative levels, apply a separate envelope to each harmonic and then manipulate the frequency of each of them to emulate the way in which they behave in real life. What's more, there would need to be some way of controlling the sound so that it changed in accordance with a user's playing technique, exactly as a "real" instrument does.

Building a sound from scratch in this way is known as *additive synthesis*, and while in theory it is technically possible, in practice it is extremely difficult and expensive to implement. Modern resynthesis techniques can build up sound from its constituent frequencies, but this is a rather specialised subject and not very relevant to the way in which most affordable synthesisers work. Of course, all of this can change overnight, as breakthroughs in technology are frequently followed by dramatic price reductions.

Despite the apparent impracticality of additive synthesis, there are methods of approximating the behaviour of real instruments, and although early attempts in this field didn't produce a particularly accurate representation of the original sounds, they did have a certain musicality. No such instrument yet built satisfies all needs, however, and it can be argued that the relative strengths and weaknesses of modern instruments are also what makes them interesting.

analogue synthesis

Mainstream synthesis started with the analogue synthesiser, so called because it relies entirely on analogue circuitry in which oscillators, filters and envelope shapers are controlled by electrical waveforms and voltages. It isn't necessary to know how any of these work in detail, but it's helpful to be able to visualise the process of synthesis as a series of simple building blocks.

Analogue circuitry doesn't posses the inherent stability of modern digital designs, so parameters such as tuning on analogue instruments tend to drift a little, especially in response to significant changes in room temperature, but the subtle detuning effects that this causes are thought to contribute to the warm, organic sound produced by analogue instruments. Although few modern instruments are based on analogue circuitry, many attempt to emulate it by digital means, and it's a valuable exercise to look at the basic building blocks of a typical analogue synthesiser, as they're almost identical in concept to the components inside modern digital instrument.

To the musician brought up on modern polyphonic instruments (ie those that can play multiple notes simultaneously), it might seem curious that, originally, analogue synths were all monophonic and had no velocity sensitivity. In other words, the note produced was always at the same level, no matter how hard the key was struck, and you could only ever produce one note at a time.

subtractive synthesis

Analogue synthesis is a form of subtractive synthesis because the process starts out with a harmonically rich sound and filters are then used to reduce the level of unwanted harmonics. Subtractive synthesis is therefore very much like sculpture - you take a large block of material and then trim away anything that isn't needed until the block is transformed into a statue.

Unfortunately, the original tools available for sonic sculpting were far less precise than the chisels and scrapers used by a sculptor. Indeed, subtractive synthesis is something like trying to create a sculpture using a clumsily wielded shovel! In other words, the available tools are not sufficiently refined to enable us to produce a sculpture that captures anything like the detail of real life. At best, subtractive synthesis produces a caricature of the sound being imitated, although with some types of sounds the simulation can sometimes be more attractive than the real thing.

Modern S&S (Sample and Synthesis) instruments also work on the subtractive principle, but instead of starting out with electronically generated waveforms, they use electronic samples (short recordings stored in microchips) of real instrumental sounds that are then further modified by filters and envelope shapers.

building blocks

Any subtractive synthesiser can be thought of as comprising a number of quite separate building blocks that can be wired together in a variety of ways, depending on the desired result. Indeed, the early modular analogue systems were precisely that - arrangements of electronic circuitry in separate sections that could be linked together with short patch cables. The

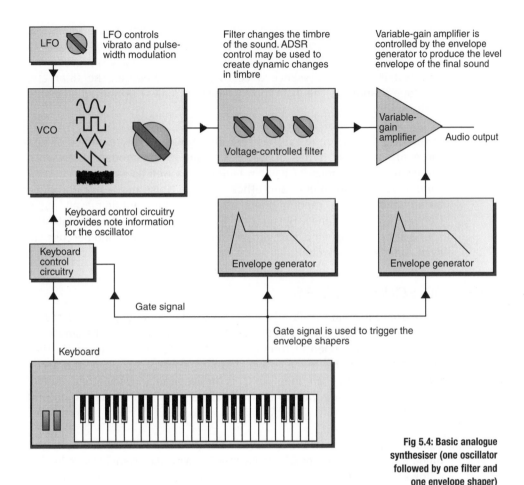

LFO controls vibrato and pulse-width modulation

Filter changes the timbre of the sound. ADSR control may be used to create dynamic changes in timbre

Variable-gain amplifier is controlled by the envelope generator to produce the level envelope of the final sound

Keyboard control circuitry provides note information for the oscillator

Gate signal is used to trigger the envelope shapers

Fig 5.4: Basic analogue synthesiser (one oscillator followed by one filter and one envelope shaper)

result often looked like a madwoman's knitting, but the sonic results could be wonderfully abstract. The term *patch* as it applies to synthesiser sounds originated from these early patch-cord systems.

The basis of any subtractive synthesiser is the oscillator that produces the raw sound, the block from which the sonic statue will be sculpted. In the case of an analogue synthesiser, the raw materials are simple repeating waveforms, whereas a modern synthesiser might use a recording of a real sound as its starting point. A very basic analogue synthesiser might comprise one oscillator followed by one filter and one envelope shaper, as shown in Figure 5.4. The oscillator generates the starting waveform that gives the sound its pitch and harmonic structure, and this harmonic structure is further shaped by means of a circuit known as a *filter*. The filtered sound is then controlled in level by means of an *envelope shaper* to determine the speed at which the level builds up after a key is pressed and how fast it decays to silence once the key is released. The filter and envelope shaper are the main tools used to trim away unwanted elements of the sound.

In the original analogue synthesisers, there was usually a choice of just three or four basic types of waveform, but in the modern S&S synth there's usually a choice of basic waveforms as well as samples recorded from acoustic instruments and other sources. Noise generators produce broad-band hiss, a random electrical waveform containing all audio frequencies at all times. By filtering noise, it's possible to simulate the sound of breathing, wind, surf, steam engines, helicopters and percussion, even rudimentary cymbals.

sine and square waves

There are four main oscillator waveforms used in analogue synthesis: sine wave, square/pulse wave, triangle wave and sawtooth wave. The sine wave comprises a fundamental frequency with no harmonics, so no further modification can be made, other than to control its pitch and level. However, it makes an ideal LFO (Low-Frequency Oscillator) control waveform for adding vibrato or tremolo because of its smooth, natural characteristics.

Square waves and triangle waves, on the other hand, contain the fundamental plus a series of odd harmonics, with the triangle wave having a lower harmonic content than the square wave. Both produce a characteristically hollow, reedy tone, but the square wave sounds brighter than the triangle wave. If the mark/space ratio of a square wave is changed, the resulting pulse waveform produces a different harmonic series and is useful for creating reed-like tones.

Although the square wave is one of the basic waveforms used in analogue synthesis, the pulse waveform, its close relative, is arguably just as important because many acoustic instruments generate an asymmetrical waveform. The square wave is so called because the "period" of its high state is exactly the same as the period of its low state – it has a 1:1 mark/space ratio, where the mark is the time at which the voltage is high and the space is that when the voltage is low.

If the mark/space ratio is altered, the sound becomes thinner and more buzzy as the mark/space ratio is increased. The harmonic content changes and, instead of having a square wave, a pulse wave is produced, which is particularly useful for creating buzzy reed tones. Many synths allow the mark/space ratio to be modulated using the output from an LFO running at just a few cycles per second, which produces a very interesting result called *pulse-width modulation*.

If you were to use two square-wave oscillators running at exactly the same frequency and then modulated the pitch of just one of them using an LFO to produce vibrato, the result would be a simple but effective chorus effect, and if you were to examine the waveform, it would look exactly the same as a single square wave having its mark/space ratio modulated. Consequently, pulse-width modulating a single oscillator provides a useful way of fattening up the sound of an unsophisticated synth, as the result sounds just like two slightly detuned oscillators playing at the same time.

sawtooth waves

The sawtooth wave comprises the fundamental plus a series of both odd and even harmonics and is used to create string, brass and many synth-pad sounds. To produce a different mix of harmonics, the oscillator waveforms may be applied in different proportions. Figure 5.5 over the page shows the main waveform types available.

Although it's educational to examine the harmonic structures of both real and electronically generated sounds, it's arguable whether a knowledge of the subject is of much practical benefit to the synthesist. Most synthesists work by ear, and even though it can be shown mathematically that a square wave has a very similar harmonic series to the sound produced by a clarinet, the reason why you ultimately choose to use the square wave as the basis for your clarinet patch is because it sounds right.

key gate

In a synthesiser, the action of pressing a key tells the circuitry which pitch to produce, but it also produces a gate signal to tell other elements of the synthesiser - such as envelope generators - when a key has been pressed and when it has been released. In MIDI terms, this corresponds to a Note On and a Note Off message. If we were to set up a synth so that the oscillator sound appeared at the output as soon as a key was pressed and stopped again when a key was released, the result wouldn't be unlike that produced by a simple organ. It's only when the sound is filtered and given a new envelope that things get interesting.

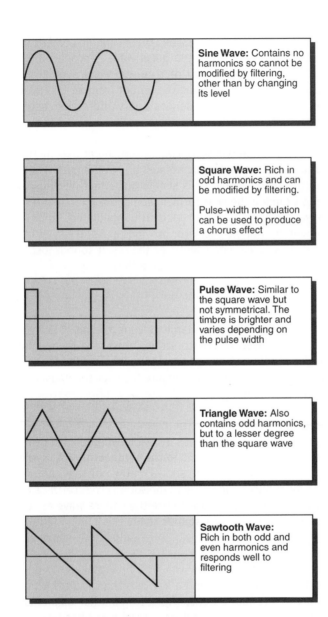

Sine Wave: Contains no harmonics so cannot be modified by filtering, other than by changing its level

Square Wave: Rich in odd harmonics and can be modified by filtering.

Pulse-width modulation can be used to produce a chorus effect

Pulse Wave: Similar to the square wave but not symmetrical. The timbre is brighter and varies depending on the pulse width

Triangle Wave: Also contains odd harmonics, but to a lesser degree than the square wave

Sawtooth Wave: Rich in both odd and even harmonics and responds well to filtering

Noise: Random waveform that contains all frequencies. Heard in isolation, it sounds like hiss

Fig 5.5: The main synth waveforms

portamento

Not all acoustic instruments produce neat chromatic pitches; some can slide from one note to another - for example, the trombone and violin. This effect is emulated in synthesisers by the *portamento* control. When this is applied, whenever a new key is pressed, the oscillator pitch will glide from the old note to the new note over a finite period of time, rather than changing abruptly. In most instruments, the portamento time is adjustable from instantaneous to several seconds per octave of glide. A fairly fast glide is useful in simulating brass sounds, especially trombone, while slow rates are useful in creating special effects.

LFOs

I've already mentioned low-frequency oscillators once or twice, so I guess that now is as good a time as any to introduce them formally. The simplest LFO is a sine-wave oscillator running at just a few cycles per second, and the modulation wheels on modern synths usually default to using an LFO to create vibrato. They do this by allowing the LFO to modulate the pitch of the oscillator. An LFO may also be routed to the filter-envelope generators to modulate timbre or output level, and modulating the output level of a patch using an LFO produces a tremolo effect. By using the control that determines the amount of LFO, the modulation depth applied to the pitch or level of the sound can be set to a musically suitable value so as to emulate the vibrato applied by a violin or flute player.

more about oscillators

Running two oscillators together at nominally the same pitch produces a rich, dynamic sound, while a slight degree of detuning allows the phase of one oscillator to drift, producing a natural chorus effect. It's also possible to tune one oscillator higher or lower than the other by, for example, an octave or a perfect fifth. This can produce very fat sounds, especially when combined with suitable filtering.

oscillator sync

Many analogue synths using two or more oscillators are able to synchronise one of their oscillators to the other, which can be used to create a dynamic, aggressive and quite distinctive sound. In Phase Sync mode, one oscillator is designated the master and the other the slave, and these may be tuned to the same frequency or to any interval, but the slave oscillator's waveform will always "restart" whenever a cycle of the master oscillator's waveform is complete. Although originally developed for analogue instruments, some digital instruments also have phase sync capabilities.

If the slave's oscillator's tuning is increased manually while the master remains constant, the slave can be heard to jump from one harmonic to the next, accompanied by an interesting change in timbre. A popular use of this effect is controlling the slave oscillator from the pitch-bend wheel of the synth but leaving the master unmodulated. Then, as the pitch-bend wheel is turned, the output signal runs through a series of harmonics, resulting in a sound much more complex than that which can be achieved by simply adding the oscillator outputs together as normal. Phase sync is popular for creating searing lead-solo sounds.

digital synthesis

Although analogue synthesisers eventually evolved to become polyphonic and, later, to become controlled via MIDI, the basic waveforms remained the same until sample-based synthesisers were developed, in the early '80s. The main conceptual difference between the two types of synthesis is that, instead of a simple electronic waveform, the starting point for a modern S&S synth is a sampled sound, such as a sustained violin note, a flute or even a human voice. These devices may still be thought of as oscillators, because in most cases the sound continues for as long as the key is held down. The exceptions are percussion instruments, whose sounds may be allowed to decay naturally.

filters and envelopes

Regardless of the type of oscillator being used, the resulting signal is usually passed through a filter and invariably through a level-envelope shaper. On modern digital instruments, the filters and envelope shapers are all implemented using microcomputer technology, but the block diagram for arranging these remains the same as that for an analogue instrument.

The character of a natural sound is determined largely by its harmonic content and its envelope (ie the way in which the level of the sound changes over time). As we've seen, percussive sounds start suddenly and then die away, whereas a bowed sound might start quite slowly and then sustain at a more or less fixed level. The envelopes of real sounds can be very complex, but in the early days of synthesis it was felt that an adequate approximation could be achieved by using a basic, four-stage ADSR (Attack, Decay, Sustain, Release) envelope generator controlling a VCA (Voltage-Controlled Amplifier), where the envelope shaper was triggered by the action of pressing a key. An ADSR envelope is shown in Figure 5.6.

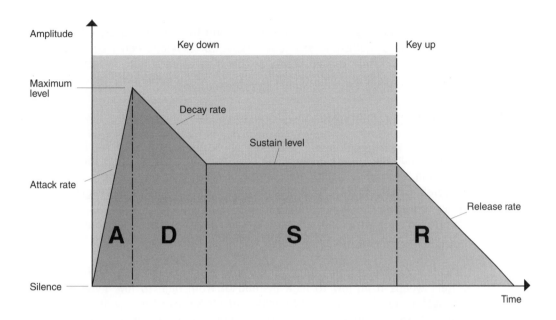

Fig 5.6: ADSR envelope shaper

The Attack portion of the envelope is simply the time it takes for the amplitude to reach its maximum level, so for percussive sounds the attack time should be as short as possible. Once the sound has hit maximum, it starts to decay at a rate set by the Decay time setting. The sound then continues to decay until it reaches the Sustain level (another user-variable parameter) and it remains at this level for as long as the key is held down. Once the key is released, however, the sound resumes its decay, this time at a new rate determined by the Release setting. If a new key is depressed before the envelope generator has completed the Release phase of its envelope, the old Release level is abandoned and a new envelope is initiated. This type of envelope generator, and more complex variations of it, are often found in modern digital synthesisers. (It is important to note that, while Attack, Decay and Release controls determine the rate at which the envelope settings change, the Sustain parameter is a level, not a rate.)

complex envelopes

Modern synths often have envelope shapers that control much more than four stages, the reason being that many sounds cannot be accurately synthesised using only a simple four-stage envelope. For example, a brass-ensemble sound may contain several staggered attack transients, corresponding to several performers starting to play at slightly different times. Using a multistage envelope shaper, an envelope could be created with several closely spaced spikes at the start of each note (as shown in Figure 5.7), a feat quite impossible to a single ADSR generator.

filter envelope control

We nearly always associate envelope generators with level (amplitude) control, but they have a much wider range of creative uses, the most common alternative being the control of filter frequency. Filters will be covered in more detail later in this chapter, but for the moment imagine the filter to be just a remote-controlled tone control. If the filter's frequency is controlled via an envelope generator, a huge range of tonal sweep sounds can be created, ranging from a slow, lazy change in timbre to a resonant twang.

It's also possible to invert the output of the envelope generator so that the filter sweeps from low to high instead of from high to low. Even fairly modest analogue synths tend to have controls for inverting the direction of the filter sweep, although on very basic models you may find that the same

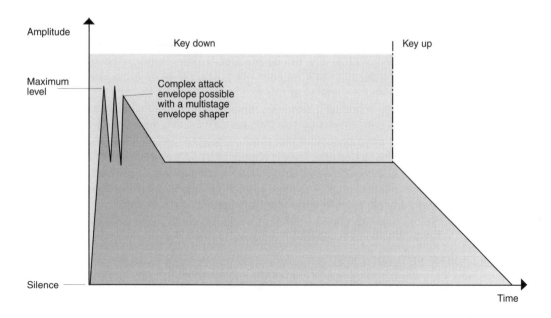

Fig 5.7: Multistage envelope showing multiple attack spikes

envelope generator is used to control both the amplitude of the envelope and also the filter sweep, restricting the range of sounds that can be produced. Even so, the filter-invert option helps to squeeze the most sonic variation out of what is available.

delay vibrato

When an acoustic instrument is played naturally, it's quite common for vibrato to be added after the note has started sounding. This can be duplicated on a synth via the vibrato-depth controller wheel, but it's also possible to use a delayed LFO to achieve a similar effect. In this case, when a key is pressed, the LFO level will build up gradually so that the sound starts off unmodulated and then the vibrato depth increases as the LFO envelope moves towards its maximum level.

envelope control of tone oscillators

An envelope may also be used to modify the oscillator pitch. This has an obvious application in creating sci-fi-type oscillator sweeps, but used more subtly it may also be used to put the finishing touches to a patch simulating a natural instrument. For example, some wind instruments tend to go slightly sharp when they are first blown, and this characteristic can be imitated by setting up an envelope with fairly fast attack and decay rates and then feeding just a small amount of this signal into the oscillator's pitch-control input. As the envelope rises at the start of a note, the pitch will be forced slightly sharp, returning to normal as the envelope finishes its Decay phase.

Applying a more drastic measure of envelope pitch control can be useful when setting up oscillator sync effects. In the above example, two oscillators are used, one set to track the keyboard pitch normally and the other with a generous helping of additional envelope control to produce a long pitch bend of several semitones. When the second oscillator is synchronised to the first, the envelope shape will control the way in which the harmonic structure changes whenever a key is pressed. A long envelope will produce a harmonic sweep effect, whereas a short envelope could be used to create a harmonically rich attack to the sound.

filtering

Although some very basic modern synths dispense with filters altogether and instead include ready-filtered sounds within their menu of basic waveforms, a filter is very useful. Firstly, simply mixing the basic sine, square (pulse) and triangle waveforms doesn't provide a broad enough range of timbres, and secondly, real sounds very often change in timbre as the sound develops. For example, a plucked string produces a sound that is initially rich in high-frequency harmonics, but then, as the sound decays, these harmonics die away faster than the fundamental. To simulate this effect with a filter, it's necessary to have one that can be made to vary its characteristics in a controllable way, and the solution is to use an envelope generator to control the rate at which the frequency of the filter increases and decreases.

Like oscillators, filters may be controlled from a keyboard (ie the higher the note played, the higher the filter frequency), from an envelope generator or from an LFO, resulting in a filter characteristic that changes rather than remaining static. Cheaper synths tend to share the same envelope generator for the filter and for the output level, while more sophisticated models have separate envelope generators for each function. Obviously, being able to set up one envelope for the filter and a different one for the amplitude provides a lot more flexibility.

types of filter

Most synthesiser filter circuits operate as high-pass, bandpass or low-pass filter types, based on those used in original analogue instruments, although more complex filter types are possible. If an instrument has only one type of filter, it will invariably be of the low-pass variety, which means that it passes only frequencies below the frequency at which the filter is set. The slope or sharpness of the filter will usually be 12dB per octave or, in some cases, 24dB per octave, depending on the make. The more decibels per octave, the sharper the sound of the filter. The two types produce a subtly different sound, which is one reason why two synths offering apparently identical facilities might sound quite different.

A filter like the one described above, with no other controls, would sound much like any other form of EQ, allowing the user only to soften bright sounds, but the addition of a Q or resonance control greatly increases the user's creative potential. Essentially, increasing the Q or resonance of a filter causes it to emphasise harmonics at the filter's cut-off frequency, rather like a wah-wah pedal or the mute of a trumpet. If the filter frequency is then varied, the familiar filter-sweep sound is produced. The graph in Figure 5.8 shows the effect of changing the resonance of a low-pass filter. By juggling the starting frequency of the filter with the rate, depth and direction of sweep, a wide range of dynamically changing timbres can be created.

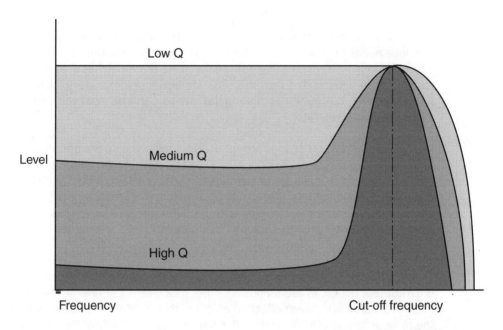

Fig 5.8: Graph displaying the effect of varying
the resonance of a low-pass filter

filter applications

Just because a filter has variable frequency and Q parameters, it doesn't
mean that every patch you set up has to be based on a fierce filter sweep. For
example, to produce a mellow string pad, you might choose a couple of
slightly detuned, gently modulated sawtooth oscillators as your source and
then use the filter as a simple top-cut control in order to reduce the high-
frequency content of the sound. In this mode, the filter isn't being controlled
from the envelope at all; it's set up as a purely static filter. In this case,
increasing the level of Q slightly would produce a sharper, more tightly
focused sound that would cut through a mix well, but if the level of Q is
increased too far, the sound will become obviously resonant and the illusion
of a string sound will break down. Adding a little keyboard control to the
filter's control input makes the filter frequency dependent on the note you're
playing, which can be useful if you're trying to simulate an instrument that
sounds brighter on the higher notes and more mellow on the lower notes.

brass sounds

Brass sounds tend to make use of filter sweeps where the filter opens fairly
rapidly (but not percussively so) as soon as a note is pressed but then closes
down again over a quarter of a second or so, resulting in a bright attack

followed by a more mellow sustain period. The attack time of the filter envelope needs to be adjusted by ear so that it matches the time it takes for a typical brass instrument to "speak". Convincing brass patches are easiest to achieve on a synth that provides separate envelope generators for both filter and level, but quite passable imitations can still be achieved with a single envelope generator.

Most classic synth-bass sounds are set up in a similar way to the brass patch but require the oscillators to be set to a lower octave. Fashionable techno-bass sounds tend to make use of rapid attack times and fairly high Q settings, and if the direction of filter sweep can be inverted, this produces interesting alternatives. A fast release time on both the filter and VCA envelopes helps create a tight, well-defined bass sound, whereas longer release times are better suited to more atmospheric music or deep bass sounds.

Classic filter-sweep sounds tend to use a Q setting that is so high that the filter is almost (but not quite) oscillating and either a long attack or release in order to create a dramatic sweep effect. In all cases that involve envelope control, the manual tuning control on the filter determines the starting state of the filter and the envelope level sets the range of the sweep.

The filter can be controlled from a number of sources, limited only by the patching arrangements of the particular synth used. One very popular effect is achieved when a random stepped waveform is fed into the control input of the filter. If the filter is adjusted to a high Q setting, the result is a kind of wah-wah that jumps instantaneously from one random position to the next at a user-defined rate.

polyphony

The advent of polyphony really signalled the beginning of the end for analogue instruments because, although it's possible to build polyphonic analogue instruments, every oscillator, filter and envelope shaper must be duplicated for every note that is to play simultaneously. In practical terms, few analogue synths were built that provided more than eight-note polyphony, and ultimately it became clear that going completely digital was the only feasible solution. Similarly, the patching systems that worked so well on the old modular synths would be completely unmanageable if the same patch had to be duplicated eight times in order to obtain eight-note polyphony.

The modern digital equivalent of the old analogue patching system is usually a button-and-menu-driven system, and although this isn't as convenient as a panel full of knobs to which you have permanent and full access, it does make very powerful instruments cheap to build. Digital control systems also made the manufacture of programmable synthesisers possible for the first time, enabling the user to save patches for instant recall rather than having to write down all of the settings in a book.

modern synthesisers

MIDI is now fitted as standard to virtually every serious electronic keyboard and instruments tend to come with a wide variety of factory-preset sounds built in as well as user memory that can store newly created sounds. A typical instrument will have a four- or five-octave keyboard that responds to velocity data and pitch-bend and modulation wheels will be provided for performance control and there will be provision made to allow you to plug in a sustain pedal. As with the majority of MIDI instruments, the notes that can be played on a modern synth aren't limited to the physical size of the keyboard; notes above and below the range of the keyboard can be played via MIDI or by using any on-board octave-transposing facilities.

on-board effects

It's common for synthesisers to come complete with built-in digital effects such as reverb, chorus and echo/delay, providing the user with a wealth of means of adding life and realism to a performance. Usually, there's a choice of types and combinations of effects, and users with the inclination to do so can edit their effects, changing things like reverb decay time, echo delay time and so on. Because the majority of effects produce a stereo output, most synthesisers are fitted with stereo outputs, although some top-end models may have multiple outputs so that the various sounds can be mixed via a studio mixing console. Multiple outputs are really only applicable to multitimbral modules. (See Chapter 6, "Multitimbral Modules", for more information on this subject.)

S&S synthesisers

At the time of writing, the majority of synthesisers work on the sample-and-synthesis method, where digitally stored waveforms similar to those used in analogue machines plus digitally stored samples of real instruments, voices and sound effects are used as the basic building blocks of sound. With this method, several sound sources can be layered together and processed via filters, envelope shapers and so on, and the results that can be obtained from such instruments are initially very impressive. The variety of sounds that these instruments are capable of producing ranges from imitations of vintage analogue synthesisers and acoustic instruments to abstract sounds, sound effects and choirs. Piano sounds based on samples can be very convincing, as can string- and brass-ensemble sounds. However, S&S synths don't do a great job at creating certain solo sounds, such as violin or saxophone sounds, because the real instrument can be played in so many different ways and yet the synthesiser creates each note from the same basic sound. Skilled use of performance controls and inventive sound programming can help overcome this problem, but there is no completely satisfactory solution.

All General MIDI instruments are based on sample-based synthesis, and the chips used in computer soundcards also tend to use it, too. Despite its limitations, this is a very flexible, easy-to-use and cost-effective method of synthesis, but, as mentioned earlier, nothing stands still in this business – it will eventually be superseded by something better.

physical modelling

Instead of creating the sound by way of oscillators and filters, physical modelling instruments use sophisticated models to emulate the behaviour of real acoustic instruments. If this seems rather abstract, it's not dissimilar to the way in which a flight simulator is used to model the way that a real aircraft behaves.

A clarinet simulation would involve simulating the vibration of the reed, the resonance of the tubular body of the instrument and the effect that the flared end of the tube has on the sound. This is a very complicated technology, but the advantage is that the modelled instrument can be made to behave much more like the real thing. For example, a physical model of a flute might change its harmonic structure when played hard to make it sound like a real flute being overblown, whereas playing very quietly will result in more wind noise resonating in the tubular body. A violin emulation would need to model the behaviour of a bowed string, the resonance of the violin body and the decay of the sound once bowing has ceased. A drum, on the other hand, requires the modelling of a tensioned membrane and a resonant shell, with the quality of the final sound depending on the accuracy of the mathematical model and the skill of the sound designer. Figure 5.9 shows a conceptual block diagram of a physical-modelling instrument.

Different mathematical models are required for different instruments, but it's possible to model convincingly many acoustic instruments by this method. Furthermore, various aspects of different instruments can be combined to

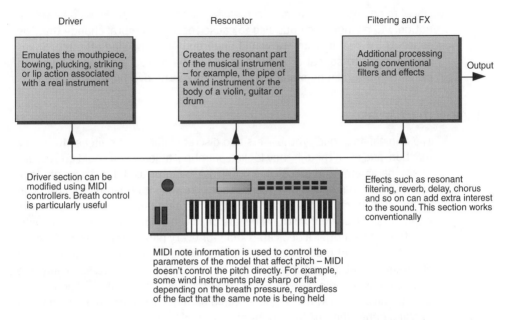

Driver

Emulates the mouthpiece, bowing, plucking, striking or lip action associated with a real instrument

Resonator

Creates the resonant part of the musical instrument – for example, the pipe of a wind instrument or the body of a violin, guitar or drum

Filtering and FX

Additional processing using conventional filters and effects

Output

Driver section can be modified using MIDI controllers. Breath control is particularly useful

Effects such as resonant filtering, reverb, delay, chorus and so on can add extra interest to the sound. This section works conventionally

MIDI note information is used to control the parameters of the model that affect pitch – MIDI doesn't control the pitch directly. For example, some wind instruments play sharp or flat depending on the breath pressure, regardless of the fact that the same note is being held

Fig 5.9: Block diagram of a physical-modelling instrument.

produce the sounds of instruments that don't exist in real life and yet still respond like true instruments. For example, you could have the reed of a clarinet, the body of a flute and the bell of a trumpet, or you could create a double-sized sax. You could even build a bowed flute or a violin with a reed! Because of the complexity involved in physical modelling, the number of user parameters is usually limited, although some instruments contain software-editing packages for those people with the expertise and patience to design and construct their own sounds. The most powerful physical-modelling instruments tend to be monophonic, but this makes perfect sense if you're modelling a monophonic wind instrument such as a flute or saxophone.

performance control

The secret of a producing a convincing performance when using any synthesiser is to make full use of real-time control, but on a physical-modelling instrument you can use several real-time controllers to vary the aspects of the sound that would change if the instrument's "real" counterpart were being played. For example, if you were playing a flute patch, you could use a breath controller to control the level of the sound, aftertouch to change the harmonics of the sound or to add "growl" and the modulation wheel to add both vibrato and tremolo, while the pitch wheel could be set up not only to change pitch but also to cause the same timbral change that the sound of the real instrument would undergo if it was pulled off pitch. Saxes can be made to squeal or growl, violins can be played with varying bowing pressure, flutes can be made breathy or the can be overblown and so on.

user interfaces

The original analogue synthesisers had discrete knobs and switches for every function, and even though they looked daunting, at least you could go straight to any parameter and adjust it. In contrast, modern digital instruments look much simpler, but behind the scenes there are still lot of parameters that can be adjusted, if you've the patience to try to create new sounds of your own. Although some current instruments are build with knobs on their front panels, only the simplest offer a dedicated knob for every parameter. More commonly, a small number of multifunction knobs can be used to access a small number of parameters at a time. Indeed, many instruments provide access to only one parameter at a time, selected using buttons and a visual display window (usually via a menu system). The selected parameter is then changed in value by using either the Up/Down buttons or a single rotary control.

Most keyboard synthesisers provide a number of buttons to allow the user direct access to sound patches and to change between banks of patches. Patches are often named, with the name being shown in the display window, and if new sounds are created by the user, they can be given new names.

By using a limited number of controls and a menu-access system, very powerful instruments can be built relatively inexpensively. The trade-off is that, on these instruments, sound editing is time consuming and not always intuitive. Software-editing systems are available for many types of synthesiser, providing more comprehensive parameter displays and access by way of a computer screen and mouse, although users who don't have the time or patience to create sounds from scratch may find it easier to make minor modifications to existing factory-preset sounds or even buy new sounds from third-party sound-design companies. Depending on the model of synthesiser, new sounds may also be available on memory cards or floppy disks.

software editors

Because most modern synths employ a menu-and-button-driven user interface, it's often easier to edit their sounds on a computer screen, where several parameters can be seen and adjusted at once. Level and filter envelopes may also be presented graphically, and the user will be able to use the mouse to drag them into new shapes, making for more intuitive editing. However, buying a software editor for every instrument you own can be expensive.

Universal synth editors adopt a modular approach, by which software modules relating to the various synths in circulation can be loaded in and used. Such a software system may initially be more expensive than a single synth editor, but the benefit is that you gain the ability to edit dozens of different models and makes of instrument.

Editing systems tend to include librarian facilities so that, if you fill up your synth memory with new sounds, you can store them on disk. This will allow you to build up a vast library of different sounds for your various instruments which you can then transfer to your synthesisers as needed. To use an editor/librarian system, it's necessary for the MIDI Out of the instrument being edited to be connected to the MIDI In of the interface serving the computer, and the MIDI Out of the interface must be connected back to the MIDI In of the instrument. This provides for two-way communication between the instrument and the computer so that patch data and instructions can be sent in both directions.

more performance control

I've already mentioned modulation wheels, pitch-bend wheels, and sustain pedals as means of implementing performance control, but there are numerous other options, some more popular than others. Pedals are practical, as they require no hands, but not all keyboards are designed to accept a pedal input. Meanwhile, add-on boxes that convert volume pedals to MIDI pedals are available commercially, as are MIDI pedals themselves.

Aftertouch is a useful performance control that comes built into many keyboards, although it tends to act on all of the notes being played at one time – only very few high-end keyboards have note-independent aftertouch. Essentially, aftertouch works via a pressure sensor beneath the keyboard that converts downward pressure into MIDI data, which can then be used to control parameters such as level, brightness, pitch, modulation depth and so on. However, it also generates a lot of data, so it's best to switch it off at the keyboard if you're not using it. The pressure response of most keyboards tends to be a little uneven, and you'll often find that you have to press quite hard to get any response at all, but there are occasions when aftertouch can really add life to a performance, so try it, if you have it, just to see what it can do. The parameter effected by aftertouch is programmed as part of a synthesiser patch or program.

Joysticks are also fitted to some instruments, and these are useful devices inasmuch as they can control two parameters at a time – one by vertical movement and one by horizontal. Often, these can be assigned to any of the regular MIDI controllers, which means that you can decide which parameters they will affect.

Ribbon controllers are rarely fitted to modern instruments, but they seem to be making a bit of a comeback in some circles. A ribbon controller is a flat ribbon fitted above a conductive strip so that, when you press down on the ribbon, it makes an electrical contact. As you slide your finger from one end of the ribbon to the other, the electrical resistance of the contact changes, just as if you were using a normal slider, so you can control any function dynamically. Unlike a slider, however, as soon as you remove your finger from the ribbon, the contact is broken and the original condition is restored. Ribbons are useful for controlling such things as level, pitch, vibrato, filter brightness and so on.

Breath controllers are relatively inexpensive and have been around for a long time, but they never became really popular, possibly because they look rather foolish and cause users to dribble! In fact, most modern keyboards don't even have a breath-controller input, so if you want to use one, you'll either need to buy a third-party breath-control interface box or use a synth module that has its own breath-control input. The breath controller itself is a headset with a simple mouthpiece attached into which the performer blows. A pressure sensor converts breath pressure to electrical information, which is subsequently used to generate MIDI-controller data. Anything that can be controlled via a MIDI controller can be controlled via a breath-control unit, although most people have them set to controller 7 in order to provide overall volume control. This is uncannily effective for articulating wind sounds, but it is also useful for adding "feel" to the sounds of other instruments, such as bowed strings. The new generation of physical-modelling synthesisers respond exceptionally well to breath control, and this alone could be sufficient incentive for more people to experiment.

chapter 6

multitimbral modules

Today, virtually every synthesiser, expander module and soundcard synth chip has some multitimbral capability – ie, the ability to play several different sounds at the same time, where each different sound or musical part is controlled by a different MIDI channel. If you wanted to create a mind's-eye model of a 16-part multitimbral synth module, you'd probably be thinking along the lines of 16 separate synthesiser modules built into one box. Up to a point, this is an excellent analogy, but what you have to remember is that these "virtual" modules are not entirely separate, and in many ways their operation is linked. At their simplest level, they all operate from the same power supply, so you can't turn them on or off individually. Also, even though the sounds that they produce may appear to be generated separately, on the more affordable models these sounds will probably be mixed to stereo inside the machine, so there is no way of accessing them separately. Some machines have four or even eight outputs to which different voices or parts can be assigned, but a 16-part multitimbral module with 16 separate outputs would be prohibitively expensive to build.

level and pan

To help overcome the limitations imposed by having all sounds pre-mixed inside the module, the user invariably has control over the sound levels and pan positions of the individual parts, although on some of the cheaper modules (and on all soundcards) these parameters may be accessible only via MIDI from a sequencer or a suitable software-editing package. In addition, simple effects such as chorus and reverb are often included, even in very inexpensive modules and soundcards, and although the same effect setting applies to each part, the effect level can be set by the user, allowing a useful degree of creative freedom. More advanced synths and expanders may incorporate effects-processing sections to rival those of stand-alone multi-effects units.

polyphony

A more important consideration is that of polyphony, and this is one area where the "virtual" synthesiser elements of a multitimbral instrument are really linked. Polyphony is a term used to describe the number of notes that may be played at the same time, and in the case of a multitimbral module you may find the following analogy helpful. Imagine that the musical notes that the unit can produce are coins stored in a single box. If the unit has 24-note polyphony, then there are 24 coins in the box. When one of the parts is required to play a note, it borrows one of the coins when the note starts to play and keeps it until the note has ended, at which point it returns it to the box. Clearly, this is fine until all 24 notes are playing at once, because then there are no more coins left in the box.

If a 25th note is played while the other 24 notes are still playing, you might expect nothing at all to happen because the "note box" is empty, but that would be musically unacceptable, so a rather more practical system is adopted. Instead of new notes failing to play, the usual solution is to "steal" a note from one of the parts already playing, and to help disguise the theft it's normal for the voice-allocation system to steal whichever of the notes was played earliest.

Even this apparently fair system can cause problems, however, especially if your song starts with a long, droning note, because in a note-robbing situation this is the one most likely to be taken, and that would leave an obvious hole in the music. For this reason, most modules use a system whereby a minimum number of notes are reserved for use by each of the parts so that, if robbing does take place, it is less likely to be noticeable. For example, if one part is playing a pad chord and one of the notes in the chord is robbed just as it's dying away, this is less likely to be a problem than if the whole chord stops playing. It's often possible for the user to change the number of "sounds" reserved for each part so that important parts have more notes at their disposal. Figure 6.1 shows a representation of a multitimbral sound module with only eight parts, for reasons of simplicity, as these days 16-part multitimbrality is more commonplace.

effects

Because the sounds from the various parts are often mixed together internally to produce a stereo output, some means is required for adding different amounts of effects – such as chorus or reverb – to each part. Virtually all multitimbral synthesisers have built-in digital effects, although very often the same effect or combination of effects is applied to all of the "parts" of the instrument. For example, a General MIDI instrument will provide reverb and chorus for all 16 parts, but the same chorus and reverb settings will be used throughout. However, to make this more flexible, each part provides control over effects levels, and in the

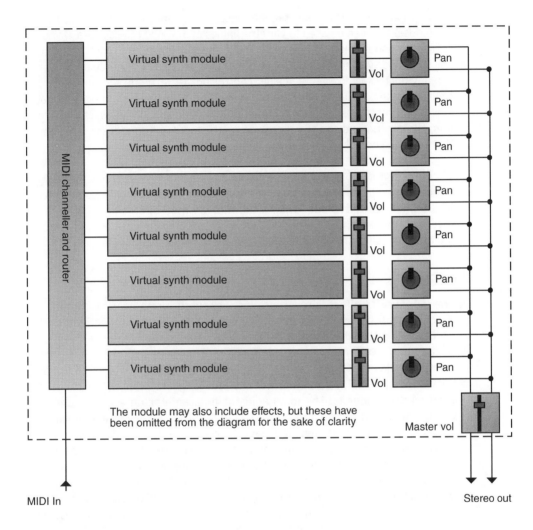

Fig 6.1: Representation of a multitimbral module

case of GM instruments the minimum requirement is for independent control over chorus amount and reverb level. These are adjusted using MIDI controller information, and the relevant controllers will be shown in the MIDI instrumentation chart for the instrument. More experienced sequencer users will find it a simple matter to insert controller information at the starts of songs, usually during the count-in bars, so that the effects levels are set up automatically. As a rule, the higher the controller value, the greater the level of effect.

Most serious sequencers now provide onscreen faders (which are moved via the mouse) that can be used to vary the values of any kind of MIDI data. If your sequencer handbook mentions this facility, check it out, as it's much easier to adjust settings via faders than to enter numbers. Emagic's Logic Audio includes a ready-built GM mixer that makes controlling a GM module or soundcard simplicity itself, while some software allows the user to configure additional faders and control just about any function that can be accessed over MIDI, so there's really no end to the number of synth-module or soundcard functions that you can control via MIDI, if you put your mind to it.

The list of possible studio effects grows daily, or so it seems, but the main effects you're likely to come across are listed below, along with some hints about where to use them. While a GM module may offer only chorus and reverb, a more sophisticated MIDI instrument may include one or more multi-effects sections capable of studio-quality effects processing.

reverberation

The most useful effect is reverberation, or reverb for short. Reverberation describes the pattern of complicated echoes and sound reflections that occur when a sound is heard in a real space – for example, a concert hall or a cathedral. Different types of space produce reverb with different characteristics, so most reverb units provide room, hall and chamber simulations as well as emulations of the studio reverb plate, which is often used on drum sounds. The main adjustable parameter on a reverb unit is decay time – ie the time it takes for the reverb to die away to inaudibility – but you may also find that you have control over the brightness of the reverb. More sophisticated units offer control over many more parameters, such as the reflection density of the reverb or the pre-delay time between the sound and the reverb that follows it. Indeed, one of my studio units has 99 different reverb parameters to adjust. However, you'll be pleased to know that, in most instances, control over the type, decay time and brightness of reverb is quite enough to get the job done.

delay

Delay is simply another term for echo, and if you feed some of the echo back to the input of an echo device, it recirculates, causing many repeat echoes before finally dying away. The number of repeats and the speed at which they die away are set using the Feedback control, while the time between repeats is controlled via the Delay Time parameter. You may find that preset effects are good enough to use as they are, without any editing, but you might like to consider the useful musical trick of setting a delay time to a multiple of the tempo of the song. This will cause all repeats to be perfectly in time and will help reinforce the rhythm.

Stereo delays are also sometimes provided, where the repeats alternate between the left and right speakers. This is sometimes known as *ping-pong delay*.

chorus

Chorus is a simple effect that takes a signal and mixes it with a version of itself that is delayed slightly and subjected to a slow modulation of pitch. The result sounds much like two performers playing the same part. Chorus is most effective in thickening pad parts or string-ensemble sounds. The two important parameters are depth and rate.

flanging

Flange is a similar effect to chorus, except that the delay times used are very short and some of the output is fed back to the input. The result is a psychedelic whooshing sound that you'll recognise as soon as you hear it. The relevant controls here are speed, depth and feedback, with feedback determining the strength of the effect. Flanging works best on harmonically rich sounds such as bright string pads, although it can also be used on drums and cymbals. However, because it is such a dramatic effect, it should be used sparingly.

phasing

Phasing was originally a guitar effect and it produces a sound that is similar to flanging but rather more subtle. Slow sweep rates are most effective, and the effect works well on sustained pad sounds, electric pianos or plucked parts. The main controls are speed, depth, and intensity.

rotary speakers

The electric-organ sound is inexorably linked with the rotary-speaker cabinet, the most famous being the Leslie-speaker/Hammond-organ pairing. The rotary speaker system uses a combination of rotating horns and baffles and is used to create a complex tremolo effect that contains elements of both pitch and level modulation. A two-speed motor drives the baffles and this is controlled by a kneeswitch or footswitch. Because of the mechanical inertia of the baffles, changing speed takes a second or two, and this "run-up-and-down" time is an important part of the effect.

Most effects units include an electronic simulation of the rotary-speaker effect, some of which are more successful than others. Some are little more than a chorus effect, while others are very authentic. Most, however, include the speed-change "run-up-and-down" characteristic of the original. Although designed to be used with organ, this effect works well on a whole range of sounds, including other keyboard sounds and electric guitar – John Lennon even used it on vocals! The rotary-speaker section of the Native Instruments B4 drawbar organ plug-in (mentioned in Chapter 12, "Software Instruments"xxx) can be used as an independent effect to process any of the audio tracks in a MIDI-plus-audio sequencer.

advantages of multitimbrality

Multitimbral synth modules have many advantages, although they need to be used with sequencers for the most to be made of their considerable features. The main advantage is that of cost – it's obviously cheaper to buy a single multitimbral module than eight or 16 separate MIDI instruments. There's also a convenience advantage, in that a single unit is compact and easy to connect up, and if it has a mixed stereo output, as most have, you can get by with a relatively small mixer.

A further advantage is that most modules (including all GM instruments) have on-board drum and percussion sounds, which means that you don't have to spend more money on a drum machine or drum sound module. In the case of GM modules, the drum part is set to MIDI channel 10, but this cannot be relied upon for non-GM machines, which tend to handle their drum sounds in a number of different ways, so it's important to read your instrument handbook.

The newer breed of GM- and Roland GS-compatible sound modules enable users to exchange MIDI song files in the knowledge that their songs will play back on any GM module with the right sounds, regardless of the manufacturer. Equally importantly, the drum mapping will be consistent, so you won't find that a snare drum on one machine plays back as a cowbell on another. (See Chapter 2, "General MIDI", for more details.)

using modules

On a practical level, just because a machine is described as being "16-part multitimbral", it doesn't mean that you have to use all 16 parts. Indeed, it may be better to use just two or three parts from each of a number of different modules in a composition to avoid the possibility of note robbing and to provide a wider variety of available tone colours. This is particularly true of earlier machines, some of which had very limited polyphony.

voices and tones

One of the problems facing anyone coming to terms with multitimbral synths is the manufacturers' jargon, particularly as different manufacturers tend to use different jargon. It's fairly logical to call the various virtual synth modules parts, because these equate fairly well to the different musical parts that they may be called upon to play. But what do we call the sounds of the notes that these parts play? Indeed, *sounds* seems like a good word to me, but Roland, for example, call them *tones* – and life still isn't simple, because a tone may be built up from more than one basic sound. Roland call their basic building blocks of sound *voices*, and their quoted polyphony relates to voices, not tones. In other words, if you play a sound or tone that is made up from two voices layered together, that counts as two voices of polyphony, even though you can only hear one note playing.

facilities

The most basic multitimbral sound module or soundcard will provide between eight and 16 parts, although GM modules must provide a minimum of 16 parts as standard. (See Chapter 11, "Interfaces", for more information on what facilities to expect.) Some modules aimed at the computer-music market also include a built-in MIDI interface, which represents a cost saving and makes setting up easier. All GM and most non-GM modules include digital effects and, apart from some modules designed to be used exclusively with computers, front-panel control should be provided for selecting sounds, as well as for determining part level and pan and effect settings. On programmable machines, it's also usual for the front-panel controls to provide access to sound-editing facilities.

chapter 7

samplers and sampling

Samplers have become a mainstay of the modern music studio, but if you're not familiar with them, you can think of them as essentially just another type of synthesiser where the source waveforms can be recorded and edited by the user. In the case of a regular synth, the sound waveforms are chosen by the manufacturer and stored in ROM (Read-Only Memory), which means that you're limited to using permutations of the source sounds provided for you. Although one of the appeals of the original samplers was that you could go around the house hitting pans and blowing milk bottles to create samples of your own, many users also make extensive use of the many commercial libraries of ready-made samples available on CD-ROM.

hardware samplers

Once a sound has been recorded into the sampler's RAM (Random Access Memory), it can be played back at varying pitches under the control of a MIDI keyboard or sequencer. In this respect, playback is just like using a regular synth. For a sampler to play back a sample at a higher pitch than that at which it was first recorded, it has to speed up the sound, with the result that the sample also plays back faster. Exactly the same thing happens with tape – if you double the tape speed, everything happens twice as quickly and the pitch goes up by one octave. Conversely, if you drop the pitch by slowing down the sample, the sound will go on for longer.

Because RAM (which is where samplers store the sounds loaded into them) only works when power is supplied, most samplers forget everything when switched off, which means that some form of permanent sound-storage system is required, and this is true of both hardware and software samplers. Most budget hardware samplers and more professional older models offer floppy-disk storage as standard, with hard-disk storage available as an option. Stereo audio files sampled at 44.1kHz require around 10Mb of storage per minute, so clearly what can be fitted onto a 1.44Mb floppy disk is very limited, although new models tend to come with hard drives already fitted. Software samplers, on the other hand, save their samples to the computer's hard drive and load them into its RAM for playback.

software samplers

Software samplers work in essentially the same way as their hardware counterparts, except that they use the computer's own RAM to load and play back sounds and the sound comes via the computer's audio interface or soundcard rather than from the back of an external hardware unit. Some software samplers can also "stream" samples from a hard disk in real time, which means that the lengths of the samples that can be played back is no longer limited by the amount of free RAM available. Probably the best known name in this area is the Tascam (formerly Nemesis) GigaSampler. On these devices, a short section at the start of each sample is held in RAM to enable the sampler to respond quickly when a note is played, after which audio data is streamed from the hard drive as required. Of course, streaming from disk increases hard-drive activity, which may reduce the number of conventional audio tracks that you can play back, but on the positive side it has made possible some very elaborate sound libraries, such as those for grand pianos in which every note is sampled for its full length over a range of playing intensities (what synth players would call velocities), with and without dampers.

To my mind, software-sampler plug-ins have a number of advantages over their hardware counterparts, not least being that the user interface is often presented onscreen as a traditional synth-style control panel, complete with knobs, faders and buttons. Furthermore, these may be automated by recording their movements in real time. Figure 7.1 overleaf shows the user interfaces from Emagic's EXS-24 VST and Steinberg's Halion samplers. Both interfaces are much more user-friendly than poking about with a postage-stamp-sized LCD display, a rotary dial and a handful of buttons!

When using a software sampler in its traditional Instrument mode, there is a limit on the amount of polyphony available, just as there is with hardware synths, but in most cases you can specify the amount of polyphony that you need, although, as you might imagine, polyphony eats up processor power. With some models, the filter section can be switched off when not required in order to conserve processor resources. Note that, while some software samplers are available as VST plug-ins, others (such as the Emagic EXS-24) are designed to work only in the manufacturer's host software (in this case, the Logic Audio sequencer).

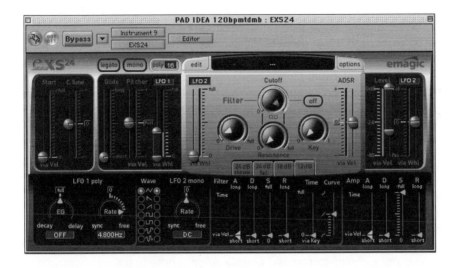

Fig 7.1: EXS24 (above) and Halion screens

uses of samplers

Before delving deeper into exactly what goes on inside a sampler, it will be helpful to look at the two main ways in which people use them in music production. If you sample single musical notes, such as strings or organ sounds, you can play the sampler much like any other synthesiser, the beauty being that you're not restricted to the internal sounds supplied by the manufacturer. The other great thing is that absolutely any sound can be sampled and used as a musical instrument; one of the first things that people do when they get their first sampler is to go around the house hitting and scraping things and recording the results.

To make a sampled sound musically useful, a sampler needs to work polyphonically so that you can play chords, and the sounds need to respond to the common MIDI controllers, such as pitch bend, modulation and sustain. Most modern machines are also multitimbral in the same way as conventional synths, within the limit supported by their maximum polyphony.

The other popular way of using samplers is to record not just individual notes but whole musical or rhythmic phrases, and this way of working forms the cornerstone of modern dance-music construction. A typical application might be to sample a four-bar drum rhythm and then trigger this on the first beat of every bar to provide a continuous rhythmic backing. Only one MIDI note is needed to trigger the loop, which makes this a very economical way of working, in terms of polyphony, although long loops need more RAM than samples of individual beats.

sample memory

One thing that you soon discover after having bought a sampler is that you could always use more sample memory. Because sampled sounds are held in RAM, the maximum sampling time is always limited by the amount of memory available. If you're using your sampler multitimbrally, the available sample memory is divided between the various sounds loaded in at any one time. Software samplers use the computer's own RAM and a fully expanded, top-of-the-range sampler may hold several minutes' worth of samples, and it makes sense to fit as much RAM as you can afford, now that it's so cheap.

Because RAM is finite, various strategies are routinely adopted to make the most of it, although the falling prices of memory have made some of these more or less obsolete. At a full audio bandwidth of 20kHz, with a 44.1kHz sampling rate, one minute of stereo sound takes up around 10Mb of RAM.

If you can make do with mono, this immediately doubles the amount of sampling time available, and if you can tolerate a lower audio bandwidth by setting a lower sampling rate then this time can be extended again by a factor of two or more. However, the capacities of both hardware and software modern samplers are so great that operating at a reduced bandwidth really shouldn't be necessary any more.

looping

The other time-saving strategy used when sampling sustained musical sounds such as strings or flutes is to play back part of the sample in a continuous loop, which allows the sound to be sustained indefinitely. Most sustained sounds have a distinctive attack portion, but as they start to decay the sound becomes more consistent. Listen to something like a flute or a string section playing a sustained note and you'll notice that very little changes after the initial attack. This being the case, there's no reason to sample the whole sound being played; you simply need to sample the first few seconds and then use the sampler's editing facilities to create a loop so that the middle part of the sample repeats itself continually until the key is released. The length of the original sound will probably be too short if you want to hold a string pad down for 24 bars in one go, but looping it will allow you to sustain your notes for as long as you like. Obviously, there's little point in trying to loop short or percussive sounds, but you can loop long percussive sounds, such as the decay of a gong or cymbal.

There's another good reason for looping sounds, and that's to get around the way in which the lengths of notes change as you play higher or lower on the keyboard. Once a sound is looped, its level never has to decay to silence because you're always looping around the same section of sound, as shown in Figure 7.2, which leaves you free to shape the decay of the note using familiar ADSR-style envelope shapers. These work in samplers in exactly the same way as they do in synthesisers.

crossfade looping

Sometimes, no matter how careful you are, you'll find that the point at which you've looped a sample remains audible as a change in tone, a change in level or even a click. Clicks occur when the shapes of the waveform at each side of the loop "edit" point don't match up perfectly. Fortunately, crossfade looping can eliminate clicks in just about any situation. Most serious samplers have a crossfade-loop facility that uses internal editing algorithms to overlap the start and end points of the loop

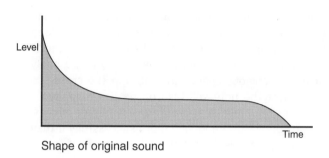

Shape of original sound

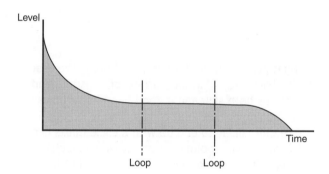

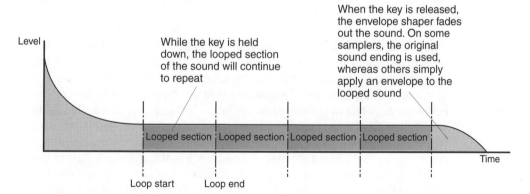

While the key is held down, the looped section of the sound will continue to repeat

When the key is released, the envelope shaper fades out the sound. On some samplers, the original sound ending is used, whereas others simply apply an envelope to the looped sound

Behaviour of sound after looping

Fig 7.2: Looping a sustained sound

and then smoothly fade one into the other, instead of the loop point being a sudden transition between beginning and end.

The crossfade should normally be made as short as possible, or the sound may appear unnatural, but at the same time you need to make it long enough to hide any unpleasant glitches, such as clicks or abrupt timbral changes. However, if the start and end points of the loop are too badly matched, you may hear a very obvious change in timbre at the crossfade point, while if the loop is short the note will take on an irritating, cyclic quality that gets more obvious (and faster) at progressively higher pitches. Slowly decaying sounds can sometimes be looped more successfully if they are compressed before being sampled, as this will maintain a more consistent level, but unless you have access to a studio compressor, this may be beyond your control.

looping problems

The basic idea behind looping is pretty straightforward, but finding the best sounding loop points can be tricky for a whole variety of reasons, and creating "invisible" loops requires both skill and a good ear. Firstly, unless the waveform shapes at the beginning and end of the loop match up in level, shape and phase, you're quite likely to end up with a click. Clicks can be minimised by looping at zero-crossing points (points at which electrical signals cross over from being positive to negative or vice versa), but if the waveform levels and shapes don't match pretty closely, you may still hear a glitch.

If you take too long a section to form your loop, you may find that the sound's own natural decay means you have a difference in level between the start and end of the loop, which will be audible as an unnatural modulation. This might lead you to believe that, the shorter the loop, the smoother the result will be, while the reality of the situation is that even apparently steady sounds are constantly evolving in their harmonic textures, and if you take too short a section to create your loop, you end up with something that sounds more like a bland electronic tone than a real instrument. Part of the skill in getting good loops is to choose the optimum loop length, but although that takes practice and experience, it's not as difficult as it sounds and is definitely easier on samplers equipped with waveform displays.

Sounds to be looped should always be sampled without vibrato or any other form of modulation because the modulation rate will change depending on the note being played. Also, it's harder to loop a sample with vibrato because not only do you have to match up the basic waveforms but you also have to ensure that you're looping a whole number of complete modulation cycles, or you'll end up with a repeating hiccup in the vibrato.

Finally, stereo sounds are a little more difficult to loop because a good waveform match on one channel may not correspond to a good match on the other. Where stereo looping is essential, crossfade looping is almost always necessary to hide the join. Also, when your stereo sample includes panning, you should take special care that you don't get an abrupt jump in the stereo image every time the loop repeats.

envelopes

To recreate the effect of a sound's natural decay, samplers include envelope shapers - just like those found in synths - to allow you to modify the envelopes of your sampled sounds. In most cases, the attack of the original sound can be left as it is, although you can always modify it if required - for example, a fast-attack string sample can be turned into slow strings by decreasing the attack time. With looped or sustaining samples, a new decay has to be created in order to prevent the sound from stopping abruptly when the key is released. If you've sampled an organ sound, an abrupt stop is OK, but most instruments have a slower decay time, which can easily be duplicated by using the Release phase of the envelope shaper. At its simplest, this will mean that the sound will remain constant in level while a key is held down and then fade out at a pre-determined release rate when the key is released. Of course, you can use the envelope generator more creatively to set up any envelope you like, just as you can on a conventional synth. Similarly, some samplers offer complex, multisection envelope generators and may even be able to generate two or more different loops within the same sample. For the sake of simplicity, though, I'll be sticking to the basic features here.

Filters are very often included as part of most basic samplers' armouries and may be modulated by envelopes, keyboard position, loudness and all of the other sources found in a typical synthesiser. By combining volume envelope shaping with envelope filtering, source sounds can be changed quite dramatically.

triggering

If you have a sound that plays through from start to finish without being looped, you'll find that there are different ways of triggering it. For example, if you hit the same key twice and you want the original sample to carry on to its natural conclusion while the newly triggered one plays over the top, you'll need to select the "one-shot" Trigger mode. On the other hand, if you want the original sound to stop and then trigger again from the beginning for that clichéd "N-N-N-N-Nineteen" effect, you'll need to choose Retrigger mode. Again, most samplers support these basic triggering modes, but there may be slight differences in the terminology used.

multisampling

So far, I've covered the rudimentary principles of sampling, but I haven't yet touched upon the way in which sounds become very unnatural when transposed too far from their original pitches. The reason why this occurs is all to do with the *formants* or resonances that characterise each instrument or voice. Most instruments and all voices have very distinctive formants, such as those created by resonances in the human vocal tract, the body of a guitar and the pipe of a wind instrument. Although the note being played may change, some of these resonances stay more or less fixed, so if you increase the pitch of a note by speeding it up, you also increase the pitch of the formants and make the instrument sound smaller – hence the Mickey Mouse effect when you speed up vocals. It's sometimes possible to use this unnatural quality very creatively, but when you're trying to capture a "real" instrument, such as a piano, you have to move only a few semitones away from the note's original position before it starts to sound quite alien. This is where the very important concept of multisampling makes an entrance.

If a sampled piano sounds natural for, say, only a couple of semitones on either side of its original pitch, the only way to maintain a natural sound is to take several samples of the original instrument sound at different pitches and use each sample over a limited part of the keyboard. This is a technique known as *multisampling*, and the zones of the keyboard covered by each sample are known as *keygroups*. The more keygroups you have, the more accurate the sound will be but also the more memory you'll need to hold all of the samples. Pianos tend to be close to the top of the list of critical instruments, while strings, flutes and brass instruments can all be stretched a little further before they start to sound artificial. As I said, a sampled piano sounds natural for only a few semitones either side of its original pitch, so the only way to get it sounding "real" over the whole keyboard is to take several samples of the piano for each octave. These individual samples can then be arranged to play across the sampler's range, with no individual sample being moved more than a few semitones from its natural position. The best piano libraries use a separate sample for every single note of the keyboard (88 notes means 88 samples), and there may be alternative samples at different playing intensities as well as samples taken with and without the sustain pedal. Figure 7.3 shows how a keygroup may be built up.

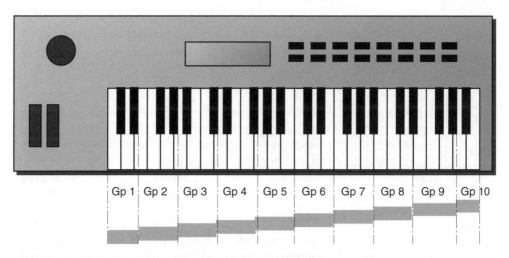

Keyboard divided into groups, in this case with five semitones per group. One sample is used to cover each group, which means that no sample ever has to play much over one tone away from its original pitch. This results in a more natural sound than using just one or two samples to cover the whole range of keys. The number of multisamples required depends to a large extent on the characteristics of the instrument being sampled

Fig 7.3: Creating a keygroup

Only experimentation will tell you how many samples you need to create an acceptable-sounding instrument, but I find that sampling one note per octave is generally OK when I'm creating samples from synthesiser sounds. Plucked sounds seem to be among the least forgiving and ideally need sampling two or three times per octave.

To make use of samples recorded at different loudnesses, velocity switching or crossfading may be employed, which simply means that you take two samples – a loud one and a quiet one – and then use key-velocity data to control which one plays. Velocity switching is the most efficient option, as it doesn't affect your overall polyphony, while crossfading to a louder sample as you play harder sometimes sounds more progressive, as you get a more gentle transition, but it also halves your polyphony, as two samples are playing at the same time.

making your own samples

An important point to note about sampling is that, because it is a digital process, it's important to sample the signals at the highest possible level in order to get the best signal quality and the lowest noise. However, if you go too far and clip the signal, the chances are that it will sound pretty dreadful, as digital samplers have no margin of safety like analogue recorders do. If the sound you're trying to sample isn't repeatable, it may be better to record it to tape first and then sample it, which will allow you to try again if it doesn't work out the first time.

Before you can record your own samples, you're going to need a microphone, and if your sampler doesn't have a mic input then you'll need to use a mixer or something similar as a mic pre-amp. Having said that, almost any decent dynamic vocal mic will do for most basic sampling jobs, especially when the result is to be used as a percussive element; you'll only benefit from using a studio capacitor mic when sampling really high-pitched sounds, such as triangles.

Once the notes or phrases have been sampled, you can trim the starts and ends, normalise the levels (if necessary) and then think about looping, in the case of single-note samples. If you're working with a software sampler and the source sounds are noisy, you may also want to run denoising software to clean up the sounds – for example, to remove hiss and hum – before you go on to edit the samples.

Hardware samplers often include mic-level as well as line-level inputs, making it possible just to plug in a mic and record a sample. You'll still have to take care over your recording levels, though, just as you would with any other digital-recording device, and if you're creating multisamples from the same instrument you should ensure that you play at the same loudness for each sample. Once you've loaded your samples, save them to disk before going any further and then you can assign them to keygroups. If the notes sound right when played in their keygroups, you can move on to looping them where necessary, but bear in mind that some hardware samplers change the original sample rather than creating a new version. This is one reason why you should back up your sounds directly after sampling, because if you don't then an unsuccessful looping session could destroy all of your hard work. If you've backed up your samples and a loop goes wrong, you can simply reload the original from disk and try again.

The way in which you record samples using a software sampler such as Steinberg's Halion or the Emagic EXS-24 will depend on which soft sampler you have. Some models allow you to sample directly using VST samplers, although Emagic's EXS-24 VST (which, as you may have guessed, is the sampler I use most of the time) requires you to record the samples in your host program's waveform editor before importing the result into the sampler. This is less clumsy than it sounds, as the waveform editor can be opened directly from within the Sample Edit window. Once in the sampler, the loops can be adjusted in length, crossfaded and - where multiple samples have been made at different pitches - arranged into keygroups. Furthermore, you don't have to reload the samples in order to change the crossfade settings. Some software samplers (the EXS-24 included) make keygrouping easy for you by offering an automatic zoning function that sets up keygroups based on the samples given to it. You still have to carry out any looping manually, but this function certainly speeds up the process.

using samplers as recorders

When samplers first came onto the scene, the primary aim was to sample individual notes or sounds so that you could play them in much the same way as you'd play any other keyboard instrument. Now that longer sampling times are available, it has become popular to sample whole musical phrases that can be played back from a single key. Probably the first application of this type was to sample whole sections of vocals, allowing the engineer to copy a good chorus from one part of a song and then fire it into the mix when the next chorus came around. However, it was quickly realised that there was enormous creative potential in working in this way and that, if several complete drum rhythms were sampled at the same tempo and then each one was assigned to a different key on the keyboard, you could effectively play an entire drum part simply by holding down the appropriate keys. (It is slightly confusing that musically meaningful sections sampled in this way are referred to as *sample loops*. These are quite different from looped samples, which were covered earlier in the context of extending the lengths of samples.) After that, it didn't take long for a whole genre of loop-based recording to spring up based on the capabilities of the sampler.

looping drums

Samplers usually allow you to loop drum parts or other phrases so that they play continuously, but when you're working with a sequencer there's a strong likelihood that the timing of a drum loop will drift away from the tempo of the sequencer over a period of time. A far better option is not to loop your drum rhythm within the sampler but simply to retrigger it every bar, or however long the pattern is, by using a note from the sequencer quantised to the first beat of the bar. You can match up the sequencer tempo to the tempo of the drumbeat pretty easily, and it doesn't really matter if there's a tiny discrepancy because every time the drum rhythm is retriggered, it's brought back into perfect sync. The same is true of other

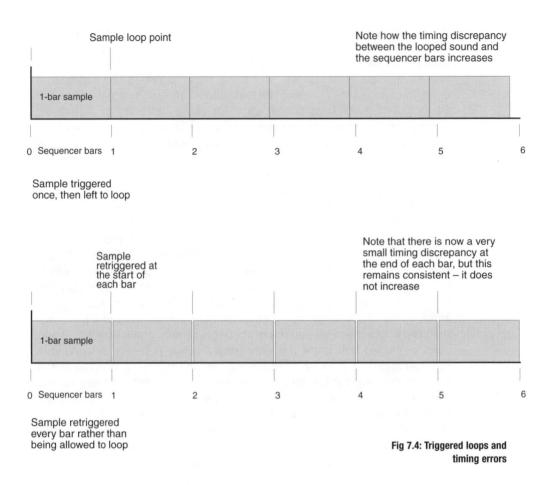

Fig 7.4: Triggered loops and timing errors

rhythmic elements, such as guitar riffs and even long vocal sections - it can be better to break them down into shorter phrases and then trigger each phrase independently. Figure 7.4 shows how timing errors can occur if you don't trigger your rhythmic sample loops from the sequencer.

groove manipulation

One of the problems with samplers is that it's difficult to use them to change tempo without changing pitch, but there are a couple of initiatives that help out in this area when it comes to working with drum loops. The most common are Propellerhead's REX format and Spectrasonic's Groove Control, both of which work by breaking up drum loops into their individual beats so that the rhythm tempo can be changed over a wide range without the pitch of the individual beats changing with it. There are technical differences between these two systems, but the most significant is that Groove Control samples are available only in commercial libraries while you can create your own REX file samples using Propellerhead's ReCycle software. ReCycle has various automatic and semi-automatic tools for dividing drum rhythms into separate beats, after which the result can be saved as a REX file for use in any REX-compatible software.

Both systems rely on sliced using loops, with MIDI notes being used to trigger the different slices. This means that, for every drum loop you load, you'll also need the corresponding MIDI file to drive it. Naturally, these are supplied along with the samples, and with Groove Control these are conventional MIDI files. Groove Control developers usually add ambience and lengthen the slices so that the groove can be slowed down considerably without odd-sounding spaces appearing between beats. Conversely, as the loop is sped up, the samples get shorter, so as to reduce overlap. Groove Control MIDI files can be imported conventionally into any sequencer, while REX files must be supported by the application in which they are used.

changing the feel

As supplied, the Groove Control MIDI data determines the feel of the drum groove, but it's easy to change the feel of a pattern by using the Quantise and Swing features of the sequencer. This ability to experiment opens up lots of creative possibilities, since you can layer and combine nearly any groove from any of the Groove Control libraries and then adjust the feel of them so that they work together. Groove Control library loops can also be used as playable drum or percussion sample kits, because each slice is allocated to a different MIDI note. All you need to do is note which keys on your keyboard trigger which sounds.

Until REX files and Groove Control came along, studio musicians were pretty much restricted to using drum samples as they came or suffering the side-effects of time-stretching. These days, however, using samples provided in the REX or Groove Control file format provides much greater flexibility, in terms of both tempo and the ability to change elements of the sound and feel, so for anyone involved in rhythm-based music, this is an area to explore further.

experimentation

It's extremely instructive to experiment with sampling your own sounds - even the most innocent everyday objects can yield interesting results when played back at different speeds. Once you've got past the obvious blown bottles, sewer-pipe didgeridoos and metal kitchenware, you start to find that steel garage doors make great snare drums, bouncing balls can be tuned down into monster kick drums and innocent wooden banister rails can sometimes blossom into very organic marimbas.

instrument sample libraries

So far, I've covered just the essentials of sampling, but once you get into sampling you'll discover a lot of things for yourself. However, one thing you'll soon find is that life is too short to make your own grand-piano samples, so standard orchestral and instrumental sounds are best obtained from a sound library. If you have a sampler that can read CD-ROMs, this makes life easy, as virtually all modern samplers can be connected to a CD-ROM drive or have one built in.

The wealth of sample libraries that are now available is amazing. Not only are all of the standard orchestral and instrumental sounds available, sampled to a very high standard, but you'll also find a huge supply of grooves, loops, sound effects and samples of classic analogue synths. The most popular sample format at the moment is for the Akai S1000 and S3000 machines, and most serious VST samplers can import these formats using the host computer's CD drive. Other common formats include Roland, E-mu and Akai S5000/6000, while there's also a trend towards supporting the less expensive SoundFont II format developed by Creative Labs as well as formats proprietary to software samplers such as GigaSampler and Sampletank.

Once you start to follow the CD-ROM route, you'll probably be pleasantly surprised at how easy it is to get your hands on fully produced, ready-to-play sounds. Furthermore, if you're using a software sampler, you'll probably find that sample sets that took a minute or two to load into a hardware sampler load into your software sampler in seconds once they've been transferred to your hard drive. If your software sampler has the facility to create categories for your samples, make use of it or you'll soon find your hard drive full of oddly named samples and you'll have no idea what they sound like. I know this because I've done it!

Samples provided on CD-ROM are already set up in programs that contain their looping information, key mapping, envelope settings and so on, so you really just need to load them and play. The majority of CD-ROMs are supplied formatted for Akai samplers, but because of the popularity of these machines most of their major competitors (both hardware and software) also make it possible to load Akai-format disks. If you're after stock sounds, well-produced drum loops or exotic ethnic bits and pieces, it's far easier to buy the sounds than it is to sample your own. Creating your own samples is fun, and it's a central part of what sampling is all about, but there are few people with the time and skill to produce something like a perfectly multisampled grand piano.

Sample CDs in audio-only format are a useful source of new sounds and have the benefit of being significantly cheaper than CD-ROM sample libraries. Also, you can play them directly into the analogue inputs of your sampler using a domestic CD player. All you have to do is set the record levels, and if you're lucky enough to have a sampler with a digital input and a CD player with a digital output, you can pipe the data in digitally (at 44.1kHz only, of course). If you go via the analogue inputs, keep in mind that the sampler is really a digital recorder and that overloading the input will result in very unpleasant distortion. Even so, you should always get the level as high as you can without running into clipping, as this will produce the best signal-to-noise ratio.

organising samples

The hard work starts after you've sampled the sounds from CD – now you have to name your samples, create loops where appropriate, sort out crossfades and put all of the samples into keygroups so that you get a smooth transition from one sample to the other as you go up the keyboard. You may also have to create keyboard zones so that sounds can be velocity crossfaded or cross-switched. I don't know what you consider to be fun, but as far as I'm concerned, unless the sample is marvellous beyond belief, life is simply too short to do this kind of job on a typical hardware sampler. Some software samplers make the job rather easier, but creating a good set of multisamples still takes time and care, so once you have something you can be proud of, back it up!

A much easier alternative is to use CD-ROM libraries, as discussed earlier. Of course, first you have to confirm that your sampler can work with a CD-ROM drive; even those fitted with SCSI sockets for the connection of external drives can be very fussy about the makes and models drives with which they are prepared to work, so if you're in any doubt you should contact the technical-support line relevant to your make of sampler and ask for advice.

Most good sample-library CD-ROMs cost as much as the drives that they are slotted into, if not more, but I have to say that, when you actually get around to using CD-ROMs, it's a real luxury, because the samples load up into neatly named programs, ready looped and keygrouped and complete with appropriate envelope settings so that all you need to do is load them and play them.

However, I can't guarantee that you'll find all of the samples on any particular disk any more exciting than your credit-card statement!

compatibility

The samplers of at least three of the major manufacturers – Akai, E-mu and Roland – are supported by a vast library of both in-house and third-party CD-ROMs, so it comes as no surprise that each has developed an operating system allowing CD-ROMs made for their competitors' machines to be used as well as their own. Some of the software-sampler formats are also becoming more commonplace, such as GigaSampler and the Creative Labs SoundFont and SoundFont II formats. However, because every sampler has slightly different parameters, facilities and characteristics, the degree of translation isn't always perfect. Sometimes the only difference is a change in tonal quality, but there are occasions when you need to edit the samples to make them fully usable. For example, the EXS-24 software sampler from Emagic makes no attempt to import the filter settings from other formats, so you have to set up your own after importing the samples. Note too that you can't carry out a straight translation between a sampler that supports multiple loops during the decay of a note and one that supports a single loop; you may be able to import the basic samples, but you'll probably need to sort out a suitable loop point yourself.

sample storage

If a sampler's basic memory provision of 16Mb is inadequate, you might well ask, what use is the integral 1.44Mb floppy drive for storing samples, especially for machines that don't have the provision to save longer samples over multiple disks? The answer is that, while floppy-disk-sized samples were once commonplace, modern libraries tend to be much, much larger, so most of the time the floppy drive is pretty useless as a sample-storage medium. For any serious storage, you'll need a hard drive or a high-capacity, removable media drive. If you're looking at second-hand samplers, don't even consider one that can't be hooked up to a hard drive.

When it comes to choosing a specific model of drive, I think that I would put quietness of operation at the top of my needs list, rather than speed of data transfer. Any hard drive is going to load up a typical set of samples fairly quickly, but some models are intrusively noisy. If you're going to buy any type of removable drive, however, it might be a good idea to check with any musicians or local studios with whom you are likely to collaborate with a view to settling on the same model. Not only does this guarantee compatibility but it also provides you with the opportunity to co-operate in ordering blank media in bulk, which can result in significant savings.

sample-editing software

Even with all of the bolt-ons you can attach and a selection of sample CDs at your disposal, you're still going to want to do some sampling of your own (I hope!), and it will soon become clear to you that working from the front panel of a typical hardware sampler isn't the easiest way of doing things. Looping samples and setting them into keygroups is more easily managed onscreen, and unless you have one of the very few samplers that supports a computer monitor then you might be tempted to check out the software sample editors on the market. Powerful sample editors are available for both Mac and PC platforms, as well as for some of the less prevalent machines, and some of these are generic whereas others are dedicated to a particular model or range of samplers. Again, the tech-support line for each make of sampler is a good port of call if you're seeking advice on compatible editing software.

MIDI can be used to transfer samples from a sampler to a computer and back again, but this is very slow. A better and faster option may be to use a system that can communicate over SCSI, but SCSI support has been dropped from most current computers and adding SCSI cards can be problematic. In my view, if you're working with a sequencer and you have a fairly powerful computer, your money will be much better spent on a good software sampler, as you'll find it much easier to use, it has its own built-in sample-editing software and it has access to all of your computer's spare RAM for sample-storage purposes.

creative sampling

While only a real die-hard sampling fanatic would dream of attempting to multisample an entire grand piano, what often really makes a recording stand out is the use of something that's a little out of the ordinary. In the early days of sampling, people would blow over milk bottles, sample the result and then play it back over the whole span of the keyboard. It didn't matter that it sounded like a penny whistle at the top end of the scale and a demonic foghorn at the bottom; that was part of the magic of the sound and, for me, part of the magic of sampling.

With rhythm playing a more important part than ever in contemporary pop music, the sampler provides the perfect opportunity to capture unusual sounds for use in a rhythmic context. The great advantage here is that the sounds don't need multisampling, fine-tuning or looping, and so, aside from a little topping and tailing, they're ready to use as soon as you've saved them to disk and loaded them into a program. The usual method of assigning percussion sounds is to place each one on its own key of the keyboard with the sample set to play at its original pitch, rather than pitched by keyboard position. Having said that, of course, it's sometimes useful to put the same sample on two or more keys to make playing rolls and fills easier.

improvising

The most exciting thing about sampling is that you don't need any real instruments in order to create some really powerful sounds. There's a multitude of natural sounds that can be captured and then manipulated, and usually all you need to do is adjust the pitch, sharpen the attack by truncating the leading edge of the sample, if need be, and adjust the decay rate. Here are some examples of noises that can be turned into great percussion sounds. If you have a DAT (Digital Audio Tape) machine, MD (MiniDisc) recorder or even a good cassette recorder, it's best to record a series of sounds to tape first, as then you only need to sample those that sound as if they're going to work.

- Slamming an up-and-over garage door – This produces a powerful sound that reverberates around inside the garage, so you'll get a different result depending on whether you're miking from inside or outside. You'll probably want to trim the sound and use only the bang at the end, and you might also find that the decay time is too long, in which case you can reduce it by using the sampler's envelope controls. Try the sound at different pitches for kick- or snare-drum substitutes.

- Slamming doors: An ordinary interior door can produce a gratifying bang if closed with sufficient vigour. Leaving a window or another door open may help, as this prevents air pressure in the room from cushioning the slam.

- Bouncing a plastic football on a hard surface – This is the UK version of miking a bouncing basketball. Tuned down, it makes a wonderful kick-drum sound, especially with the addition of gated reverb.

- Suitcases – We've all heard of drums that sound like suitcases, but if you get the right suitcase, you can make it sound just like drums. Try hitting it with different things, including a rolled-up newspaper or a wooden mallet. Keep the mic fairly close and watch the recording levels to make sure you don't run into clipping.

- Soggy paper – For this, you'll need a lump of soaked newspaper pressed into a ball. Hurl it at various surfaces and record the results. It can be surprisingly effective, but it isn't recommended indoors. Again, this makes a passable kick-drum sound.

- Baking foil – Hold up a sheet of baking foil and hit it flat-on with a wooden spoon or similar implement. You'll probably tear it, so try to get this one right first time. If you get the mic close enough and pitch-shift the result downwards, it should sound like an old reverb plate being shot!

- Snapping wood – A simple length of wooden beading can be snapped in half to provide a satisfying substitute for a techno snare sound. You'll probably have to drop the pitch quite a bit, unless you're strong enough to break logs!

- Bits of wood – Hitting a couple of offcuts together should produce a nicely resonant *thunk* that can be shifted up to give you a clave sound or down to sound like marimbas or log drums. You can play the resulting sound over a couple of octaves, and if you're lucky you might have captured enough of the pitch to tune it.

- Domestic radiators – Most radiators ring if you knock them, and by hitting them with a felt beater or even a rolled-up newspaper you can capture a useful sample that, when pitch-shifted down, sounds like a weird gong. Pitch-shift the sound up and you have an alternative cowbell. The same applies to most metal containers, so look around your house and see what's around.

- Speaker cones – Tap any speaker cone (gently!) and you'll hear a noise, but on larger speakers, such as those used in studio monitors or instrument amplifiers, the chances are that the noise will be a deep thud, not unlike a kick drum. Mic at close range, drop the pitch further, if necessary, and you have another kick-drum sound.

- Vacuum cleaners – OK, so they're not really percussive, but if you sample anything that uses an electric motor and then drop the pitch you'll find that you have something that sounds like a monstrous generator. If you can tune the pitch to match the song, you can trigger short bursts of sounds to produce a techno/rave gated-bassline feel.

- Spanners – Large spanners suspended on cotton or fishing line produce excellent bell-tree sounds, although to really capture these at their best you'll need a capacitor mic. The spanners can be tapped with any metal object or banged together, and if you drop the pitch, you can end up with some quite moody Tibetan gongs or bells.

- Plastic waste pipe – Plastic piping makes a great didgeridoo, and even if you can't manage the circular breathing, you can loop the sample to give the impression that you can breathe out forever. Larger-diameter waste piping can be played with a table-tennis bat to produce tuned percussion. Just hit the open end of the pipe with the bat.

Once you have your sound, you may need to add some effects to make it sound more impressive, and virtually any percussive sounds will benefit from having some reverb added. If your sampler doesn't have internal effects, a cheap outboard effects unit can be used in conjunction with your mixer. Take note, however, that, although you could sample sounds with reverb already added, the reverb time will appear to get longer towards the bottom of the sample's pitch range and shorter towards the top, so adding the reverb later will produce a more natural sound.

separate outputs

Hardware samplers usually come with at least one stereo output and often with the option to add more by way of a plug-in card. This will allow you to route different parts (when using the instrument multitimbrally) to different outputs, and on more advanced machines you may even be able to separate samples used within the same part. This is particularly useful when you want to separate the kick, snare and the rest of the drums in a kit so that you can apply different processing to each. Some software samplers offer the ability to route to different sequencer mixer busses, but at the time of writing some did not. If you just want to separate parts, this isn't a problem, as you can open multiple sequencers on different tracks and then route them accordingly. Separating the parts of a drum kit is a little less straightforward, but you can still do it – copy the drum MIDI data to two or more tracks, open a sampler on each track and then delete all of the notes that you don't want the track to play. For example, on the snare track, you'd delete all of the MIDI notes except for the snare hits and so on. You can then process the different sampler tracks separately, using plug-in effects.

Some software samplers also provide the facility to use multiple outputs, but this is by no means universal and may depend on the host software's routing abilities, if the sampler is a plug-in. A workaround is simply to open up two (or more) sampler plug-ins on different tracks and then split the part between them, according to what you want to route where. For example, one sampler could carry all of the parts of a drum kit apart from the kick drum, which could be moved to the second sampler track and routed to a different mixer channel. This would allow reverb to be added to the main body of the kit without it being added to the kick drum.

miking for sampling

By now, you should have some ideas of things to sample, but you may be unsure about how to mic up the sounds or how to treat them afterwards. You don't really need a fancy mic, unless you want to make high-quality recordings of bright sounds, but the position of the mic is fairly important. My usual approach, when recording this kind of sample, is to set up the mic around a foot away from the object being struck and then to change its position if this initial setting doesn't produce the desired result. As a rule, you'll only need to use longer mic distances if you're miking up something large, like a garage door or a radiator, and because you're not after a natural sound, the only criterion is whether the sound works or not, rather than the quality of the recording. If you have a mixer, a good technique is to listen to the output of the mic over headphones as you physically move the mic around the sound source. This is a very quick and easy way of finding the "sweet spot" (ie the optimum mic position for recording).

By recording to tape first, you can experiment with recording levels and sort the good sounds from the bad before you get down to sampling. If the sound you've recorded has too slow an attack, you can either truncate it, so that the first few milliseconds of the sample is thrown away, or you could consider adding another sound. For example, if you create a sample of a bouncing ball and then decide that it doesn't have enough bite, you could trigger the sample at the same time as a short percussive sound from a drum machine (or another sample) and mix the two together. The mixed sound can then be recorded onto DAT, MD or some other medium and subsequently resampled. Sounds that work well alongside kick-drum samples are things like fingersnaps, claps, rimshots and other short sounds. The trick is to mix these ancillary sounds low enough so that they merge with the sample to create a new sound. Sequencers with audio facilities provide a simple way of layering and manipulating raw sounds prior to sampling.

Once you've started to experiment, the list of possibilities is endless, and because you can amplify the sound to any level you like, the most insignificant event can form the basis of a huge-sounding sample - a snapping twig could become a monster snare drum, a kitchen cleaver slammed into a cabbage can give you yet another kick drum and a length of scaffolding can provide the basis for tuned industrial percussion.

summary

The sampler is both a creative tool (if you're sampling new sounds for yourself) and a superb device for playing back commercial library sounds. If you use a sequencer with audio capabilities and your computer is powerful enough, you'll probably find a software sampler plug-in easier and faster to use than its hardware equivalent. Because of the envelope-shaping, filtering and modulation facilities provided by a modern sampler, it can do everything a sample-based synthesiser can do but with the benefit of using longer source-sound samples.

chapter 8

alternative MIDI instruments

MIDI was originally developed for use with keyboard instruments because electronic circuitry likes the certainty of switches and a MIDI keyboard is really just a row of switches. It's very easy to generate unambiguous note messages from a MIDI keyboard – you just need to monitor what the keys are doing and (in the case of velocity data) how fast they are doing it. Individual contacts under the keys tell the microprocessor controlling the keyboard which note is being played and velocity information is determined by the very simple method of using two sets of staggered contacts and calculating how quickly the second one closes after the first. Aftertouch is also quite simple – a pressure sensor runs underneath the keyboard so that, when the keys are depressed firmly, a control signal is generated.

However, not every musician plays a keyboard, so alternative *controller instruments* were developed, some of which have enjoyed more success than others. In fact, many instruments have been manufactured or adapted to generate MIDI information, including (but not limited to) guitars, violins, wind instruments, drums and even accordions. The electric guitar is still the most popular contemporary instrument, however, so I'll tackle that one first.

guitars and MIDI

Making a guitar work properly via MIDI is a huge technical challenge, as guitars don't naturally lend themselves to MIDI – unlike the electronic keyboard, the notes are created by strings vibrating, not by oscillators being turned on and off with switches. In order to generate MIDI information, there has to be some means of knowing which note is being played. Early attempts at this included the construction of guitars with electrical connections fitted to each fret (which made the guitar a bit like a one-handed organ, from the player's perspective), and then there were wired frets coupled to picking detectors, but the problem with switching systems is that they are unreliable (sweaty fingers and all that!) and they can't provide any accurate information when it comes to string bending. All kinds of ingenious systems were tried – optical devices for reading the angle of string bend, ultrasonic SONAR-type circuits for determining the length of string that was being fretted and numerous other innovations, none of which was ever entirely successful. Even if they *had* worked properly, the majority of players wanted something that would work with their own guitars.

Fortunately, Roland took the challenge very seriously and – prior to introduction of MIDI – developed two very different guitar synthesisers. When MIDI came on the scene, Roland moved over to building guitars that generated MIDI data, but even their first efforts involved the use of a special guitar. It's only when they developed the GK2 split pick-up, which could be fitted to any guitar, that the system had any chance for mass appeal. Roland's solution – which has been adopted by some of its competitors – was not to use switches or wired frets but instead to use special circuitry to measure the pitch of each string. The signal from a conventional guitar pick-up is too complex to analyse when more than one string is sounding at a time, which is why a split pick-up (in effect, one pick-up per string) is needed. Using this system, each string can be monitored independently of the others.

On the Roland system, once a note is picked, a circuit tracks the frequency of the string and passes the information to a small processor that generates the required MIDI data. A level-threshold system decides when the string has been picked and when it stops vibrating. Unfortunately, the first part of a plucked note comprises mainly unpitched pick noise, and then, when the string does start to vibrate, there's a short time delay before the circuitry can figure out the pitch. Modern circuits track the pitch pretty quickly, but tracking is always slower on the lower strings (because of the lower frequencies involved), leading some players to complain that the delay on the bottom couple of strings puts them off.

A further problem is that guitar sounds are harmonically complex, and if a harmonic is played then the circuitry may lock onto its frequency rather than onto that of the fundamental pitch of the string. In fact, accidental mistracking occasionally plagues even the best systems. To compound the difficulties, there's no "key-up" event to tell the note when to end, so if the player doesn't terminate the note by damping or lifting off his or her finger, there's no telling when the note will stop; it all depends on the sustain of the guitar. When the level of the note has fallen below the detection threshold, it is deemed to have ended. Similarly, the very action of lifting a finger off a string can cause the open string to vibrate just enough to cause an accidental retrigger. In reality, it's important to play more cleanly when working with a MIDI guitar than when playing a conventional electric part, but if used with a sequencer – which will allow you to fix mistakes afterwards – they can constitute a practical method of recording MIDI information. Also, because it uses markedly different chord voicings to a keyboard, the MIDI guitar can produce less obviously "keyboardy" results.

pitch bend

One way in which designers of modern MIDI guitars have found to improve note-tracking is to use MIDI pitch-bend controller information to continually correct the pitch of a tracked note. Not only does this mean that finger vibrato and bends can be followed accurately, but it also reduces the time it takes to track each note, as the system can make a quick guess at the pitch and then amend this information using the pitch-bend data as soon as the waveform settles down. Hammer-ons tend to be implemented entirely via pitch-bend information, so if you're working with a sequencer, the notes you see on the Edit page may be a little different from those that you actually played. For example, a hammer-on/-off trill will be shown as a single picked note followed by pitch-bend data.

MIDI Mono mode

To enable each string of a guitar to be used for independent note bends via MIDI, each string must be handled by a different MIDI channel. The most guitar-like results are achieved with a synth that can work in MIDI mode 4 (Omni Off/Mono), which in effect puts each guitar string in control of its own monophonic part of a multitimbral module. A guitar string can play only one note at a time, of course, so this is a good way of working.

Even when there is no intention of bending notes, it's essential to stick with the one-channel/one-string approach if hammer-ons and slides are to be tracked accurately, and because guitars notes can be bent and hammered over a wide range, it's often best to set a pitch-bend range of one octave (on both the guitar controller and the synth) instead of the more usual two or three semitones preferred by keyboard players.

However, there are occasions when it can be advantageous simply to plug the guitar synth into a module set to Poly mode. Although bends, hammers and slides can't be employed when playing multiple consecutive notes in Poly mode, working in this way does provide a reasonably reliable way of triggering simple parts, such as block chords or straight melody lines.

guitar set-ups

It's important that any guitar that you intend to use with a MIDI guitar synth system is set up properly. This means that the split pick-up should be mounted as close to the bridge of the guitar as possible and that the spacing between the pick-up and the strings should be around 1mm when the string is fretted on the highest fret. Of course, this set-up may differ slightly from model to model, so consult your handbook carefully. It's also important that the strings pass over the centre of each section of the divided pick-up in order to avoid crosstalk between adjacent strings. Fret buzz causes tracking problems, so very low actions and guitar synths don't mix. Note that some pick-up systems come with a choice of screw-fixing or self-adhesive sticky pads. The latter are clearly the best choice when working with a guitar that you don't want to modify, but in my experience actually screwing in the attachment makes the system work more reliably and certainly makes it easier to adjust the height of the pick-up. If you can arrange the screws to pass through the scratchplate of the guitar, it may be worth buying a replacement scratchplate that you can then use with the divided pick-up so that, when you come to sell the guitar, you can refit the original scratchplate and hide the screw holes.

A number of major manufacturers now make both electric and acoustic guitars with built-in divided pick-ups that are compatible with both Roland and Yamaha MIDI guitar systems. Although these are fairly expensive, they nicely skirt the issue of having to modify your own guitar.

Having established that guitar synths prefer to track cleanly vibrating strings, here are a few playing tips:

• Avoid playing harmonics and play as cleanly as possible using even picking strokes.

• Conventional fast strumming doesn't work well, as the notes are too short for the synth to lock onto reliably, so try an arpeggio or a simple finger-picking pattern instead.

• Instruments such as pianos have rigidly fixed pitches, so similarly don't bend notes or use your guitar's vibrato arm. Also, if your MIDI guitar system has a Bend Off option (sometimes called Chromatic mode), this might produce better results.

• Don't think like a guitar player; think as though you're playing the instrument you're imitating. For example, if you were playing a solo flute patch, you wouldn't play chords, as flutes are monophonic. If the sound you're using has a slow attack, play slow, uncomplicated parts to let the sound develop. If the slow attack throws your timing, listen to the sound of your pick on the strings and take your timing cues from that.

- If your guitar synth has a noticeable delay on the bottom strings, try playing the part one or two octaves higher and then use your sequencer's Transpose function to bring the pitch of the synthesised sound back to where you want it. (Having said that, the systems I've tried that were made after the year 2000 have all had surprisingly fast tracking).

- Because you never know exactly how long a plucked note will last, use the sustain pedal for long chords.

- Don't sit too close to CRT computer monitors, as most MIDI guitar pick-ups react to interference from the screen, resulting in erratic note-tracking and -triggering. LCD monitors are better for all-round use near guitars.

MIDI guitars with sequencers

The following guidelines might be useful to anyone using a MIDI guitar in conjunction with a sequencer or with external expander modules:

- Always ensure that your guitar synth and any expander modules you're using are set to the same MIDI pitch-bend range (usually twelve semitones, as opposed to the more normal two or three semitones used by keyboard players).

- To record a guitar part that has complex string bends, the sequencer must be set to record on all six MIDI channels simultaneously. Consult your sequencer manual to find out how to do this. Less sophisticated sequencers may not have this option.

- Double-triggered or very low-velocity notes can often be removed automatically by your sequencer. Check the handbook to see what labour-saving functions are available to you.

- Make full use of any sustain-pedal functions available to you when playing held chords. Such functions as "Note Length Quantise" and "Force Legato" can also be used to good effect to create certain musical styles.

mental approach

Getting to grips with different sounds is something that electronic-keyboard players have always had to do, but guitar players are conditioned to expect every sound that they play to have an instant, percussive attack. Give a rock-guitar player a brass patch with a slow attack and he'll probably complain that the synth can't keep up with him. What he really means is that the attack time of the instrument is too long to allow the notes to develop at the speed at which he's trying to play. A tuba player isn't likely to attempt double-time triplets, so why expect a tuba synth patch to be able to?

the future of MIDI guitars

Because of their historic tracking and delay problems, MIDI guitars aren't as popular as they were once expected to be, but their development continues to progress and they're becoming cheaper and more reliable with every incarnation. Some designers have employed neural-net technology to help their systems recognise and correct common playing problems, and this is an area that could bring great benefits in the future. Ultimately, the guitar is a much more expressive instrument than the keyboard, so I'm hopeful that we will eventually see a more widespread use of MIDI guitars in music production.

MIDI violins

MIDI violins usually work on a similar principle to MIDI guitars, inasmuch as they have a separate pick-up for each string, but as violins don't use metal strings, the pick-ups are more likely to be piezo-electric devices. Because of the possible interference that bow noise can inflict on the tracking process, ingenious multiple-pick-up systems are sometimes employed and elaborate electronic filtering is used to strip away harmonics so that the fundamental frequency is less difficult to detect. There are systems available that can be fitted to a regular violin as well as electric violins with all of the necessary pick-ups and electronics built in.

wind controllers

Various wind controllers have been built at one time or another, most relying on switches or touch sensors to duplicate the functions of the keys on a clarinet or similar instrument. These switches provide the note information in much the same way as the keys on a regular keyboard, but a special mouthpiece capable of measuring breath and lip pressure provides additional controller information in order to add more life to the sound. The instruments may also be fitted with sliders, modulation wheels or ribbon controllers that the player can operate with his or her thumb, while other refinements include octave switches.

Played well, the wind controller is a most impressive instrument, and if used in combination with one of the newer physical-modelling synths or modules, the results have a stunning realism about them. Like real wind instruments, these controllers are monophonic, although you can still set your synth to play parallel intervals, such as fourths, fifths and octaves.

drum controllers

MIDI drum systems have been around for many years because they're not too difficult to design, compared to other controller systems. Usually, a synthetic rubber pad is used instead of a real drumhead, and this is fitted with a special pick-up that monitors how hard the pad has been struck. Impacts are converted by a processor into MIDI Note On and Off messages of differing velocities in accordance with how hard the pad has been struck.

A separate floor-mounted pad is often used in conjunction with a conventional bass-drum pedal for producing bass-drum sounds, and a regular footswitch or volume pedal often serves as a simple hi-hat open/close controller. Cymbals and hi-hat sounds can be triggered by the same types of pads as those that trigger the drum sounds, although more sophisticated systems use cymbal-shaped pads with positional sensors that allow two MIDI-controlled sounds to be crossfaded as the player plays across the surface of the pad – for example, a cymbal might have a bell sound near the centre and a ride-cymbal sound near the edge.

drum pads

Drum pads are available as full-sized kits complete with stands and fittings to replace conventional drums or they may be presented as a number of smaller pads fitted to the surface of a briefcase-sized unit. This latter type is more practical in the home MIDI studio and most have inputs to accept pedals and bass-drum pads.

Although full-sized drum pads were traditionally solid surfaces with rubber coatings, some now use tough nylon mesh heads that can be tensioned to give the same playing response as real drums and the mesh heads produce very little stick noise. It's possible to use two or more sensors in this type of drum to produce a different sound when playing away from the centre of the drum or to trigger rimshots. By recording the MIDI output of the drum "brain" into a sequencer, the original performance can be recreated, complete with all of its nuances.

The most advanced pad systems allow the user to send out sequences of notes from specific pads, either in programmed or in random order, and if these are assigned to slightly different cymbal sounds, for example, the sound will change every time the pad is struck, making for a more natural sound. The same trick can be used to make snare-drum rolls sound more natural.

practical sequencing

So far, I've talked a lot about MIDI and sequencing, and hopefully you'll have tried out a couple of things just to convince yourself that MIDI really does work, but now it's time to tackle a practical recording session using your sequencer. Be sure to keep the manual close at hand, as every sequencing software package handles things slightly differently.

Before you start work, though, the first thing you should do is make sure that you're in a comfortable working position, as sessions at the sequencer can go on for much longer than originally planned. Sitting at a poorly positioned computer for any length of time will soon result in back ache, neck ache and wrist ache, none of which help the creative process of writing music. Even though you may think that you do most of your work with the mouse, you should nonetheless put the computer keyboard in a position where typing feels comfortable. You'll also need to be able to reach your music keyboard from your sitting position, so you'll need to be comfortably placed in relation to that, too.

Even a high-resolution computer monitor can cause eye-strain so try to position the screen so that it's at least two feet away from your eyes. You should also use adequate ambient lighting in your studio so that you don't get dazzled by the screen. An anti-glare filter might help, but as long as you follow the above guidelines and don't set the screen brightness too high, you shouldn't have any problems. If you do find your eyes getting sore, consider buying a pair of VDU operator's spectacles to filter out any glare and ultra-violet light that may be coming from your monitor screen. (These goggles do the same job as an anti-glare screen but are rather cheaper, especially if you have a large monitor.) Better still, buy an LCD monitor. They're now relatively affordable, take up less desk space and don't generate nearly as much electromagnetic interference as the old glass monitors. (This is particularly relevant if you plan to record electric guitar anywhere near your monitor.)

You should always use a mouse mat, not the table top or the back of a book. (This may not apply to optical mice.) Apart from making the mouse run more smoothly, this will also extend its life by reducing the amount of dust that accumulates on the ball and internal rollers. If you're really short of desk space, consider forking out for a trackball; some people really like working with these, while others hate them. Whatever your feelings on the matter, at least you won't keep running out of mouse mat with one of these!

sequencer familiarisation

MIDI sequencing starts at your controller keyboard, which is connected via its MIDI Out to the MIDI In of your MIDI interface or soundcard. (If you're one of those people who are hanging onto their antique Atari STs, the interface on these is built into the computer.) If your keyboard includes a synth section (rather than just being a dumb master keyboard), switch to Local Off mode and plug a MIDI cable from the sequencer's MIDI Out to the keyboard's MIDI In. If you have other MIDI modules in your system, you can daisy-chain these in any order by feeding the MIDI Thru of one piece of gear to the MIDI In of the next module. If you're using virtual instruments, of course, these have the benefit of needing no MIDI interface and no wiring. Your sequencer will have a display (possibly in the transport window) that indicates when MIDI data is being received.

If you haven't done so already, plug everything in, check all of the connections, make sure that your synthesiser is plugged into a suitable amplification system and switch everything on, making sure that the volume is turned down when you do so. Once everything is powered up, turn up the volume until you can hear things properly. When you're satisfied that everything is OK, load up the sequencing software. If you haven't used a computer before, take some time to read the manual, then try a few exercises just to get used to the mouse. Make sure that you know how to start the machine and how to shut it down - don't just pull out the mains plug when you're done or you'll risk losing data or even corrupting your hard drive. You'll also need to know how to format and use floppy disks (on those computers that still use them), how to open and close files and, in the case of Macs and PCs, how to open, close and move windows. Only when you're happy with these basic computer operations should you attempt to do any sequencing.

the Arrange page

Although every sequencer package on the market has a slightly different user interface, most of the successful models bear more than a passing resemblance to Steinberg's Cubase sequencing software, on which the main page shows the sequencer tracks running from left to right across the screen. The appearances of hardware sequencers tend to be a little less

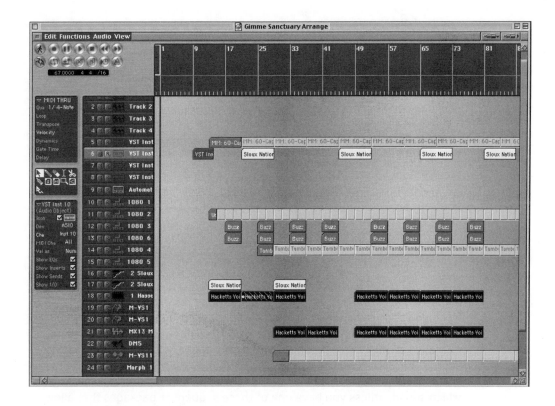

Fig 9.1: Arrange page of a typical software sequencer

consistent, but the basic principles of selecting and recording tracks, playing back sequences and editing are roughly comparable. The Arrange page of a typical sequencer is shown in Figure 9.1.

Each sequencer track can usually be set to record on any MIDI channel – you don't have to use track 1 for MIDI channel 1, but to start with it might be less confusing to set up track 1 to channel 1, track 2 to channel 2 and so on. If you have a system that comprises both an external MIDI module and a soundcard, you'll find that you also have a choice of sound source for each track. For example, if your PC system has a simple SoundBlaster card, this is likely to show up in the form of a choice between the on-board AWE32 synth and MIDI, where the MIDI option constitutes the external MIDI connection to your sound module.

Mac users don't usually have access to internal MIDI soundcards, so if you have a Mac the normal choice will be between MIDI instruments or virtual instruments (where applicable), unless a multiport MIDI interface is fitted. If you have an older Mac with a multiport interface, you'll get a choice of 16 channels on, for example, MIDI ports A, B, C and so on, probably prefixed with an M or P to indicate whether the interface is plugged into the modem- or printer-port sockets. If you have a really big MIDI system, of course, you might have an interface plugged into each port. Bear in mind, though, that the maximum number of ports that an external multiport MIDI interface is capable of supporting is usually eight with a full 16 MIDI channels per port, although some top-end interfaces offer almost double this number.

On newer models of Macintosh, the MIDI ports will operate via USB and will be numbered. Although interfaces with more than eight ports are uncommon, it's often possible to connect multiple USB interfaces if more MIDI ports are needed.

program selection

Having set your tracks to the MIDI channels that you wish to use, you should enter a MIDI Program Change number in each track, which will force your synth module or soundcard to play the sound program of your choice. Most General MIDI soundcards can have their patch names displayed within the sequencer's Arrange page, which makes choosing sounds a little easier. If not, you'll need your synth's manual open on the patch-chart page so that you can see which number corresponds with which sound, unless you have one of those sequencer packages that allow you to type in the patch names of all of your synths. This may be a tedious job first time around, but you'll be thankful later when you can call up every synth patch by name rather than by number. If you have to work with program numbers, it will help to have a photocopy of the General MIDI patch list pinned to your wall.

tempo

Now adjust the tempo to suit the music you wish to record. You can always change the tempo after recording, so if you're not a great player you may want to set this slightly slow in order to make the job of recording easier - you can always speed it up again once you're finished. Once you've started recording, the computer will play a simple metronome click via either the computer's own speaker, the audio interface or your MIDI drum sounds. After a count-in of one or two bars (depending on what you've set up in the sequencer's Preferences section), the currently selected MIDI track will record everything that you play into it.

Personally, I find click tracks very limiting to play to - I'd rather play to a drum rhythm - so if you find your timing wandering, you can record a simple drum pattern first and use this as your metronome. You can even save it as your default song, which means that you won't have to create a guide-drum part every time you start a session. If you're using a General MIDI sound module, of course, the drums will be on channel 10, and switching to different program numbers may give you a choice of different-sounding drum sets, depending on the module or soundcard you're using. Something simple with bass, snare and hi-hats is usually fine, and don't worry if it's not exactly what you want for the final version because you can always replace it or edit it later. However, unless your timing is really good, you should quantise it so that all beats line up to the nearest 16th note, for a 4/4 time signature. Different time signatures may require different quantise values, and most sequencers offer a selection of different quantisation values from a pull-down menu.

Important: All of the better sequencers have fully undoable quantise functions so that you can unquantise your work or apply a different quantise value at any time. However, some less sophisticated sequencing software doesn't let you fully undo quantising, so if you have such a system, save a back-up of your song file to disk before quantising just in case you try quantising your work and you don't like the result!

drumming made easy

If you find playing drum parts difficult, here's a tip: create three or four sequencer tracks, all set to the channel of your drum sounds (usually channel 10), and record your drum part in layers. First put the bass drum part on one track and then, when this is OK, record the snare drum part in isolation on the next drum track. When these are both working together, key in your hi-hat part. (It sometimes helps if you actually drum on the keys with your forefingers instead of trying to play the drum rhythms as if you were playing a piano.) Refer to the drum map in your sequencer manual to find out which drums are on which keys. In fact, it might be a good idea to consider sticking labels on the keys to identify each drum sound.

Most sequencers have facilities for merging data on different tracks - on Cubase and similarly styled programs, this takes the form of an icon in the tool palette resembling a tube of glue. The usual method of merging data is to select the tracks to be joined by holding down the shift key, click on the desired tracks until they are all highlighted and then click on any one of them with the glue tool. If you want to tidy up your drum tracks after you're sure they're OK, simply merge them all into one track. This will leave the Arrange page looking less cluttered.

copying and looping

Obviously, you don't want to have to tap in the drum rhythm for the whole length of the song that you plan to write, so your best bet is to create just one or two bars and then copy that part as many times as you need. Some sequencers (like Logic Audio) allow you to loop sections so that they play indefinitely while other programs (like Cubase) have a Copy menu into which you can enter the number of copies required. These copying and looping functions are immensely useful, especially in pop music, which tends to use a lot of repetition.

the next track

Once your guide-drum part is tapping away happily, choose a new track and play whichever keyboard part is most appropriate – possibly a chordal part or a bass line. Now that you have your drum part, you can turn the original metronome click down or off if it's distracting you.

When you get to the stage where you've played in two or three tracks, have a listen to your performance to make sure that the timing feels OK. If you're a good player, you'll almost certainly get more feel in your performance by not quantising it, but if you're a bit on the sloppy side you may feel it needs tightening up. Before you dive straight for the Quantise button, however, have a look at your manual to find out if your sequencer supports percentage quantising. Fortunately, most sequencer software has this facility. (See "Quantisation" in Chapter 3, "Introducing Sequencers, for an explanation of this term.)

moving your music

Another very powerful feature of sequencers is that you can move data around. For example, you may put together a composition but then decide that the synth solo should start a couple of bars later than it does. This is no problem in a software sequencer, because all you have to do is use the mouse to drag the sequence to a new position. What's more, if you want to copy it to a new position without changing the original, there's usually a keyboard shortcut whereby you can hold down a key and then drag a copy to its new location. (These keyboard shortcuts vary from package to package, so check your manual to see how your system works.) This technique is invaluable for copying repeated sections, such as verses or choruses, as you only have to record each section once and then you can drag around copies and experiment with alternative arrangements. A hardware sequencer will offer the same functionality but, instead of working within a visual environment, you're more likely to have to define the start and end locations of the section that you want to move or copy and then enter the location to which you want it to be moved or copied.

divide and conquer

Before leaving this section, I should mention the tool that appears in the form of a knife or a pair of scissors, usually found in the tool palette. This is provided so that you can cut up a recorded sequence into two or more parts. You may simply want to divide an eight-bar section into two four-bar sections so that you can copy or move the individual parts, but you can also use it to chop up an improvised solo into good parts that you want to keep and less good parts that you want to reject, for example. You can then delete the rejected parts and arrange the remaining sections (duplicating them if necessary) in any order you like to form a new and technically perfect solo.

Although there's a lot of similarity between leading sequencer software packages, the tool palettes tend to differ slightly. Make sure that you know what all of the tools on your sequencer are for and practise using them.

more on editing

At this stage in the proceedings, the idea is to become familiar with the sequencer, not to record a hit single, so rather than trying to perfect that solo synth part, let's move on to explore some of the editing tricks that can performed on the data you've just recorded.

Find the Transpose command, select the part that you want to transpose, move the melody part up or down an octave and then play it back to hear how it sounds. The Transpose command comes in very handy if you want to create a part that's outside the range of your keyboard, but you might also find that the part you've recorded simply sounds better when played back an octave higher or lower. A useful trick is to copy the data from one track to an empty track set to a different MIDI channel, set it to a different sound and then raise it or drop it by an octave. This will give you two different instruments playing back the same part an octave apart.

the Grid Edit page

The other editing process with which you should familiarise yourself is the fixing of wrong notes. Once again, most sequencer packages have a Grid Edit window of some kind in which the notes are represented as bars on a grid that depicts time (in beats and bars) in one direction and pitch (in

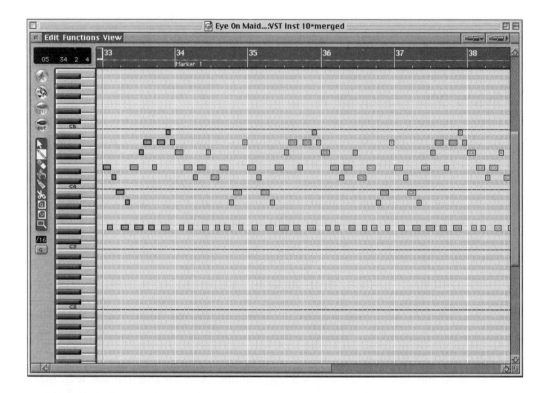

Fig 9.2: Grid Edit page from a popular sequencing package

semitones) in the other. This is sometimes called a *piano-roll editor*, where a piano-keyboard graphic is used to depict the pitch axis of the grid. (Figure 9.2 shows the Grid Edit page from a popular sequencing package.) To correct wrong notes in a Grid Edit page, it is necessary only to drag them by clicking, holding and moving the mouse until they are at the right pitch or timing position. Even if you can read music notation, the Grid Edit page will actually give you more information than a conventional score as it shows precisely where each note starts and stops and it may also show you how loud each note is.

the MIDI Event list

If you're not comfortable with grid editing, you should also have a MIDI Event list that represents your composition as a long list of MIDI events, each marked with its own beat and bar location. Values in this list may be changed either by typing in new values or by using the mouse to scroll up

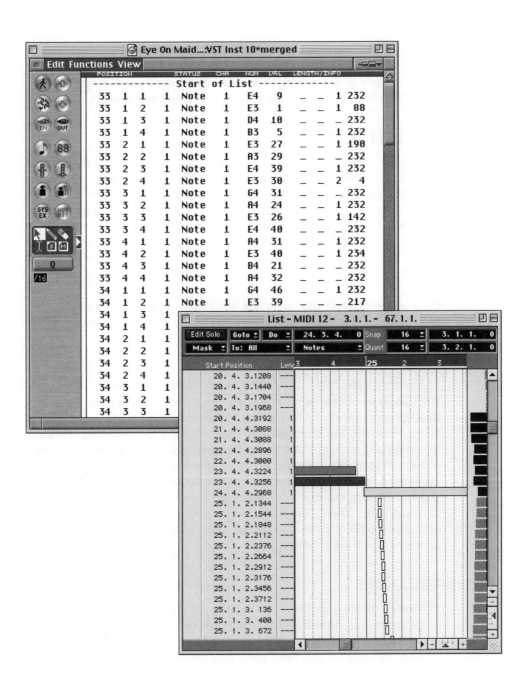

Fig 9.3: MIDI Edit lists

and down through the available values. As different packages adopt slightly different methods, it's important to refer to your manual when trying out any of the editing techniques discussed here. Figure 9.3 shows the MIDI Event lists of a couple of typical sequencing packages.

the Score Edit page

Finally, the more musically literate user may prefer to edit notes on the stave, and the majority of serious sequencer programs allow for this. On the Score Edit page, notes may be physically dragged to new pitches, deleted or inserted, and the more advanced packages allow you to prepare a full multipart score ready for printing. For music notation to make sense, however, you'll need to enter the correct key and time signatures for each song. Figure 9.4 shows the Score Edit windows from a couple of typical sequencer packages.

Once you've finished your song and any editing that needs to be done has been done, don't forget to save everything before switching off the computer or all of your work will be lost.

bad news and good news

The bad news is that what has been described so far represents only a small proportion of what a powerful sequencer package is capable of doing. However, the good news is that, once you've mastered the basic recording and editing skills that have been discussed so far, you'll know enough to start making serious use of your sequencer. Most of the time, you'll need to use only a fraction of your sequencer's available features; you can explore the more sophisticated functions as and when you feel that you need them. However, you're bound to come up against the occasional difficulty, so I've listed here some of the more common problems and their solutions.

troubleshooting

• Two or three modules can usually be daisy-chained without any problem, but more than three may cause you to suffer from stuck or missed notes. If this happens, use a MIDI thru box on the output of your sequencer and feed each module from a separate output on the box.

Now let's assume you've wired your system up properly, but no sound comes out. Here are a few things to check – some obvious, some less so.

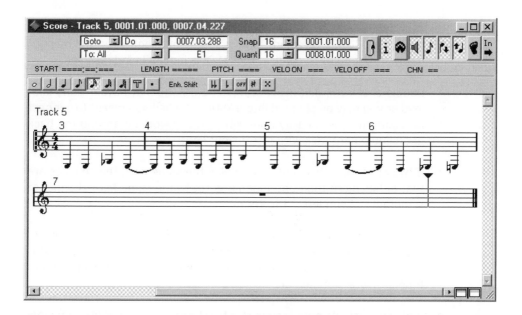

Fig 9.4: Score Edit window

- It sounds obvious but check everything is switched on and that the MIDI cables are pushed in firmly. If you're using modules that have both Multi and Single modes, make sure that Multi is selected for multitimbral operation. Also, make sure that the volume controls on your synths and on the amplification system you're using are turned up. Use the "MIDI Received" indicators on your sequencer and on your hardware modules to confirm that MIDI is indeed being received.

- Double-check your MIDI cable connections – you may have a faulty MIDI lead or you may be plugged into a MIDI Out when you meant to connect to a MIDI In. This is easily done when you're working around the back of an equipment rack with insufficient light!

- If two or more instruments try to play the same part, the chances are that either more than one module is set to the same MIDI channel or something's been left set to Omni.

- If your master keyboard plays its own sounds when you're trying to record using the sound of another module, make sure that Local Off is really set to Off. Some instruments default to Local On status every time they are switched on.

- If playing a single note results in a burst of sound, rather like machine-gun fire, or if you get stuck notes or apparently limited polyphony, you may be suffering from a MIDI loop. Once again, the most common cause of this is that the master keyboard has been set to Local On when it should be on Local Off.

  Note: If you have an older keyboard with no Local Off mode, you'll probably find that your sequencer allows you to disable the MIDI Thru function on the channel on which your master keyboard is transmitting. This should get you out of trouble.

  If you're unlucky enough to have neither facility, your best bet is to record with the MIDI In physically disconnected from your master keyboard – in other words, using only the sounds generated by your external modules. When you've finished recording, you can then reconnect the master keyboard's MIDI In and use it to play back one or more of the recorded parts. Fortunately, few people buying a new system will come across this limitation.

- If the sequencer records OK but the wrong sound plays back, you may have forgotten to enter a MIDI Program Change number into your sequencer track. Alternatively, if your synthesiser hosts multiple soundbanks, it may be set to the wrong bank. In such cases, include a Bank Change as well as a Program Change message at the start of the track to set up the correct sound.

saving your songs

If you're using an older computer without a hard drive, such as an Atari ST, you'll need to have a formatted floppy disk to hand in order to save your work, whereas if you're working on a machine with a hard drive, you can save your song file to disk in exactly the same way as you would save any other kind of computer file. It also makes sense to save your material every few minutes, just in case there's a crash, but if you regularly use a computer for other tasks, you won't need to be reminded of this. Each sequencer has its own file format, so you can't normally change song files from one sequencer platform to another, although there are a number of exceptions where software manufacturers have built in facilities that will allow you to import song files from other makes of sequencer.

standard MIDI files

To facilitate file transfer, most sequencers will allow you the option of saving your work as an SMF (Standard MIDI File), and these can be freely swapped freely between platforms. Commercially available song files are invariably in SMF format, usually on PC-formatted disks, and Atari ST computers can read SMFs from PC disks while older Apple Macs need to have either System 7.5 running or use a PC-to-Mac conversion program such as AccessPC. More recent Macs can all read PC-formatted floppy disks, either via the internal floppy drive (if fitted) or via a peripheral USB floppy drive.

Note that SMFs support only the basic 16 MIDI channels – they can't handle the additional channels you get from using a multiport MIDI interface. Transfers are still possible 16 tracks at a time, but this is a tedious job. When emailing files to a Mac or PC user, use a suitable file-compression utility, such as DropStuff or DropZip, respectively, in order to preserve the file type.

automating MIDI

This next section is just a little more advanced, so if you don't feel like trying it out yet, that's OK. However, it's easier to do than it is to read about, and I'm sure you'll find that it opens up many interesting possibilities.

As you've learned already, MIDI controllers can be used to adjust many different parameters relating to a musical instrument, the most useful in a mixing situation being main volume (controller 7) and pan (controller 10), but you aren't limited to automating volume and pan during a mix; you can, in theory, change any parameter of an instrument that is assignable to a MIDI controller, including portamento rate (controller 5), sustain pedal (controller 64) and, where supported, criteria such as filter frequency and resonance. These latter parameters aren't defined controllers, and it's up to individual manufacturers to determine if and how they are implemented, so it's a case of looking in the back of the manual to see exactly what you can access via MIDI. It really is worth looking into those apparently tedious back pages once in a while!

Automation also extends to virtual instruments, and in most cases this is easier than controlling a hardware instrument as the MIDI data generated by moving any of the virtual controls when the track is in Record mode is recorded directly. Composers of dance music particularly appreciate the ability to manipulate and record filter settings in real time.

automating patch changes

The other fundamental component of MIDI mix automation is the Program Change command. If you have a limited number of MIDI instruments, it can be very useful to be able to change sounds in the middle of a song. Most sequencers will allow you to enter a new Program Change command directly from within the MIDI Event list, enabling you to decide at exactly which bar and beat the change should take place. Sometimes you need to be careful of where you insert the command in order to get a graceful changeover of sounds but the vast majority of synths help you out by retaining the old patch sound for any sustained notes - these don't change until they are released, even if newly played notes have switched to the sound of the new patch.

If you have a sequencer that doesn't let you enter Program Change commands directly - and to be honest, I can't think of anything even semi-serious, offhand, that doesn't allow you to do this in one way or another - you can instead use the Program Select buttons on your master keyboard to send a Patch Change command at the appropriate time. The patch change will be recorded into your sequencer, just like any other MIDI event, and if it isn't in quite the right place you can always go into the MIDI Event list and move it. The same applies to any other physical controls on your synth that send MIDI controller information: the movements can all be recorded in real time.

Even if you don't intend to change patches during a song, you should still insert Program Change commands at the start of each track, ideally during the count-in period, so that all of your instruments are automatically set to the appropriate patches before playing commences. Some sequencers handle this for you automatically so you don't need to do this by hand, but it's still useful to be aware of it.

It also pays to be aware that, if you copy a track so that you can use it with a different MIDI instrument, any embedded Patch Change information (and any other recorded MIDI controller data) will also be copied, so don't forget to update any copied Program Change numbers before continuing work or you might find totally inappropriate patches being called up. I've fallen for this one more times than I'd like to admit! Furthermore, if you don't need any of the controller information you've copied over, select it in the MIDI Event list and delete it.

practical MIDI automation

When it comes to using controller information to set up volume and pan effects, you first have to make sure that your instruments respond to these messages. This may sound obvious, but there are a few older instruments out there that are totally oblivious to master volume (controller 7). The only way of fading out with one of these is either to pull down the fader by hand or to doctor the MIDI note velocity data in your sequencer's MIDI Event list so that the notes actually become quieter. Fortunately, such instruments are comparatively rare.

Thanks to modern sequencer design, there are now many ways of entering controller information. In the early days, you had to add controller numbers and values to the MIDI Event list or record them in real time, but now there are often more intuitive graphic methods available. If you have a keyboard with assignable data sliders or wheels, you have an even more convenient way of sending controller data in real time without having to edit it afterwards.

hardware controllers

The trouble with the computer mouse is that it can control only one thing at a time, whereas the traditional studio engineer can often operate a couple of controls simultaneously. Fortunately, you can get the same degree of flexibility by using a hardware controller with a software sequencer. A hardware control surface translates the action of conventional knobs and faders into MIDI messages that control the virtual knobs and faders on your sequencer's Mixer page or indeed any MIDI parameter that you set them up to control.

There are several different types of controller available at all kinds of prices, the simplest being the familiar MIDI fader/knob box. Some of these use only knobs and are designed mainly for synth editing and control, whereas those designed for mixing tend to come with faders as well as

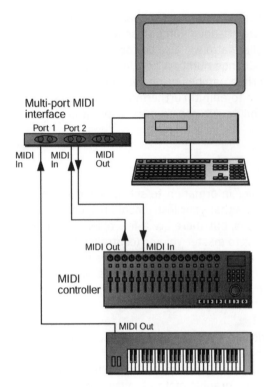

Multi-port MIDI interface

Port 1   Port 2

MIDI In   MIDI In   MIDI Out

MIDI Out   MIDI In

MIDI controller

MIDI Out

Fig 9.5: Set-up displaying bi-directional MIDI connections to a controller

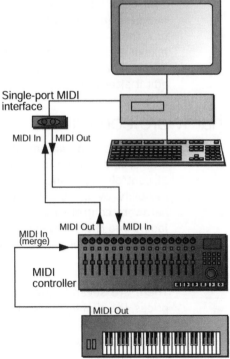

Single-port MIDI interface

MIDI In   MIDI Out

MIDI In (merge)   MIDI Out   MIDI In

MIDI controller

MIDI Out

knobs. A useful addition for guitar players working alone is an assignable footswitch jack for hands-free punching in and out.

Budget controllers use standard, non-motorised knobs and faders, which makes them relatively inexpensive to build, and most allow you to define the type of MIDI message being sent by each control. For example, if you wanted to control the channel fader levels on a typical sequencer mixer, you'd probably need to set each fader to a different MIDI channel and have it send MIDI controller 7 data over the range 0-127 while knobs could be set to send MIDI pan data (controller 10) and so on.

For controlling only level and pan in a mixing situation, a simple fader box will do the job effectively enough, but it's more useful if you can configure the faders as aux sends or use them to control EQ or plug-in parameters. For this to work, the controller needs to be programmable in much the same way as a synthesiser or effects pedal, so that patch 1 might configure the faders to control volume, patch 2 might assign them to aux send 1, patch 2 might assign them to aux send 3 and so on. This means that the addition of a display of some kind is required, as well as the inclusion of further buttons for programming and perhaps a data wheel, so such a device is understandably more expensive than the most basic type of controller.

Setting the fader and knob assignments for each patch is simple enough but can take a long time. To make this job less tedious, some controllers come with templates for the controlling of common sequencers or for editing the more popular synthesisers. Many also include a MIDI Learn mode, in which case they need a MIDI In as well as a MIDI Out to facilitate bi-directional communication. The usual arrangement is that, once a fader has been put into Learn mode, moving any onscreen knob or fader with the mouse will automatically assign the selected fader to operate that particular parameter. This MIDI set-up is shown in Figure 9.5a and requires you only to connect the controller's MIDI Out to a MIDI In port on the sequencer and a sequencer MIDI Out to the controller's MIDI In (assuming that the computer uses a multiport MIDI interface). However, it's not uncommon for MIDI controllers to offer some kind of MIDI merge facility so that the controlling keyboard can feed into the sequencer via the controller without the need for a multiport MIDI interface. In this kind of arrangement, the controller-keyboard and fader-control data are merged before being sent to the sequencer, as shown in Figure 9.5b. Where a built-in MIDI merge function isn't available, a standard MIDI merge box can be used to combine the controller and keyboard outputs before feeding them to the sequencer's MIDI In.

While MIDI fader boxes of the type described here are cost effective, the faders on them don't physically move unless you move them yourself, so if you use any mix-level automation or switch to a different bank, the faders are likely not to match the current value of the parameter to which they are assigned. In some systems, the fader takes control of the assigned parameter only when you move it through the position that corresponds to the current parameter value, which helps but isn't a complete solution, although it does prevent the sudden jump in controller value that would otherwise occur if the data changed to reflect the fader position as soon as the fader was moved.

Manual fader systems are most useful when they're spending most of their time doing one job, such as controlling levels and pans or controlling a specific synth, but if you need to be able to switch functions frequently, they're less than ideal.

A better (albeit more expensive) solution is to use a moving-fader controller that is either designed specifically for use with a specific piece of software or comes with a choice of personality templates that includes the sequencing software you're using. Emagic's Logic Control and Steinberg's Houston are examples of such dedicated controllers.

Because the kinds of systems described here employ moving faders that move to the correct value whenever you change functions, you gain the ability to switch banks quickly and seamless, moving from fader control to aux or EQ at the press of a button. Other benefits include tape-style transport controls, Mute and Solo buttons, track-record arming buttons and even the ability to access and edit plug-in instruments and effects. Having the right hardware controller can make a huge difference to the usability of a system and can make using it feel much more like using a traditional, mixer-based studio, particularly when you're trying to set up an automated mix.

level tricks

Even if you don't need traditional fade-outs or -ins, using controller 7 is a useful way of tailing off a long sound that otherwise ends too abruptly, especially at the ends of songs. You could achieve this by editing your synth patch, but the controller 7 workaround is generally a lot easier and arguably more precise. Equally usefully, controller 7 data will allow you to vary levels during the course of a song, just as you would with an automated mixing console. The easiest way of entering data in this case (if you don't have a hardware MIDI fader unit or a bank of assignable faders on your master keyboard) is to create an onscreen fader assigned to the appropriate controller and MIDI channel or to use your keyboard's assignable faders, if you have them. Some players like to use a MIDI volume pedal that generates controller 7 data to add expression to their parts. This method is particularly effective with string sounds and similar pads.

Most of the current computer-based sequencers allow you to create your own new onscreen faders that can be moved via the mouse to send any type of MIDI data imaginable, and if there are functions present on your sequencer that you want to use regularly, it's best to save these as part of your default song so that you don't have to re-invent the wheel every time you start to write a new tune.

When automating things like level and pan using controller data, you have to remember that, if you implement a fade-out at the end of a song, those instruments will still be turned down the next time you run the song and will remain down until new controller information is sent. That being the case, don't use controller data just to fade out the last few seconds of your song but also insert controller data at the beginning of the next, during the count-in bar, to set your starting levels. The same is true of pan: if everything goes out stage left, it will stay there until either the instrument is reset or new controller information is registered. Embedding controller information at the start of a song is a good habit to get into, and once again you can do this in your default song so that you only have to do it once. You can always make any required changes once the song has been loaded.

Pan effects can work very nicely when synchronised to the tempo of the song, and an easy way of doing this is to create a short section of pan information and then either copy it or loop it. You could save a few examples as part of your default song and then either use them or dump them when the song is loaded up.

Because it's so easy to automate instruments in a MIDI mix, you'll probably find that you're able to do things that were never before possible, and although you may go over the top at first, don't be reluctant to experiment – it's only because users have constantly pushed at the boundaries of MIDI's capabilities that we have such a powerful MIDI specification available to us today. What's more, all of your automation data is saved with your song so you can recreate exactly the same mix at any time.

advanced uses of controller 7

Controller 7 acts exactly like a conventional volume control, enabling you to turn the levels up or down during a single sustained note – something that you can't do simply by changing the note's velocity data. In practice, this means that, if you have the patience, you can actually create envelopes for sounds by using controller 7 data, and one neat trick is to emulate a keyed "gating" effect by using controller 7 values of 0 and 127 to create a full-on or full-off effect. In other words, you can use controller 7 to switch your sound on and off rhythmically in order to create a contemporary "chopped" effect. For example, if you take a four-beat bar in which each beat is one-eighth of a bar in duration and set controller 7 to a value of 127 at the start of each beat and take it down to 0 at the end of each beat, your synth patch will beat four to the bar. With a little imagination, you can design your controller data to create interesting rhythmic effects, and you can, of course, use intermediate controller values if you want the level to pulse rather than switch on and off hard.

transferring sequencer files

I mentioned earlier that standard MIDI song files provide a means of transferring data from one sequencer to another, and within their limitations they can work extremely well. In fact, there are three different types of MIDI file: format 0, where the entire song is saved as a single sequencer track; format 1, where the sequencer tracks are kept separate; and format 2, where the song is saved as a series of patterns. Format 1 is probably the most useful and is the most commonly encountered. However, when you load up a format 1 MIDI file, you may find that the tracks don't come up with their original MIDI channel numbers and sometimes lose their names, too. It all depends on how the sequencer that created the data stored its information. Fortunately, restoring order is usually fairly straightforward. However, as I said earlier, standard MIDI files don't convey MIDI port information; they can be used to store a maximum of only 16 different MIDI channels. However, you can get around this limitation by, in effect, copying the contents of each MIDI port as a separate song SMF and then pasting them into a new song in order to reconstruct the original.

If you need to transfer a file to or from a hardware sequencer or from a non-standard computer platform, you may find the disk formats to be completely incompatible, in which case it may be possible to transfer files by playing them out of one sequencer and recording them into another. However, there is slightly more to this technique than meets the eye and to get it to work properly you should proceed as follows:

• Connect the two sequencers together with MIDI leads such that the MIDI Out of each machine feeds the MIDI In of the other. This two-way connection is necessary in order to ensure accurate timing of the transferred information. If your source song uses multiple MIDI ports, it's best to copy one port's worth of data at a time.

• Set the sequencer containing the song that you want to copy to External Sync mode. The sending sequencer must be clocked by the receiving device to ensure optimum timing accuracy while the receiving sequencer is left in Internal Sync mode. If the receiving device has what's known as a soft MIDI thru function, switch this off to minimise the amount of data being sent via the MIDI Out along with the MIDI Clock data.

• Set the receiving sequencer to record MIDI data but choose a slow tempo, again to maintain optimum timing accuracy. The reason why timing accuracy is such an issue here is that all of the data for all of the tracks is being recorded at once and sequencers are better at outputting lots of tracks than they are at receiving them. That's why it's safest to transfer multiport data a port at a time, even if both sequencers are equipped with multiport MIDI interfaces. A tempo of around 50bpm should be OK, and of course you can change this to the correct value once you've captured the data.

• Start the receiving sequencer recording and the transmitting sequencer will automatically start and run in sync with it.

• If you still find that the timing is insufficiently accurate, repeat the procedure with all of the source sequencer tracks muted except for one, which will enable you to send one track at a time. When the recording is complete, select a new source track and a new destination track and repeat the procedure until all of the tracks have been recorded. This is a trifle slow and tedious, but if it's an important song, the effort may be worth it.

tidying up

Finally, if you managed to transfer all the data in one go, you'll find that your whole song occupies a single track in the destination sequencer. Most modern sequencers have a "demerge by MIDI channel" function which will automatically sort out the data into separate tracks with reference to MIDI channel number. You'll probably still need to identify which instrument is supposed to be playing each part, but if the original file contained program information, this should have come over, too. If you don't have a function like this on your machine, you can look forward to picking through the data manually, which is a time-consuming procedure. One way of doing this is to copy the song track to all 16 tracks and then edit one track at a time, discarding any data not on the MIDI channel appropriate to that track. By working like this, you'll end up with all MIDI channel 1 data on track 1, channel 2 data on track 2 and so on. Figure 9.6 shows how two sequencers can be connected to facilitate data transfer as described here.

advanced user tips

- Create a default song (ie an "empty" song file that has your instruments already set up and ready to go) and store a copy on a locked floppy or as a locked file on your hard drive so that it can't be overwritten by accident. A typical default song contains the MIDI channel and track assignments for your different instruments, suitable "vanilla" starting patches, any user-definable options that the software might provide and various MIDI-status functions such as MIDI thru, MIDI click and so on. Setting this up manually every time you start a new song is obviously a chore you can do without.

  In some instances, it can help to create a number of different default songs for different applications. Again, lock these so that they can't accidentally be overwritten.

- Create your own guide drum parts. Rather than use the default metronome when recording, program a simple drum part to work against instead. This will provide you with a better "feel" of your piece and you'll also find it easier to keep time. Most modern rhythms are based on four beats to the bar, so if you're using a conventional metronome, you're playing directly over the top of it, which in turn makes it difficult to hear. By adding a suitable hi-hat pattern, you're much more likely to stay in time. Rather than start from scratch every time you start working, it pays to save your guide-percussion parts either in a separate song or as a part of your default song so that they're always available whenever you start a new song. If you use several rhythm types on a regular basis, either save them all in the same default song, so that you can erase the ones you don't need, or create separate default songs for each.

- Use your computer keyboard. Just because most jobs can be tackled using the mouse, some things are faster and easier from the keyboard – as long as you can remember the shortcut keys. A useful trick is to print out all of the main keyboard commands and put the print-out under a transparent mouse mat. Failing that, take the low-tech approach and pin it to the wall.

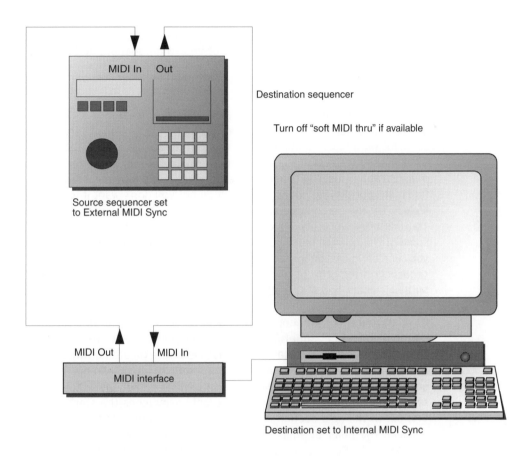

Destination sequencer

Turn off "soft MIDI thru" if available

MIDI In   Out

Source sequencer set
to External MIDI Sync

MIDI Out   MIDI In

MIDI interface

Destination set to Internal MIDI Sync

Fig 9.6: Sequencer-to-sequencer transfer

- Copy important documentation. The trouble with most MIDI systems is that you end up with a stack of manuals a foot thick. It helps enormously to photocopy the lists of preset patches for all of your instruments and also to type out the names and descriptions of your user patches and memory-card contents. These sheets may then be put into plastic sleeves and clipped into a single binder or pinned to the wall.

- Use custom screens. Some programs, such as Logic Audio, have a built-in system for saving and accessing various screen layouts or *screensets*, as they're known. In a program where several windows might need to be open at once, this can be a real time saver because a single key can bring up a screen layout that you've previously specified with all of the windows properly sized and positioned exactly in the right place. The smaller your monitor, the more you'll appreciate this function; without it, you spend most of your time opening and closing windows, dragging them about the screen and resizing them so that you can see everything that you need to.

- Don't over-quantise. Those who criticise electronic music for its robotic feel have probably heard the result of too much quantisation. It's true that some forms of music demand a rigid, robotic approach to timing, but if you want to keep the feel of the original performance, it may be better not to quantise at all – just use the sequencer as you would a tape recorder. If you feel that your playing needs tightening up but you don't want it to sound lifeless, try the percentage-quantise function, if your sequencer has one. This will bring your playing closer to the nearest tick but will still leave some of the original feel intact. On a more practical point, it also helps if you don't rigidly quantise everything because doing so makes the sequencer attempt to play lots of notes at the same time. This creates a MIDI bottleneck and may lead to timing errors in a busy mix.

- If you have a part that needs to be played "free" (ie without any specific tempo reference), simply turn down the click track, turn off all quantisation and record the part just as if you were recording with a tape recorder. If you have to make this part match up to a more rigidly quantised section that follows, you can either move the whole free section backwards or forwards in time until it matches the start of the first bar of the next section or insert a couple of radical tempo changes between the point at which the first section ends and the where next section starts. Putting in a fraction of a bar of very low tempo will create a longer gap whereas speeding up the tempo for a while will reduce the amount of time between the two sections.

- Be paranoid about backing up your work. Computers have a habit of crashing or locking up when you least expect them to, so save every few minutes. If you're using an Apple Mac, you'll probably develop a nervous twitch that makes your left hand press Command + S automatically. When working with a hard drive, back up important work at the end of each session. Modern hard drives are reliable, but they're not infallible – in the case of a serious drive crash, all of the data on that drive is toast! Reliability issues aside, computers occasionally get stolen, and often the data on them is worth more than the computer!

- Keep a notebook. Paper may be low tech, but when you come across a six-month-old disk filled with MIDI files named something like "Ideas 1-99", a few notes can be worth their weight in gold.

- Don't re-invent the wheel. If you've created your own MIDI control data for cyclic panning, or if you have an assortment of killer drum fills, hoard them. You can create your own MIDI equivalent of clip art so that, instead of always working from scratch, you can copy and paste various useful odds and ends from a library song. Other things worth keeping are MIDI messages used to reset the pitch-bend range after patch changes on obscure instruments such as Roland's old CM32P, which always defaults to a twelve-semitone bend range after a patch change. You might also want to save major and minor chord arpeggios (which can be transposed and copied). The list is endless. The only rule is not to waste time repeating the same action.

chapter 10

sequencing with audio

Originally, MIDI sequencing and hard-disk recording existed side by side as two quite separate disciplines, but their convergence was inevitable. The result is the complete integration of MIDI sequencing, digital direct-to-disk multitrack audio recording and automated digital mixing within a single operating environment. What was less predictable in those early days was the extent to which software and instrument plug-ins would feature in the modern desktop studio. Today, instead of having racks of effects units and synthesiser modules, we can do virtually anything we need to entirely in the software domain and the concept of the desktop computer studio is a practical and affordable reality. High-capacity computer hard-disk drives are now cheaper per "track minute" of storage time than either analogue or digital tape. Using almost any modern integrated MIDI-plus-audio sequencing software, it's possible to record and play back a large number of audio tracks alongside conventional MIDI tracks and manipulate the recorded audio to an extent previously possible only when using high-end digital workstations. The purpose of this chapter is to provide an overview of what to expect from a MIDI-plus-audio sequencer. (More details concerning the use of virtual effects and virtual instruments can be found in later chapters.)

Although an in-depth description of digital audio would be out of place in this book (you should instead read *Desktop Digital Studio*, also available from Sanctuary Publishing), this chapter covers all of the basics that you need to be aware of if you're planning to use the audio capabilities of your MIDI sequencer.

the hardware

Other than a controller keyboard and MIDI interface or one of the new generation of keyboards that includes a built-in USB MIDI interface, the only other essential piece of computer hardware is the audio interface, which may be anything from a budget games-type soundcard to sophisticated external audio hardware with multiple inputs and outputs (possibly in both analogue and digital form). Soundcards usually fit into the computer's PCI slots whereas external interfaces either require an additional PCI card or plug directly into the computer's USB or FireWire ports. USB is rather slow and so really is effective only for interfaces with a maximum of six discrete audio outputs while FireWire is more suitable for professional applications where more input and output channels of audio are needed or where multiple channels must be recorded at once.

One physical limitation of a soundcard is that there's very little room on the back panels of computers for sockets so cards with multiple outputs often use a "breakout" cable that connects to the card via a small multipin connector while the other end of the cable may be fitted with regular jack or phono sockets. In my experience, very few soundcards have balanced audio inputs and outputs (see "Glossary" for a definition of the terms *balanced* and *unbalanced*) while most serious hardware interfaces are balanced as standard.

In addition to handling audio recording and playback, your soundcard/audio interface is also responsible for outputting the sound from any virtual instruments that you may be using – you can't use virtual instruments at all without some kind of audio-output capability.

drivers

In order for an audio interface or soundcard to function, it needs a piece of software called a *driver*. This acts as an intermediary between the hardware and your sequencing software and should be supplied by the manufacturer of the soundcard or interface. Games-type soundcards may or may not come with drivers suitable for use with a sequencer, so it's usually wisest to go for a card that is designed specifically for music sequencing. In some cases, the card will be manufactured or endorsed by the manufacturer of the sequencer, in which case it will come equipped with compatible driver software. Steinberg's ASIO (Audio Streaming Input/Output) driver has become widely accepted as a standard model for using third-party soundcards and it interfaces with all of the major sequencing packages on both the Mac and PC platforms as it is designed to support low-latency, multichannel audio.

latency

The term latency is one that will crop up quite often when you start to read about digital audio, so it's probably best to devote a little time to it now. When you create an audio recording, you'll probably be singing or playing along to some MIDI parts that you've recorded previously. In most cases, you'll want to hear a mix of what you've already recorded – plus what you're currently singing or playing – via headphones, and if your current performance seems slightly delayed or echo-like in the headphones, you're hearing the effects of latency. If you have a fast, modern computer and an audio interface that works with ASIO II drivers or some equally sophisticated driver, this latency may well be too low to notice, but it's always present to some extent on all computer-audio systems. (Latency is also covered in Chapter 12, "Software Instruments", for the benefit of those readers who don't feel that this chapter is relevant to them.)

Here's the quick and dirty explanation of latency: When audio is recorded into a computer, there's a small but fairly insignificant delay as it is converted from analogue to digital code, but the way in which audio data is then packaged and routed via the computer's internal bussing system to the CPU (Central Processing Unit) introduces a further delay which may vary from just a few milliseconds (ie virtually undetectable) to half a second or more (ie virtually unusable). This delay is compensated for within the computer so that all of the audio tracks play back with the correct relative timing, but when you're actually recording something latency can create an audible delay between you playing or singing something and that same sound being audible at the soundcard/interface output. Naturally, a delay that's long enough to hear (ie more than around 12ms) will distract you from your performance and throw your timing.

Modern software, quick computers and well-written drivers will minimise latency, but if you can't get it down to a manageable figure with your own system you should use a soundcard or interface that is fully compatible with the ASIO II driver standard, as this also provides "thru monitoring" by routing the audio being recorded directly to the Audio Out of the soundcard during recording or overdubbing. This means that you can't hear any computer-generated effects on the signal being recorded while you're recording it, but at least you lose the timing problems. You can always add plug-in effects when you come to mix. The reason why you can't monitor plug-in effects live when thru monitoring is that you're actually monitoring the input signal before it reaches the CPU, where the effects are generated. (Note, however, that you can't do this with virtual instruments, as they are generated by the CPU itself, although workarounds are described in Chapter 12, "Software Instruments".)

the sequencer interface

Almost all commercial sequencing software now includes some basic provision for audio recording and playback as standard and many packages include more sophisticated options, such as the ability to run plug-ins in order to extend the functionality of the basic system. These plug-ins provide audio processing such as effects, EQ, dynamics control and so on as well as software instruments like synths, samplers and drum machines. Whereas the desktop studio of a decade ago had to rely on external MIDI sound modules, it's now possible to run a studio entirely inside the virtual world of the computer, although most users still use a combination of software and hardware instruments.

Although every piece of music-sequencing software offers slightly different features, all of the major players now provide facilities for multitrack audio recording and playback and audio mixing (usually with EQ), the ability to use software-processing plug-ins (such as reverb, delay, compression and chorus) and the ability to utilise plug-in software instruments that play back through the sequencer's audio mixer.

Most sequencers follow the general paradigm established by Cubase, whereby the sequencer program handles both MIDI tracks and audio tracks in the same environment and whereby both types of track can be divided, moved and copied in similar ways. Tracks may also be used to drive virtual-instrument plug-ins. Figure 10.1 over the page shows the Arrange window of a typical MIDI-plus-audio sequencer, with the audio, MIDI and virtual instrument tracks clearly visible.

platforms

The majority of professional MIDI-plus-audio software is designed to run on either Apple Macintosh or PC platforms. At the time of writing, the Apple Mac platform still seems to be the preferred choice of most professionals, as it is generally easier to set up and maintain, although the relative cheapness and widespread ownership of PCs has prompted software designers to work very hard to bring their PC programs up to the same level of sophistication as their Mac versions. With the exception of Cakewalk SONAR, which is currently available only for the PC, all of the major players have released versions of their software for both platforms, and in most cases the Mac and PC versions are closely matched in terms of features and facilities. Because of the demands placed on the host computers by modern audio systems, the minimum requirement for any serious work is a Mac G4 or a fast Pentium III machine, although doubtless these specs will look quaintly slow by the time this book is next updated!

audio capabilities

A fast Pentium PC fitted with a basic consumer soundcard will typically allow you to record as many tracks at one time as your audio interface or soundcard can handle (usually between two and eight tracks) and will simultaneous play back 24 tracks or more depending on the power of the

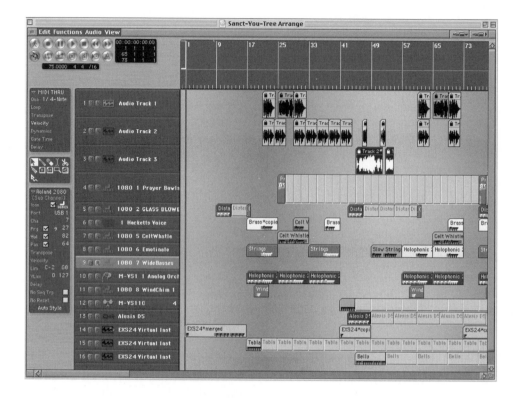

Fig 10.1: Arrange window of a typical MIDI-plus-audio sequencer

computer, the speed of the hard drive and whether or not a separate drive is used for recording and playing audio files.

Budget soundcards tend to mix all of your audio tracks to a stereo output, but there are a number of affordable cards available with multiple outputs for those who demand the ability to mix their audio sounds externally on a hardware mixer. Most general-purpose consumer soundcards are designed primarily for the computer-game and multimedia market, but most include an on-board MIDI synthesiser sound chip, stereo audio in and out sockets and a MIDI interface. However, in order to avoid problems with unacceptably high latency, you should choose a card with an ASIO driver or one that has a low-latency driver designed specifically for the software with which you plan to use the card. You should also be aware that games-type soundcards can also be very complicated to set up, as the audio signal has to be routed through them using their own support software in addition to your sequencer software. My advice would be to spend just a little more on a card that is designed specifically for music sequencing rather than for games and one that you know is fully compatible with your choice of music software.

moving and modifying

Once you've recorded your audio tracks (which can be stored onto your hard disk in the same way as any other computer data), they can be moved, copied and pasted in much the same way as has been previously discussed for MIDI tracks, although there are obviously some things that you can do to MIDI data that are either immensely difficult or impossible to do to audio. For example, you can't just click a button and directly transpose your audio or quantise it as you can with MIDI notes – both of these processes are trivial in the MIDI domain but to achieve the same effect with audio signals would involve complicated signal processing. Even so, many of these seemingly impossible tasks can be done (albeit only to a limited extent) thanks to the signal-processing capabilities included in the sequencer software (although side-effects caused by the processing itself are often audible). For example, audio can be pitch-shifted or changed in length and even quantised to a degree, provided that the amount of change is modest. As a rule, small pitch shifts or time stretches – say, less than 10% – can be handled quite adequately, but larger degrees of pitch shift or time stretch produce unpleasant and clearly audible side-effects.

One very popular innovation is the loop-based sequencer, the first popular example being Sonic Foundry's ACID. ACID used a simple drag-and-drop interface to allow the user to import rhythmic loops or audio parts that could originally have been at different tempo and in different keys. The program then applied time- and pitch-manipulation automatically to make the various parts fit together. With this kind of software, some side-effects were evident if an excessive amount of change was applied in either the pitch or time domain, but on the whole these programs handled the process very successfully. At the time of writing, similar features are also being added to the mainstream sequencer packages in order to ease the process of composing music that makes extensive use of pre-recorded loops and phrases.

signal processing

Because of the increasing power of computers, it's now possible to use software to emulate functions that traditionally required recording-studio hardware. For example, a modern audio-sequencing package may not only allow you to control the level and pan positions of the various tracks as they are mixed internally but may also provide equalisation (by way of studio-type tone controls) as well as the ability to accept plug-in effects such as reverb and delay, dynamics processing such as gates and compressors and spatial-enhancement techniques to make your mix appear to move outside the confines of the loudspeakers. All of these functions can now be handled using just the processing power of the computer itself, although some professional systems still require add-on cards carrying powerful DSP (Digital Signal Processing) chips to take the load of the host computer. Software effects and instruments that make use of the computer's own processor are said to be *host-based systems*.

Because computers get more powerful with every generation, and because of the commercial pressures of the games and multimedia markets, relatively inexpensive systems using only the computer's own processing power rival the performance of traditional studio hardware and dedicated digital-audio workstations. It's also common to see MIDI-plus-audio packages that can integrate with onscreen video so that, if you're working on the soundtrack to a TV show, you can run the video as a QuickTime movie to help you match up your cue points.

benefits of integration

Being able to record and manipulate audio alongside MIDI is very powerful advantage because you can employ such techniques as copying the best vocal chorus to every chorus position in a song or applying a little pitch shifting to a flat note to bring it back into pitch. Better still, you can use a plug-in such as AnTares' Auto-Tune to automatically correct minor vocal pitching problems. You can also import sound samples in .WAV or .AIFF audio-file format from the numerous CD-ROMs available, giving you access to drum rhythms, voices and instrumental phrases that can be worked into your own compositions. Virtually all modern dance and techno music is composed in this way, but the process is just as applicable to conventional pop music, TV commercials, new-age music and so on.

Another significant benefit of using a sequencer with integrated audio (not to mention that of not having to fork out for a multitrack tape recorder) is that you don't need to provide a means of synchronising your tape machine or hard-disk recorder to your sequencer. Not only does this save you money but it also makes the whole system easier to use. Also, when you've finished a song, it makes it easy to back up all of the relevant files in one place.

storage considerations

Multitrack audio recording requires approximately 5Mb of disk space per track for every minute recorded, assuming that you're recording 16-bit audio at a 44.1kHz sampling rate, the standard for audio CD recording. Working at 24 bits will reduce your storage time by one-third and working at higher sample rates will reduce your storage time proportionately. Most large-capacity hard drives are now fast enough to record audio, but a spindle speed of 7,200rpm or greater is recommended.

Accepting that you need at least 5Mb of disk space for every track minute, using audio within a MIDI sequence may still take up less space than you'd imagine, simply because data is only recorded where it is needed. For example, if you have a pause in the vocals for the guitar solo, you don't need to record the pause, whereas with tape recording the tape is always used, whether anything is being recorded on it or not. In addition, because you can use the same data more than once, you might find that a single 30-second audio file containing the backing vocals for a chorus is all you need in order to provide backing vocals for a whole five-minute song. Similarly, if the guitar solo is only one minute long, you'll use only one track minute of disk space. If much of your musical backing is provided by conventional MIDI instruments, you might find that the audio parts of your song add up to only a few track minutes in total. When I wrote the first version of this book, even a 1Gb hard drive was considered large enough for audio use, but now you can buy a 100Gb drive for less money, so storage space is much less of an issue than it used to be. A 1Gb drive will hold around three hours of mono audio, so a 100Gb drive could hold up to twelve hours or so of 24-track audio, making it far cheaper than tape as a storage medium.

more about soundcards

To get audio into and out of your computer, you need either a soundcard equipped with A-to-D (Analogue-to-Digital) and D-to-A converters or external hardware that does the same job. These essential bits of hardware digitise the sound from your microphone or instrument when you record and, when you play back, convert the digital data back into an audio signal that can be played through your hi-fi or desktop multimedia speakers or mixing console.

Budget soundcards tend to reproduce with less than optimum audio quality when compared with their more expensive counterparts, but as long as the signal path is 16-bit resolution the quality should still be adequate for writing demos or composing. Indeed, the most serious limitation with cheaper soundcards is often the quality of the ASIO driver software more than the audio quality. For more serious work, however, more sophisticated soundcards or external hardware is recommended, and if you need to mix your audio tracks externally, you'll need to use hardware with multiple outputs. Similarly, if you need to record more than two tracks of audio at once, you'll need a card or interface with the requisite number of inputs.

Many soundcards and interfaces include digital inputs and outputs in addition to analogue I/O (Input/Output). The norm for stereo operation is the S/PDIF standard (as found on consumer CD players, DAT machines and MD recorders), but some also support the ADAT optical format for sending eight channels of audio over a single optical link. The ADAT format (originally devised for the Alesis ADAT eight-track digital tape recorder) is extremely convenient, not only for transferring material to and from ADAT-compatible recording hardware but also for connecting audio outputs to a digital mixer, most of which now offer ADAT interface cards as an option.

choosing a soundcard

The first thing you have to decide is how many separate inputs and outputs you're going to need. If you're working alone, recording one part at a time, a card with a single stereo input will be fine, but if you need to record a group of musicians playing at once then you'll need a card or interface with multiple inputs. If you anticipate connecting to digital equipment in either S/PDIF or ADAT format, you'll need to identify the options that meet those needs, too.

Having decided on the format of card you need, you should check with the software distributor's product specialist to find out which cards work OK and which have known compatibility problems. You should also note that, although the PCI card format is the same for Macs and PCs, some card and interface manufacturers provide drivers for only one computer platform or the other, not necessarily both. PCs in particular throw up more than their fair share of compatibility problems, so if you're not familiar with computers it's often safest to buy a complete system from a specialised music retail shop with the software and soundcard already installed and tested.

Cards used for audio recording must support what's known as *full duplex operation*. In practical terms, this means that you can listen to previously recorded material at the same time as you record a new part. If the hardware doesn't support full duplex operation, you won't be able to listen to your existing audio recordings at the same time as recording new parts (although for some applications it may be enough to hear the MIDI tracks while recording). While all serious audio soundcards and interfaces now support full duplex operation as standard, you may still come across the occasional games-quality soundcard that doesn't.

specifying a system

The number of tracks that you can record and play back will depend on the type and speed of computer you're using, the type and speed of the hard drive and the sample rate and bit depth at which you're working. For these reasons, you should buy the fastest machine that you can afford. If you're not buying a complete system, check with the software and soundcard suppliers that their products are compatible with each other and with your make and model of computer. It's also a good idea to visit internet music groups to see if any other users have comments on the configuration of the hardware that you're thinking of buying.

Because PCs are built by so many different companies, and because not all use the same ICs (Integrated Circuits) on the main circuit board, you can end up in a situation where certain combinations of hardware and software either run incorrectly or fail to run at all. A little good advice at this stage can save a lot of expensive disappointment later on, but my advice to anyone but the most experienced of PC gurus is to buy the computer, hardware and software from a single supplier, ready configured. This may cost slightly more, but at least you have some recourse if things don't work properly, whereas if you buy all of the components from different suppliers and then find out that the system doesn't work, you may find it difficult or impossible to get anyone to agree to take responsibility. Worse, you may not be able to get your money back! Macintosh users tend to pay a little more for their machines, but because the hardware is all under Apple's control, incompatibility problems due to differences between models are much less likely to occur.

Realistically, a Pentium III 800MHz PC with 256Mb of RAM and a 40Gb hard drive running Windows '98 should be considered the minimum configuration for any serious work. However, don't expect to be able to use a computer-based MIDI-plus-audio system straight out of the box without first learning something about computers. In an ideal world, a system such as this would be just a tool to do a job, but you'll soon discover that learning to operate and maintain this particular tool is quite an involved business. At the very least, you'll need to learn how to open and close files, how to move files around, how to install programs, how to use the mouse and so on. Fortunately, most people now have basic computer experience, but if you don't you should try to get a friendly computer user to sit beside you for an hour or two while you're learning.

Mac users shouldn't consider anything pre-G4 for audio use and ideally one of the faster models, at that. Dual-processor machines may not offer much performance improvement when used with OS 9.x but should be far more effective when all of your music software is carbonised to run on Mac OS X.

The question of computer operating systems can be a vexing one, and again it's something on which you should seek advice. At any one time, there are usually around four different PC operating systems in common usage, but it may be that one works better with audio software than the other. Your sequencer manufacturer's technical-support line is the best place to check this if your dealer doesn't know.

Soundcards vary enormously in terms of the sound quality that they're capable of reproducing. The audio path should ideally be able to support both 16-bit and 24-bit material at sample rates of 44.1kHz and 48kHz. I don't feel that higher sample rates are particularly relevant to the vast majority of users, especially as they halve number of tracks and plug-ins that your system can support, but if you feel that you may need to use them sometimes then you shouldn't have to look too hard to find a card or interface that can support them. Their signal-to-noise ratios should be 90dB or better, and if you want to experiment with higher sample rates then you should check that both your audio hardware and software support them – there's no advantage in buying a 96kHz-compatible soundcard if your audio software supports only 48kHz.

The signal-to-noise ratio is essentially a measure of how much background noise the system produces compared to the maximum signal that can be accommodated – the higher the ratio, the less hiss is produced. The synthesiser sections that are available on most general-purpose soundcards can vary wildly, but the only way to judge the artistic quality of the sounds that they produce is to listen to them. While a low-level background hiss may not be much of a problem, a similar level of digital whine can sound much more intrusive. It's a good idea to arrange a demonstration before you buy, but in the case of soundcards that reside within computers it pays to be aware that the amount of noise that's picked up from a computer's internal electronics may vary from one machine to another.

the growing system

As pointed out earlier, a typical budget soundcard will mix its on-board MIDI synth sounds with any recorded audio and pipe both signals through a single stereo output, and this set-up is fine for composing or making basic demos. Some users install two or more soundcards in their computer, but a multiple-output card or interface is invariably a more reliable option and is certainly easier to configure. You'll probably also want to add an external MIDI synth module or two, even if you already have access to some virtual instruments. When you get to this stage, you'll also need a hardware mixer to combine the outputs from your interface or soundcard with the outputs from your external hardware instruments. This kind of set-up will also provide you with a greater degree of control over individual sounds or groups of sounds and will enable you to use hardware effects (although the availability of high-quality plug-ins makes this aspect less important than it once was). If you're using hardware synths, a mixer is an essential component of the system, although it needn't be complex or expensive.

using a separate mixer

Using a small mixer will provide you with separate control over the level, tone and pan positions of each input to the mixer, and you should also notice a significant improvement in sound quality, with more clarity and less hiss when you record via a microphone. The mixer is used to convert the mic signal to line level before you feed it into your soundcard, and even a budget mixer will have better mic amps than a typical soundcard – if the soundcard has mic amps at all. Figure 10.2 shows a typical MIDI-plus-audio studio based around a simple stereo-out soundcard and a few external MIDI synths linked to a small mixer. A domestic hi-fi is being used for monitoring and for recording the final mix. Note that, if you have a spare channel and a spare pre-fade aux send on your external mixer, you can use these to feed the mic signal to the soundcard input independent of the rest of the mixer. Here's how it works.

In many home studios, vocal and instrumental parts are overdubbed one at a time, so one input is often sufficient. On a standard mixer with no multiple busses or other fancy routing options, however, the easiest way to use a mic channel for feeding a soundcard is to turn its fader fully down and then use the pre-fade send control to send the mic signal to the mixer's pre-fade output jack. The pre-fade send control is normally used to set up monitor mixes, but in the smaller studio it can be fed directly into the soundcard input as a means of routing the mic signal separately. Essentially, the mic signal goes through the mixer channel via the pre-fade send and out of the pre-fade-send jack without interacting with anything else that the mixer may be doing, almost as though it were a separate piece of hardware. All you have to do is keep its channel fader down when mixing and also ensure that the pre-fade aux send is turned fully down on all channels when recording, except for the one being used as a mic input. The diagram in Figure 10.2 also illustrates this routing option. If fitted, the master send control is used to set

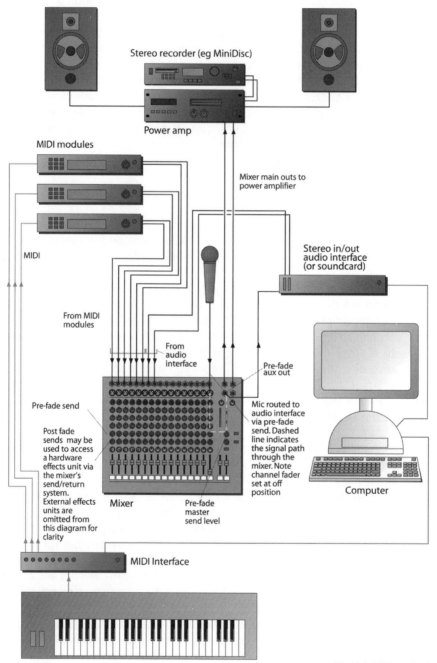

Stereo recorder (eg MiniDisc)

Power amp

MIDI modules

Mixer main outs to
power amplifier

MIDI

Stereo in/out
audio interface
(or soundcard)

From MIDI
modules

From
audio
interface

Pre-fade
aux out

Pre-fade send

Mic routed to
audio interface
via pre-fade
send. Dashed
line indicates
the signal path
through the
mixer. Note
channel fader
set at off
position

Post fade
sends may be
used to access
a hardware
effects unit via
the mixer's
send/return
system.
External effects
units are
omitted from
this diagram for
clarity

Mixer

Pre-fade
master
send level

Computer

MIDI Interface

**Fig 10.2: MIDI studio linked
to a small mixer**

the recording level using the recording software's onscreen metering system. If you don't have one fitted, use the mic channel's send control.

A further tip here is that you can turn up the mic channel fader when recording in order to hear the mic signal in the stereo mix (which you'll need to monitor via headphones while overdubbing). By monitoring the mixer channel in this way, while switching off thru monitoring on your the computer, you'll avoid the distracting effects of any system latency - although you'll also lose the ability to monitor the effects of any software plug-ins being applied to the input signal.

mixer functions

In the case of a soundcard with stereo outputs, you don't have the luxury of being able to treat each audio track independently with the hardware mixer, but you can still perform all of the necessary processing and balancing via plug-ins and the sequencer's own mixer facilities. You'll still be able to balance the outputs of the soundcard and the external MIDI modules in relation to each other.

Even with an eight-output soundcard, you won't be able to separate every sound for processing (unless you restrict yourself to playing back no more than eight audio tracks) but you can still gain a surprising amount of control over your work by routing sounds to the card's outputs in logical groups. For example, you should keep the lead vocals and solo instruments separate, if you can, route backing vocals to a stereo subgroup and so on. If your budget will stretch to it, you might even want to buy a separate reverb unit so that you can add more professional-sounding reverb to your mixes. Reverb plug-ins are pretty power-hungry devices, however, so the algorithms that they use tend to be simplified in order to prevent them from hogging too much CPU capacity. Even so, using a hardware reverb box may be worthwhile only if you have a soundcard with multiple outputs, as only then will you have the ability to add different amounts of reverb to different streams of audio.

audio drives

The hard drive is a very important component in audio recording, so it's worth saying a little more about it. Recording and playing back multiple tracks of audio to or from a hard drive makes the drive work very hard, so it helps enormously if you can use a completely separate drive for audio work. At one time, AV (Audio-Visual) drives were recommended for multitrack work because, unlike regular hard drives, AV drives are designed to produce an uninterrupted flow of data. Older non-AV drives may occasionally pause for an instant to recalibrate themselves, and this can lead to breaks or glitches in the sound being recorded or played back. Fortunately, virtually all modern, high-capacity drives are designed with AV requirements in mind, so this issue no longer arises, although it does pay to buy the drive with the fastest access time and fastest continuous rate of data transfer. As a rule, 7,200rpm drives are better in this respect than 5,400rpm drives.

Another reason for having a separate drive is that, wherever possible, audio files need to be contiguous. If they are broken into fragments, the drive has to spend time looking for the various sections, and again this can cause glitching if your system is running close to its limit. The more you save and delete files on disk, the more fragmented the available free space becomes, so new files may be recorded in shorter segments to fit the available spaces. To get around this, you should run a defragmentation program from time to time. Such programs move the files around to join up unconnected file segments and ensure that all of the free space on a disk is in one continuous chunk.

At one time, SCSI drives were recommended for audio work, and technically they are still the fastest option (at least until FireWire drives fulfil their promise of even greater speed), but a 7,200rpm IDE drive is much cheaper and is still capable of recording and playing back more than 24 tracks of audio at a time. At the time of writing, most FireWire drives are actually IDE drives in a box with a FireWire interface, so they don't work as fast as a drive designed specifically for use at FireWire speeds, but they are nevertheless easy to hook up to modern computers as external drives and they can be "hot plugged" (ie connected and disconnected without first having to switch off the drive or the computer). When using the newer-generation flat-screen Macintosh iMacs that have no facilities for adding internal cards or additional drives, using an external FireWire hard drive for audio (often in conjunction with a FireWire audio interface) is a good option. The cheapest and usually quietest option for larger computers is to fit a second 7,200rpm IDE drive inside the host computer and record audio files on that.

backing up

So what do you do with your data once the hard disk is full? A MIDI file may take up only a few tens of kilobytes, but a CD-quality audio track takes up around 5Mb of disk space for each minute of recorded data. Obviously, you don't want to leave your hard drive full of audio data, but at the same time you probably don't want to wipe the data, either. After all, what if a record company hears your demo and wants you to do a remix? One solution is to use a removable drive, but some are too slow to work with real-time audio, and if this is the case you'll have to work on your fixed hard drive and then transfer your back-up files onto the removable drive for archiving purposes. However, it is a valid option, as long as you choose a removable media of sufficient capacity.

Data DAT-tape systems such as Exobyte are also used for backing up data, and these have the overriding advantage of employing cheap media, but the save and load times are very long so you may need to back up or load in long projects overnight.

The most cost-effective option is to store your audio data on CD-R using a CD-R drive. CD-R disks can only be recorded once and hold only around 640Mb of data, but they cost only a few pence each and a typical multitrack song will fit on a single disc. Data DVD disks holds several times the capacity of CD-Rs and their prices continue to fall, so they are likely to take over from CD-R in situations where greater storage density is required.

Ironically, regular fixed hard drives have become cheaper to buy than their equivalent storage time in tape, either analogue or digital, so another option that's gaining popularity is to use low-cost IDE drives mounted in removable bays. These removable drive bays may be fitted to most computers and separate, low-cost caddies are used to hold the drives themselves. In the case of IDE drives, the computer should be shut down before the drives are changed, but other than that it's a matter of simply unplugging one drive caddy and slotting in another.

mastering

One point I haven't touched on yet is how to record the end result of your labours. The cheap-and-cheerful way is to use a cassette deck, and as long as the deck is cleaned fairly regularly and used with good-quality cassettes the results obtained with one can be surprisingly good. However, if you want to release your own cassette or CD album of your work, you'll need to mix onto something with rather better sound quality. The professional choice for 16-bit audio at 44.1kHz or 48kHz is still DAT, but a cheaper and increasingly popular option for the recording musician is to buy a MiniDisc recorder. Even though these use data compression (needed to squeeze a lot of music onto a small disc), the sound quality is very good and most people can't tell MiniDisc audio from the sound produced by regular CDs.

Finally, if you have enough spare audio tracks on your sequencer, you can mix your whole composition - audio tracks, virtual instruments and external hardware MIDI instruments – via an external mixer back into your audio interface or soundcard and record the result in stereo as a new stereo track. An advantage of working in this way is that you can then burn a CD of your finished work with a regular computer CD burner without having to re-record the audio into your system.

digital-audio fundamentals

My plan was to keep this book as simple as possible, but there are some fundamental aspects of digital recording that are important to understand if you're planning to use your sequencer to record audio as well as MIDI, and some of these also apply to the use of virtual MIDI instruments.

Digital audio equipment – computer soundcards and audio interfaces, DAT recorders, MiniDisc recorders and so on – is generally designed to accept analogue signals, such as the outputs from microphones and instruments. Converters in the audio interface must first convert the analogue input into a digital format before it can be recorded. The chain of events goes as follows: The analogue signal voltage from a microphone changes in proportion to changes in air pressure, then the analogue-to-digital converter turns these analogue voltages into numbers comprising ones and zeros. These digits are represented in the circuit by the presence or absence of a nominally fixed voltage. In essence, converting an analogue signal into digital information involves measuring the analogue voltage at regular intervals and then turning these measurements into a series of binary numbers. Every second of sound needs to be sampled and measured several tens of thousands of times a second if the end result is going to be of CD quality. If you have enough instantaneous measurements per second, the original sound can be accurately recreated up to the highest frequency limit of human hearing.

digitising

The process of measuring and digitising an analogue signal is known as *sampling*, and Figure 10.3 illustrates the process. Each sample is a snapshot measurement of signal level taken at one point in time, and the more often these measurements are made, the more accurately the curves of the original analogue signal are followed.

Sampling theory states that, if the output is to be reconstructed accurately, you must sample at a minimum rate of twice the highest frequency that you're likely to encounter. If the sampling frequency is less than twice the highest frequency, additional frequencies will be introduced based on the

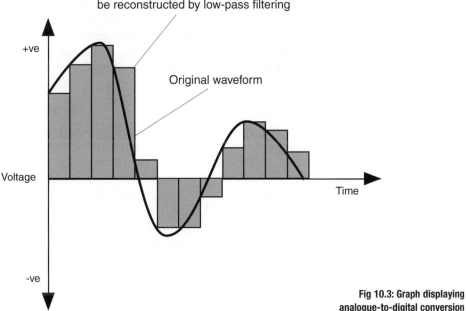

The signal voltage is sampled at regular intervals and then held until the next sample is taken. The original signal can be reconstructed by low-pass filtering

Original waveform

+ve

Voltage

Time

-ve

Fig 10.3: Graph displaying analogue-to-digital conversion

sum and difference between the sampling frequency and the audio frequency. These *aliasing frequencies* were never present in the original signal and sound musically unpleasant. To prevent aliasing, it is necessary to filter out any frequencies in the original signal that are above half the sampling frequency. Because no filters are perfect, the sampling rate must be made a little higher than twice the maximum audio frequency, which is why for an audio bandwidth of 20kHz we have a minimum sampling frequency of over 40kHz. (Audio CDs and MiniDiscs use a sampling rate of 44.1kHz.)

The accuracy with which individual samples are measured is extremely important, and the more digital bits that are used to represent each sample, the more accurate the measurement. CDs and DATs use 16-bit sampling, although many digital multitrack recorders and signal processors now use 20- or 24-bit conversion.

The numbers used in a digital system, like numbers everywhere, increment in whole-number steps, and eight bits will give you two-to-the-power-eight steps, which works out at 256. This means that your loudest signal could have 256 steps, although quieter ones will have considerably fewer, which in practice gives a rather poor level of resolution and results in what's known as *quantisation distortion*, a side-effect that sounds not unlike tape hiss. The main difference between quantisation distortion and ordinary hiss is that the former disappears in the absence of a signal (unlike most other sources of noise) whereas the latter remains. Nowadays, eight-bit sound is rarely used, other than in some non-demanding computer applications, but it serves to illustrate the point: using more bits gives a vast improvement in resolution. These days, most digital processors use 16-, 20- or 24-bit resolution converters.

Each bit in a linear sampling system equates to 6dB of dynamic range, so an eight-bit system can give you a dynamic range of only 48dB at best, which is about as noisy as a cheap cassette recorder. 16 bits gives a maximum dynamic range of 96dB, while 20- and 24-bit systems can still give practical dynamic ranges in excess of 120dB. However, for a digital system to deliver anything like its theoretical best performance, the numbers representing slices of the original analogue signal have to be replayed with exactly the same timing relationship as that at which they were recorded.

sample rates

Simply stated, the sample rate is the number of times each second that an audio waveform is "measured" during the analogue-to-digital conversion process. This sampling must be done at precise intervals and is generally controlled by a very accurate crystal clock. Provided that the same sample rate is used for analogue-to-digital and digital-to-analogue conversion, the replayed audio will be of the same length and pitch as the original.

Although the minimum sample rate for serious audio work is 44.1kHz, less critical work is sometimes done at 32kHz (which reduces the audio bandwidth to under 15kHz), while broadcasters prefer to work with a sample rate of 48kHz. Most DAT machines and soundcards support both 44.1kHz and 48kHz sample rates, but it's important to note that everything in your system must be set to run at the same sample rate or your final audio recording won't play back at the same speed as that at which you recorded it. If you're planning on making CDs, it's safest to do everything at 44.1kHz, whereas if you're producing material for broadcast, stick to 48kHz.

So-called high-resolution sample rates have been introduced that run at double the current standard sampling rates, so now 88.2kHz and 96kHz can be added to the list. In theory, these rates produce a slightly better sound quality, but in practice few people can detect a difference. My own view is that a sample rate of 96kHz will provide a sonic advantage only if you're using the most esoteric equipment to make recordings of acoustic instruments in a very sophisticated studio. The next section deals with some of the possible reasons why high-sample-rate audio might sound better, even though theory dictates that standard sample rates already go beyond the frequency limit of human hearing.

the high-sample-rate argument

The regular 44.1kHz sampling rate provides an audio bandwidth of 20kHz, which exceeds the hearing range of most humans, but there is a school of thought that suggests that recording with a much wider audio bandwidth will produce a better and more accurate sound. The 96kHz sample rate doubles the *audio* bandwidth to 40kHz, and although you can't actually hear these frequencies, there are plausible arguments as to why these recordings should sound better.

One important factor is that the very harsh filters used to block out everything above 20kHz in a 44.1kHz system - the so-called anti-aliasing filters - tend to impart their own sonic signature to the sound. This was certainly a significant factor in early digital converters, and although current designs are much better in this respect, it is thought that there may still be some audible artefacts generated by the filtering process that individuals with particularly sensitive can perceive.

Another theory is that, in real life, frequencies above the range of human hearing that emanate from different instruments interact or intermodulate to produce audible frequencies which are then recorded. However, if the instruments are separately miked using a 20kHz system, these high frequencies are removed before the sounds are combined, so some of the sonic character is lost.

Whether you use a 24-bit/96kHz or a 16-bit/44.1kHz system is up to you, but keep in mind that, for a given computer system, the number of tracks that you can run at any one time and the number of plug-ins that you can use at a 96kHz sample rate will be half that of a standard 44.1kHz sample rate.

16 or 24 bits?

Standard audio CDs use a 16-bit/44.1kHz format, so why do we need systems that can record at 20 or even 24 bits? Actually, there is a good reason. Whenever you process a digital signal by changing its level or adding EQ, it loses a little of its resolution due to mathematical rounding up or rounding down, so what started life as a 16-bit signal may end up with the same resolution as a 14- or 15-bit signal after processing. The signal will still have 16 bits, but the accuracy of the data it contains will have been eroded slightly by processing. Furthermore, a 16-bit signal has maximum resolution only when recorded at its at maximum level; quieter sounds are recorded at fewer than 16 bits, so the resolution at low levels is correspondingly coarser.

By recording and processing using more bits that you need for the final delivery medium (ie CD), you can preserve the maximum possible resolution right through to the end of the project. For example, if you work at 24 bits and leave yourself a safety margin of 4dB in order to avoid clipping when recording, the resolution has already been reduced by the equivalent of four bits. Changing gain, normalising or other processing may reduce the resolution by another bit, so what you're let with is a 24-bit signal that has the same resolution as an 19-bit signal recorded at optimum. However, this is still more resolution than you need in order to make a 16-bit CD, so you'll still end up with a high-quality product at the end of the process. But if, on the other hand, you'd done the same with a 16-bit source signal, if you'd lost the same five bits of resolution along the way you'd be left with the equivalent resolution of an eleven-bit signal, which in practical terms means a higher level of background noise and more distortion at very low signal levels.

While a small loss of resolution is of little practical concern when dealing with pop music (which generally has a very limited dynamic range), when it comes to recording acoustic music you may find that extremely quiet passages sound audibly degraded.

dithering

A recording made and mixed with a 24-bit resolution can be reduced to 16 bit using a process know as *dithering*, which preserves much more of the original dynamic range of the signal than simply truncating (discarding) the least significant eight bits. Essentially, a tiny amount of pseudo-random noise is added to the signal to dither very low-level digital information, but to prevent this noise from compromising the apparent signal-to-noise ratio of the recording it can be mathematically designed so that it appears high in the audio spectrum (usually above 15kHz), where the human ear is least sensitive. This refinement is known as *noise-shaped dithering*.

Without getting too technical, dithering allows the music to remain audible as it fades down into the noise floor, just as it does when reproduced over analogue tape. Without dither, the signal will get progressively more distorted at lower levels and then cease abruptly as the LSB (Least Significant Byte) is turned off. Most stereo-editing software packages include the facility to dither 24- or 20-bit audio down to 16 bits. It should be noted, however, that dithering should always be the last process that the signal undergoes if it is to be effective.

Although 24-bit/96kHz audio-recording rates may seem unnecessarily esoteric at the moment, not to mention wasteful of processing resources, it pays to be aware of them, especially as 24-bit/96kHz audio may become the standard hi-fi format if DVD becomes widely adopted as a high-end audio-delivery format. Most audio-recording equipment and software is now 24-bit/96kHz compatible, whether you need that resolution or not, and as storage capacity rises and processors become more powerful there will be less concern about conserving resources by working at 16 bit/44.1kHz. Already RAM (Random Access Memory) and computer hard drives are orders of magnitude cheaper now than they were a few years ago, so data storage is no longer the major cost concern it once was. However, we're still pushing computers pretty hard, when it comes to processing, and as high-resolution 24-bit/96kHz audio takes around three times as much processor power per minute as CD-quality 16-bit/44.1kHz audio, you should expect a dramatic drop in the number of tracks, plug-ins and virtual instruments that you have at your disposal if you choose to use it.

digital connections

Unlike analogue systems, on which every signal needs to be sent down a separate cable, digital systems allow two or more signals to be sent along the same cable yet remain completely separate. How this apparent magic works isn't important at this stage, but here the words *clocking* and *sync* need to be explained further.

The best way to understand what's going on is to look at an example. Lets say that you have a computer studio set-up with a digital input and you want to transfer some music from a DAT recorder or a MiniDisc player into your computer in the digital domain. The first step is to connect the digital output from your player phono connector (which is probably S/PDIF) to the digital input of your computer interface or soundcard. S/PDIF is a standard connection protocol developed by Sony and Philips for consumer digital equipment, and on some equipment it may be provided as an optical port as an alternative to, or in addition to, the phono co-axial connector. Commercial-format adaptors are available for converting co-axial S/PDIF to optical and vice versa.

When you play the DAT machine, a highly accurate crystal clock controls the rate at which the samples of data are played back in order to ensure that the material is the same length and at the same pitch as that of the original. In order to get these little slices of data into a computer, the computer's sampling clock has to be running at exactly the same rate as that of the DAT machine. If the DAT machine and computer are allowed to run independently, their clocks will always run at slightly different speeds, even if they're both set to the same frequency, resulting in clicks and crackles in the audio as the two clocks drift in and out of sync with each other. To avoid clocking problems, the DAT player is used as a master and the machine that it feeds into is set to External Clock mode, which means that its own clock is synchronised to the sample rate of the signal being received at its S/PDIF socket.

Word Clock

An alternative system to the above that is used in more professional studios, and one that I believe will become more important in the project studio over the next few years, is to use a very accurate master Word Clock generator to control all of the digital equipment in a studio. The main difference between this and simple master/slave sync is that the sample clock is fed via separate sockets, rather than relying on the clock embedded in the digital audio signal. The master clock has multiple outputs, each of which feeds the Word Clock input socket on each piece of digital equipment being used. All of the equipment is then set to Word Clock sync so that it slaves to the master clock. Once this is done, signals can be transferred from one machine to another without the user having to change sync settings or worrying about master/slave status. Word Clock usually travels via unbalanced cables terminated in bayonet-fitting BNC connectors, and as with other digital interconnects the relevant socket will normally be clearly labelled on the rear panel of the equipment. As with all other digital-clocking systems, there can only be one master – all of the other pieces of gear act as slaves and lock to the master clock.

Many semi-pro pieces of studio equipment have rather poor internal clocks that can introduce "clock jitter" into the rest of the system, causing a degradation of both audio quality and signal-to-noise ratio, so using a master clock often improves the audio quality noticeably and also simplifies the operation of a system.

Although digital co-axial S/PDIF connections use the same type of phono connectors as audio cables, it's important to use a proper digital cable if problems are to be avoided. Conventional audio phono cables often appear to work fine, but the problem is that they don't provide accurate signal transmission because audio cables don't have the correct impedance for use with digital signals. The result is an increase in error rate, although you might not hear anything obviously wrong because the receiving piece of equipment will mask minor errors with its error-correction system. If the error rate gets too high, however, these errors may result in clicks or other audible glitches.

The reason why cheap audio cables don't work properly is that digital-audio data takes up a much greater bandwidth than analogue audio. At the high frequencies involved, impedance mismatches reflect some of the signal back along the cable, and these "echoes" compromise the signal-to-noise ratio of the system such that, at some point, zeros may be misread as ones or vice versa. To do the job properly, digital cable specified for use with S/PDIF signals is required, as this minimises reflections and maintains the signal's integrity.

Some S/PDIF connections use an optical connector where the data is transmitted over fibre-optic cables rather than as electrical signals. The Alesis ADAT optical format (developed for use with the original Alesis ADAT eight-track digital tape recorder) uses the same type of connector, so it's important not to get the two types mixed up. Both systems use the same types of transmitting and receiving devices, but their data formats are very different. No damage will be done if you try to connect an ADAT interface to an S/PDIF or vice versa but no signal transmission will take place, either. The main practical difference is that an S/PDIF optical cable carries two channels of audio (ie stereo) while ADAT carries eight channels.

Optical cables also differ in quality, just as cables do, and there are two areas in such a cable where optical signals can be degraded: the termination and the fibre-optic cable itself. The optical quality of a cable (or *lightpipe* as it's sometimes called) determines the distance over which a signal can travel before errors become a problem. The terminations affect how efficiently light enters or leaves the cable, so the more terminations a signal passes through, the greater the loss will be. If you need cable lengths of more than a couple of metres, it's worth investing in high-quality optical cables.

clock sync

The concept of digital synchronisation is hugely important, so it's worth looking at it in a little more detail. Synchronisation is possible via S/PDIF because the digital data carried along an S/PDIF cable also carries the clock signal from the source machine, and this is used to synchronise the clock in the receiving device. However, the receiving device has to be placed into External Digital Sync mode for this to happen. (Figure 3.2 shows a DAT machine feeding the input of a soundcard to illustrate this arrangement.) All of the digital recorders that I've used switch to Digital Sync mode automatically if switched to digital input, and this kind of auto-switching system is very sensible, as there are no normal circumstances in which you'd want to accept a digital input while the receiving machine was running from its own internal clock (ie in Internal Sync mode). Nevertheless, some computer audio systems require you to select Digital Sync mode separately, as well as Digital Input. If you select Digital Input but not Digital Sync, you'll probably end up with clicks and glitches in the audio that you transfer.

The rule is that, unless your studio runs from a master Word Clock, the source device should run from its own clock (ie Internal Sync mode) and the receiving device should be set to Digital Sync mode. Multiple devices can be cascaded in this way, but stringing more than three or four digital devices in a chain might cause problems, as additional connections to tend to cause increased "clock jitter".

Note: More professional equipment uses the so-called AES/EBU digital interface, which can usually be identified by the fact that it uses XLR connectors rather than phonos. In any event, the sockets are normally marked clearly on the rear panels of studio equipment. Both S/PDIF and AES/EBU carry a stereo signal plus a clock, but they operate at different voltage levels and so are not compatible, strictly speaking (even though you can sometimes get away with plugging an adaptor lead between the two). AES/EBU is balanced (see "Glossary" for an explanation of this term), has a nominal level of 5v and can use conventional mic cables over short distances while S/PDIF is an unbalanced system operating at around 0.5v and requiring digital-grade co-axial cable in order to work properly. Using audio phono leads isn't recommended, even if the system appears to work normally.

The main advantage of S/PDIF is that DAT start IDs and CD track IDs are carried as part of the data format, while with AES/EBU these are stripped out. The optical version of S/PDIF (sometimes known as TOSLINK) is also useful in situations where the screen connector of a co-axial cable might cause ground-loop problems. On the other hand, AES/EBU ignores the SCMS (Serial Copycode Management System) copy-protection systems used in some DAT machines to prevent cloned tapes from being recopied in the digital domain.

sample-rate converters

In situations where you want to work at one sample rate but some or all of the source material is at another, sample-rate conversion will be necessary. This can either be accomplished by an external hardware box that takes in a digital signal at one sample rate and outputs it at another in real time, or it can be done in software. For example, if you have recordings made on a

DAT machine at 48kHz and you wish to master a CD, which requires audio sampled at 44.1kHz, you'll need to convert the audio sample rate before you can compile the CD. If you don't, the CD will seem to play OK but the audio will be slow and pitched down by a factor of 44.1:48, or around 10%.

interfaces

Although this chapter covers soundcards in more detail, it also includes information on audio interfaces that exist as external hardware rather than as PCI cards (although some still need a PCI card in order to establish contact with the host computer). While multimedia soundcards may combine audio recording with a MIDI synthesiser chip, the majority of hardware interfaces have no sound-generating capabilities – they are purely audio interfaces. Budget games-quality soundcards tend to come with fairly mediocre synthesiser chips, but it's perfectly possible to put more sophisticated synthesisers and even samplers onto relatively cheap computer cards, as is amply demonstrated in the upper echelons of cards in the Creative Labs SoundBlaster range, where the manufacturer's own SoundFont technology is used to provide high-quality sample playback. What's more, you'll often find a surprising amount of useful (and also some less useful) support software bundled with the card, including ASIO drivers, "lite" versions of the major sequencers, editor librarians, MIDI song files, mixer maps for the most commonly used sequencers and even sampling capability. However, a general-purpose card may be more confusing to configure than a dedicated audio card designed for music sequencing.

Other cards are designed to provide only synthesis and are often used in conjunction with a regular audio-only or audio-plus-synth soundcard. Additionally, some multimedia soundcards have connectors for a so-called daughterboard, a "piggy-back" circuit board that provides enhanced functionality. Adding a good-quality synthesiser daughterboard can improve the built-in sounds of a regular soundcard significantly. Usually, the output from the daughterboard is mixed with the stereo output of the host soundcard.

what is a soundcard?

A typical multimedia soundcard combines audio I/O (Input/Output) with a chip-based on-board synthesiser or sample-playback engine and a MIDI interface offering one channel of MIDI In and one of MIDI Out. Some also include digital effects that can be applied to the audio and/or MIDI sound sources (all General MIDI synth chips provide at least reverb and chorus for the MIDI sound sources, as they are part of the General MIDI specification). All basic cards will have at least one stereo analogue audio input and one stereo audio output, allowing analogue audio to be recorded and played back. These inputs and outputs go via analogue to digital and digital to analogue converters on the card so that recordings can be made in a digital format. The ASIO driver (normally provided with the card) handles the audio communications between the converters on the card and the host sequencer software. In contrast, a dedicated synth-only card (which may also include on-board effects) will normally have just an output (usually stereo), although some models also have analogue audio inputs to allow the user to make use of their on-board effects for external sounds.

The most common soundcard synth engines are based on a wavetable (ie sample-and-synthesis) synthesiser chip providing GM sounds plus the effects specified in the General MIDI protocol. An alternative form of sound generation is to use sample playback, such as that employed by Creative Labs' SoundFont system, where the sounds to be played back are stored on the computer's hard drive and loaded into the playback engine as required (much as with a regular software sampler). Both the sounds and effects can normally be edited via software catering for sound modification. Some soundcards have RAM sockets on their boards, allowing the sample RAM to be increased, if desired, although there is now a tendency for manufacturers to build cards that use the computer's main system RAM to store sample data instead. (More RAM enables you to use longer samples or play more samples at once.)

Multimedia cards designed for the PC tend to have a joystick port (for use with games) that can double as a pair of MIDI In and Out ports with an adaptor cable. All cards should come with a low-latency software driver and, as stated in the previous chapter, an ASIO driver provides the greatest degree of compatibility between soundcards and the major brands of sequencer.

On a multimedia/games card, there will most likely be audio input connections for a CD-ROM drive (allowing audio CDs to be played back via the card) and there may also be small on-board amplifiers for driving headphones or low-power desktop speakers. It's also traditional to supply a bundle of support software (including software drivers, where appropriate) so that the user can make use of the various facilities offered by the card. Other facilities found on some cards include digital-input and -output connectors (usually S/PDIF, for interfacing with DAT machines, CD players, MD recorders and so on). More advanced cards may have multiple audio inputs and/or outputs, but most of these tend to be dedicated audio cards designed for use with computer music rather than general-purpose multimedia cards. One exception to this trend is the series of Creative Labs cards that can be used with an I/O expander that fits into a spare computer drive bay to provide additional input and output capacity.

Cards with synthesiser capabilities are often able to offer techniques such as physical modelling, wavetable synthesis, conventional sampling and analogue-synthesiser emulation, although the huge advances in host-based virtual synthesis have tended to overshadow these developments. On multimedia cards, the synth engines are based on dedicated synth chips programmed to perform a specific task (not unlike the ones used in hardware synths and modules), whereas the most powerful card-based synths tend to be based on DSP (Digital Signal Processing) chips, where the instruments are still based in software but, unlike their VST counterparts, run on the card's DSP chips in order to avoid over-burdening the host computer. One clear advantage of the DSP approach is that the same card can support different types of synthesis, depending on the software being run on it.

dedicated audio interfaces and cards

Cheap audio-only cards with two inputs and up to eight physical outputs are not uncommon, but because of the lack of physical space on the back panel of a typical computer card the analogue connectors usually come via a breakout cable, with a multipin connector at one end and multiple single audio connectors at the other. Anything more elaborate tends to be presented as a separate audio interface that connects to the computer via either an included PCI card, USB (for small numbers of audio channels) or FireWire. While systems employing breakout cables are often unbalanced, most external hardware interfaces are fully balanced, which is preferable when connecting to a mixer with balanced line inputs.

Dedicated interfaces are where you're also likely to find multichannel digital interfaces such as ADAT, although the ADAT interface is fitted to some card-based interfaces, too. Clearly, having an ADAT interface is an advantage if you need to transfer material from an ADAT-compatible hardware recorder into your computer for editing or processing purposes, but it also facilitates easy connection to digital mixers equipped with ADAT interfaces. Figure 11.1 shows a basic audio set-up with the audio being mixed with the outputs from external MIDI hardware via a small analogue mixer.

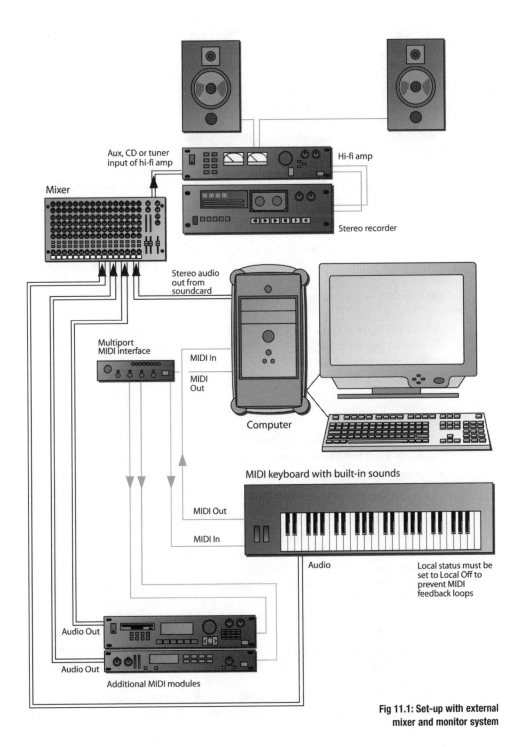

Aux, CD or tuner
input of hi-fi amp

Mixer

Hi-fi amp

Stereo recorder

Stereo audio
out from
soundcard

Multiport
MIDI interface

MIDI In

MIDI
Out

Computer

MIDI keyboard with built-in sounds

MIDI Out

MIDI In

Audio

Local status must be
set to Local Off to
prevent MIDI
feedback loops

Audio Out

Audio Out

Additional MIDI modules

**Fig 11.1: Set-up with external
mixer and monitor system**

installing cards

Because PCs have a number of expansion slots, it's sometimes possible to use two or more soundcards in the same machine, although I'd recommend against this due to the PC's vulnerability to complications. When installing any kind of computer card, it's essential to follow the guidelines that come with the card regarding precautions to be taken against the possibility of damage by static electricity, and you should always unplug the computer from the mains before removing the cover. A resistive earth strap is sometimes provided to connect your wrist to the metal frame of the computer, although I usually find it adequate to hold the computer chassis with one hand while removing the card from its protective bag with the other, thus ensuring that both the computer frame and the card are at the same electrical potential. Then you can simply insert the card into a free slot (after first removing the blanking plate), making sure that it lines up with the connector and then pushing it gently but firmly into place. A single screw normally secures the back plate via the hole where the blanking plate was fixed.

In the case of general-purpose multimedia soundcards, installing hardware and its support software isn't always the painless procedure it ought to be, although, unlike the earlier ISA cards, virtually all modern soundcards are now designed to fit into PCI slots, which means no more struggling with IRQs (Interrupt Requests) or DMAs (Direct Memory Access) on those occasions when plug-and-play doesn't work. (See "Glossary" for an explanation of these terms).

Earlier non-plug-and-play-compatible hardware was often configured by means of little jumper switches on the circuit boards, but more modern ISA cards handle everything in software, courtesy of Windows plug-and-play, which in Windows '95 and later versions of Windows is designed to look after hardware installation for you. However, it can still run into trouble when it can't find a solution to hardware conflicts caused by having more pieces of hardware installed than there are DMAs and IRQs to service them. This is because the number of available IRQs and DMAs is limited, and once they're all taken you can't add any more cards without first taking out one of your existing cards, unless you resort to engaging in complex system adjustments every time you want to change your hardware. Again, the in-depth workings of specific computers is not within the remit of this book, but with any luck you won't encounter any of these older ISA cards, anyway. If you aren't confident about installing a soundcard of either the ISA or PCI variety, get a technically competent supplier to do the job for you before parting with any money.

Modern Macintosh computers currently use PCI slots exclusively and tend to have simpler installation procedures than PCs, although you should be aware that iMacs don't have any PCI slots at all. Fortunately, external audio interfaces are available that connect via USB or FireWire, which means that no PCI card is needed, only suitable driver software. However, USB has a relatively low bandwidth, and so is really suitable only for systems where no more than four or six simultaneous outputs (at 44.1kHz or 48kHz) are needed and where a separate USB controller can be dedicated to the interface. Attempts to share the USB bandwidth by connecting two or more peripherals to the same controller can reduce the number of channels that can be played back without causing glitching or other problems.

FireWire has a much wider bandwidth than USB (although USB may reverse this state of affairs), making it possible to connect multiple eight-in/eight-out interfaces where 16 or more inputs and outputs are needed or where 24-bit/96kHz audio is being used. In theory, FireWire can handle over 100 channels of audio simultaneously, depending on the rate and bit depth of the samples. Because a FireWire connection doesn't require a PCI card slot, and because of its speed and reliability, it is becoming a popular choice for serious users.

and then there's MIDI

A basic PC MIDI music system will generally make use of the MIDI interface provided by the soundcard, and a common way of working is to use a MIDI adaptor cable (often supplied with the soundcard) that plugs into the card's joystick port. Alternatively, you can buy a hardware adaptor. These kinds of adaptors look like long multipin plugs with MIDI sockets built into them and often allow you to leave your joystick connected via a joystick thru socket. Be aware, however, that some MIDI programs get upset if a joystick is left connected, so if you're in any doubt, unplug it.

The limitation of the simple "one-in/one-out" MIDI interface is that you can only use it to drive 16 external MIDI channels, and with today's synth modules this usually equates to a single multitimbral instrument. However, remember that the internal soundcards (other than, possibly, the daughterboard) use virtual MIDI ports, as do any software plug-in instruments that you're using. This is obviously good news if you're on a budget, as you can use your internal soundcard and software synth sounds at the same time as your external MIDI module and still need only one MIDI port.

If you need more ports in order to handle additional external synths, you'll need a multiport MIDI interface offering two, four or eight sets of MIDI outputs. (These are discussed in greater detail in the section entitled "MIDI Ports" in Chapter 3, "Introducing Sequencers".) A "dumb" MIDI master keyboard can be connected simply to the MIDI In while a MIDI synth would need to be set to Local Off so that the synth section could be driven from the MIDI Out port of the computer. (The implications of MIDI Local On and Off are explained in Chapter 1, "Introducing MIDI".)

While it's clear why multiple MIDI output ports might be useful (when you have more than one multitimbral hardware synth, for example), it's not so obvious why you might need multiple inputs. One possibility is that you may want to add a hardware MIDI controller to your system, in which case this may need to be connected to its own MIDI port. However, you may also have a software synthesiser editing and librarian package. These require bi-directional communication with all of your synth modules, and so MIDI ports must be available for connecting both inputs and outputs. As a rule, the MIDI input ports can be configured to operate as a MIDI merge box (usually the default option), which in most instances is the simplest way of working.

The majority of today's multiport MIDI interfaces are designed to connect via the USB interface, supported by both Mac and PC hardware. However, when using Macintosh computers, multiport MIDI interfaces that aren't directly supported by the host software need a driver that establishes common ground between the hardware and the software. Perhaps the most common example is Opcode's OMS (Open MIDI System) protocol, although Mark Of The Unicorn's conceptually similar FreeMIDI can be used with any FreeMIDI-compatible MIDI-interfacing hardware and sequencing software.

combined interfaces

It surprises me that more people don't build combined audio and MIDI interfaces, as these would be especially useful when working on laptop computers. Fortunately, a few of these have started to appear, and these are often based around a small MIDI keyboard that connects to the computer via USB. The keyboard hardware on these devices includes audio I/O connections and has internal circuitry that functions much like a regular USB interface. However, as audio and MIDI must share the available USB bandwidth, most models offer only two-in/two-out audio operation. But if you have a powerful laptop running lots of virtual instruments and you want to make records on the beach, this is the way to go!

Note that, in order to work with Macintosh computers, keyboards and interfaces with built-in USB connectivity generally need OMS software. In most cases, OMS will be provided along with the keyboard or interface's support software. OMS should not be needed with OSX-compatible interfaces and software.

summary

Games or multimedia soundcards offer exceptional value because of their low cost, their on-board synth engines and their bundled software (which often includes a fully functional "lite" version of a major sequencer, such as Cubasis, which is a scaled down version of Cubase VST). Ironically, though, while these types of cards have the accessible price, they're often the most complicated to use, so unless you're already familiar with them and their applications, I'd strongly recommend that you use a simpler, audio-only card instead. Not only will this reduce complications but it will probably give you better audio quality.

If you take this route, you'll need a separate MIDI interface (which again will be less susceptible to problems than those built into some soundcards) and, as you'll have no card-based synthesis capability, you may choose to buy a controller keyboard and use its own sounds rather than use a dumb MIDI controller keyboard. You also have the option of using plug-in software instruments, most commonly in the VST format, and these are available in all price ranges from the freeware distributed on the internet upwards. (VST instruments and their uses are covered in greater detail in the next chapter. For further information on this subject, check out *basic VST INSTRUMENTS*, also available from Sanctuary Publishing.) Plug-in instruments have the advantage that they require no physical MIDI port to make them work, although they do drain your computer's CPU resources.

software instruments

At one time, MIDI instruments such as synthesisers, MIDI modules, samplers and drum machines were always hardware devices or rack units connected to the sequencer's interface via MIDI cables, as described earlier in this book. Progress, however, marches inexorably onwards, and today there is a fantastic array of so-called virtual instruments at our disposal, some emulating traditional hardware and others offering capabilities unavailable elsewhere. Software synthesis isn't a new subject, by any means, but it's only recently that desktop computers have become powerful enough to handle audio recording, MIDI sequencing and the software synthesis of multiple instruments at the same time. Software instruments are available in many forms, but the most popular come in the form of *plug-ins*, which can be loaded into a computer and accessed and controlled from within the host sequencer software. Alternatives exist, such as "ReWire" technology (covered later in this chapter), which provides a software patching system to integrate some stand-alone software instruments into the software-sequencer environment, but the plug-in market is where the main growth has occurred and, with few exceptions, is where the most interesting instruments are to be found.

Different sequencer packages require different plug-in formats, with Mark Of The Unicorn's Digital Performer having its own MAS format, Cakewalk's SONAR having yet a different system and Steinberg's Cubase supporting its own VST system. Emagic's Logic Audio has its own plug-in format, too, but can also host VST plug-ins, which makes it a very powerful tool. The whole plug-in concept was pioneered by Digidesign, whose original system relied solely on plug-in DSP cards for power. Specially written plug-ins could run on these DSPs, but they weren't compatible with any other system. On the other hand, VST is a very widespread, host-based format (which means that it runs on the computer's processor chip, not on a special DSP card), and it can even be used inside some non-VST-compatible sequencers using a so-called *software wrapper* to make it look to the computer like the kind of plug-in that it supports. But what exactly is VST? What does it stand for? And what can it do for your music?

the VST incentive

VST (Virtual Studio Technology) was the brainchild of German music software manufacturers Steinberg, who developed it to work with their Cubase VST MIDI-plus-audio sequencer software. In the first instance, this system provided only software effects and signal processors, but it was later extended to encompass software instruments with the introduction of the VST II protocol, which allowed plug-ins to receive and act upon MIDI data. Although software instruments are strictly VST II compatible, they're generally referred to simply as VST instruments.

One of the best things to happen to software music was Steinberg's decision to open up their VST protocol to third-party developers. This meant that third-party software companies could create new effects and instrument plug-ins that could be used within Cubase VST. Furthermore, Steinberg allowed other designers of sequencers and audio programs to make use of the VST protocol, which was good news for software-instrument developers as it meant that they had to develop only one version of each plug-in (well, actually one Mac OS version and one PC Windows version) for use in all VST-compatible sequencer programs.

plug-in diversity

Support for the VST format is by no means universal, although Steinberg's Cubase, Cubasis and Nuendo, Emagic's Logic Audio, Berkley Systems' Bias Peak and TCWorks' Spark and Spark XL are all VST compatible. Opcode's Studio Vision software (which at the time of writing is no longer being developed) also supports VST plug-ins directly, while a wrapper program is needed to use VST plug-ins inside the MAS environment of Mark Of The Unicorn's Digital Performer and Cakewalk's SONAR software can also use VST plug-ins via suitable wrapper software. It's easy to see why the VST format is so popular.

Different versions of VST plug-ins are required depending on whether the host software runs on a Mac or PC, and there are some Mac plug-ins that aren't available for PCs and vice versa.

The VST II format is able to read both MIDI and tempo information from the host sequencer, so in addition to being able to play conventional keyboard parts, the instruments may also be designed to include rhythm generators, arpeggiators and so on, all locked to the tempo of the sequencer. (Most of the descriptions here will relate to VST instruments, although the alternative plug-in formats all work in very similar ways.)

computer power

VST effect and instrument plug-ins are said to be *native* or *host based* because they rely entirely on the host computer's processor and memory for their operation. Each plug-in takes a proportion of the computer's available processing power, so every computer has a limit to how many software instruments it can run at once. There's no easy way to put a figure on this, though, as some instrument plug-ins take more processing power than others, and the load exerted on the computer also depends on the polyphony being used. With a modern, fast Mac or PC, you shouldn't find this too limiting, but I feel that hardware instruments will still be around for a few years yet.

the pros...

Software instrument plug-ins have both advantages and disadvantages, compared with their hardware equivalents. On the plus side, they don't take up valuable MIDI interface ports, and often the playback timing is far better than the timing resolution of MIDI itself. This is because, although they behave as MIDI instruments, the control system within the computer isn't inhibited by the bandwidth and speed restraints of conventional MIDI hardware. In fact, some systems boast sample-accurate playback of virtual instruments.

Another benefit is that virtual instruments appear in the same environment as your sequencer audio tracks so there's no need for a hardware mixer to combine audio and synth-based sounds. Of course, you'll still need a mixer if you have one or more hardware MIDI instruments in your system. Virtual instrument plug-ins may also be used in combination with virtual effects plug-ins, so you don't need to worry about how to route the virtual instrument through an external effects processor.

Also on the positive side, plug-in formats such as VST effects and instruments need no wiring, they don't wear out with age and there are no noisy cable problems to sort out. Indeed, in many cases, free software updates are available, which means that your instruments actually get newer as they age! The sound quality available to you is limited mainly by the quality of your soundcard, and because you're not using separate equipment boxes you don't have to buy a big rack and a load of power-distribution boards. However, one of the biggest benefits I've discovered is that both effect and instrument VST plug-in settings can be saved along with your song data, enabling you to get a mix back exactly as you saved it. Furthermore, control changes can be recorded into your sequencer, enabling you to automate things like filter resonance, filter frequency and so on. This goes down especially well with people writing dance music!

Another benefit is that you can use the same VST plug-in within several different audio tracks at the same time. In fact, you can use as many instances of it at one time as your computer's available CPU power (or your sequencer's virtual-instrument track limit) can support.

...and now the cons

The downside of any host-based software instrument is that it takes a proportion of your available computing resources, and as newer and more powerful instruments become available so the pressure to upgrade to a faster computer becomes ever more intense. Realistically, you can expect to keep the same computer for no more than 18 months to two years before it starts to look sadly underpowered!

Lack of a physical user interface may also be a concern, but personally I prefer the virtual representation of a traditional knobs-and-buttons user interface to the usual cursor controls and mini-LCD windows found on typical hardware synths. Nevertheless, if you're into making multiple real-time control changes at the same time, a MIDI hardware controller is a big benefit as a mouse can change only one parameter at a time. There's also the issue of latency to contend with, the very real demon in the virtual world.

latency

Latency is a very important concept to understand, especially if you're using VST instruments. In practical terms, latency is a small time delay that occurs between triggering a note on a MIDI keyboard and the software instrument responding. It can also be heard when recording audio into a computer-based system while monitoring the audio output from the computer. When analogue audio is recorded into a computer, the signal is converted to digital data and then routed via the computer's PCI buss and CPU before being passed on to the soundcard outputs. This takes long enough that the delay is sometimes audible. The magnitude of this delay depends on the speed of the computer, how well the software driver works and how much RAM buffering is needed in order to ensure reliable audio performance, but even the fastest computers can't avoid latency altogether (although they can help minimise it). The result is that, on a system with excessive latency, you may perceive a delay between pressing a key on your MIDI keyboard and hearing the note sounding. This latency delay is compensated for on playback, but when you're actually recording it can affect your ability to sing or play in time, especially if it's longer than 10ms or so. Fortunately, a modern computer using a well-designed audio interface and driver can deliver latency times below 10ms, so playing virtual instruments should feel as immediate as playing hardware instruments.

Placing other effect or processor plug-ins after an instrument plug-in may increase the latency further, and so, while playing the instrument alone may feel OK, adding another plug-in might make it feel "wrong". The solution is to record the instrument parts without further processing and then add the processing plug-ins later. In systems where the latency is so high that it makes accurate playing impossible, you can record your MIDI parts while listening to the sound of a hardware instrument or soundcard and then use the recorded data to play back a virtual instrument.

the importance of drivers

The amount of software-instrument latency that you experience will depend both on the power of your computer and on the software driver handling your audio I/O (Input/Output). Some games-type soundcards come with their own drivers, and the worst of these have latency values of a quarter of a second or more, rendering them quite unusable for any real-time work. Most serious audio hardware comes with more sophisticated audio drivers and one of the most common of these is ASIO (Audio Streaming Input/Output), another Steinberg development. ASIO drivers are specifically designed to handle multiple audio streams with low latency. Like VST, ASIO has become a widely adopted standard and is supported by a significant number of sequencer packages, audio-editing packages and so on. The creation of the ASIO driver is the responsibility of the audio-hardware manufacturer, so if in doubt you should check that an ASIO driver is included with your prospective purchase, unless you're using hardware specific to your sequencing software, in which case it may have its own low-latency driver.

The ASIO II revision of the format provides direct thru monitoring of audio signals being recorded (although only on compatible audio hardware) so as to prevent latency from distracting musicians performing overdubs - there's nothing worse than singing or playing guitar and hearing the sound in the headphones a fraction of a second later! Thru monitoring gets around this problem very neatly by automatically passing the card's input directly to its output during recording, bypassing the computer entirely. However, thru monitoring can't help in the case of virtual instruments, as the sound of these is generated within the computer (which means that you can't bypass it!), so there's always some degree of latency between pressing a key and hearing a sound. For a VST instrument to be playable in real time, you ideally need a system that has a latency of less than 10ms or you'll feel an off-putting lag when playing, especially when using rapid attack sounds, such as piano.

Note that some MIDI keyboards take up to 5ms to send MIDI data after a key is pressed, so this delay is added to the latency of your computer system. For this reason, a latency performance that might be just short enough for comfortable audio recording might still appear long enough to be distracting to proficient keyboard players once the delay produced by the controller keyboard has been added. If you have a system that can't achieve adequately low latency values to allow you to play comfortably, try recording the instrument part using a regular hardware or soundchip MIDI sound source as a guide and then switch the track back to the VST instrument for playback.

Audio software generally comes with some way of allowing the user to adjust the latency, usually by changing the size of a small memory buffer used to provide an unbroken stream of audio through the system. If you set the buffer size too small, the audio will start to break up or, in serious cases, recording or playback may be halted altogether, whereas if you set the buffer size too high the system will be more reliable but the latency will be high. In some instances, you can set a lower latency time when recording and then increase it when you come to play back your complete mix, thus preventing any audio glitching. Latency has no practical effect on playback, only on recording. The more audio tracks and virtual instruments you have playing back at one time, the higher the buffer size will need to be set if operation is to be reliable, and the only way you can figure out the best setting is to experiment until playback becomes unreliable and then go back to the previous buffer size.

types of software instrument

With your appetite whetted for the benefits of virtual instruments, as well as coming clean about their limitations, it's natural that you should now want to know what types of instrument plug-in are available. In fact, virtually any method of hardware synthesis can be implemented in the software world, although performing multilayer additive synthesis with separate filters and envelopes on each layer is a very processor-intensive business. A large part of virtual synthesis seems to be taken up with emulating classic analogue synths. Going back even further, you can even buy a plug-in based on the Mellotron, the original analogue-tape-based sample-playback instrument. Indeed, Figure 12.1 over the page shows the G-Media M-Tron plug-in, which includes a selection of soundbanks taken from the original Mellotron tapes. Additional sounds from the Mellotron and other vintage instruments can be bought as an optional add-on to extend the usefulness of the instrument.

Fig 12.1: G-Media M-Tron

Clearly, the easiest instruments to emulate in software form are those that already use digital technology, although the application of physical modelling has also made it possible to get very close to the sound of classic analogue instruments. Physical modelling is different to sampling in that the various elements that make up an instrument are each modelled mathematically and then an algorithm is devised to synthesise the sound. If the modelling has been carried out properly, the instrument should behave more or less like the real thing, including reproducing any imperfections or other quirks that give it its sonic identity. There are already excellent models of tone-wheel organs, electric pianos and classic analogue synths, often with built-in effects such as reverb, chorus, tube-amp overdrive and even rotary speaker cabinets. The graphically (and sonically) splendid NI B4 tone-wheel organ plug-in is shown in Figure 12.2. (For more information, see the section "Physical Modelling" in Chapter 5, "The Basics Of Synthesis".)

To me, the really exciting thing about software instrument plug-ins is that their designers can create new instruments that have no hardware counterparts. Moreover, the instruments can be given any kind of graphic user interface that the designer can dream up. A fine example of this is Native Instruments' Absynth, a multisynthesis instrument capable of an extraordinary range of sounds and with a seriously weird user interface, as shown in Figure 12.3. Absynth can draw upon a whole range of waveshapes, or the user can draw new waveforms that can then be used as sound sources. Additive and FM synthesis is also supported, along with ring modulation, comprehensive filters and effects.

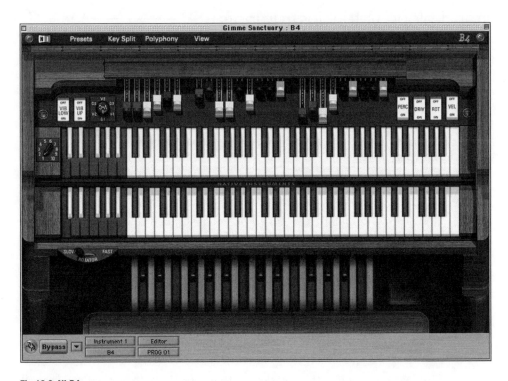

Fig 12.2: NI B4

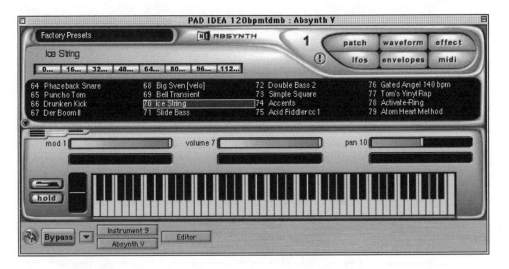

Fig 12.3: NI Absynth

stand-alone virtual instruments

There are a number of software instruments currently on the market that are designed to work as stand-alone applications rather than as plug-ins, which causes problems when you try to run them from a sequencer. Fortunately, the most successful virtual instruments are now available as plug-ins, but where this is not the case, a technology known as ReWire may provide a solution. However, in order for ReWire to work, both the host sequencer and the software instrument being used must be ReWire compatible.

ReWire

ReWire was originally developed by Propellerhead to enable their stand-alone ReBirth software synth/rhythm machine to work co-operatively with other applications (initially Cubase), but the concept was later opened up to other software developers. ReWire provides the means to transfer audio data between two programs in real time in much the same manner as a software cable carrying up to 64 or more audio channels. One of the main benefits of this system is that two or more ReWire-compatible applications can send audio out through the same audio interface at the same time.

The way in which this works is that any ReWire-compatible virtual instrument or other application can send multiple audio streams into a ReWire-compatible host program, such as Cubase VST, enabling its output(s) to be mixed along with any of the Cubase audio tracks or plug-in VST instruments. In other words, a ReWire-compatible stand-alone virtual instrument's audio output can be mixed from within a sequencer program almost as easily as a VST plug-in.

Transport control and synchronisation are also handled by ReWire, so multiple programs - each having its own built-in sequencer - can be run together in perfect sync. In the case of ReBirth and Cubase, this means that ReBirth can start and stop Cubase or instead Cubase can start and stop ReBirth.

Of course, using ReWire places an additional load on the computer's CPU, and it may cause longer latency times when used with your sequencer than the same application running on its own, but it does provide a practical means of running non-plug-in virtual instruments alongside a sequencer in a controllable manner and allows the audio output from the instrument to be routed through the sequencer's own audio mixer.

software piracy

Music-software companies seem particularly prone to piracy (the illegal copying and distribution of their software to users who haven't paid for it), and manufacturers of plug-ins seem particularly at risk in this respect. Of course, in the long term, this doesn't do any of us any good, because if no one pays for its software, the company producing it will go out of business and there'll be no new programs. There's also a real possibility of picking up computer viruses when downloading software from the internet, legitimately or otherwise, so on the whole it's best to steer clear of pirated software and also to use a virus checker if your music computer is also used to access the internet. Anti-piracy systems generally involve some inconvenience for the legitimate user, but sadly they are a fact of life – even though most get hacked in an alarmingly short space of time!

If you want something for nothing (or, at least, very little), there are altruistic programmers out there creating software instruments and even audio recorders and sequencers and releasing them as freeware or shareware, usually via the internet. Freeware is, as its name implies, completely free, whereas shareware relies on a system whereby the designer trusts the user to send him a small fee if his product turns out to be useful. Sadly, the complexity of getting $10 from Europe to the USA and vice versa often means that these guys don't get the payments they should. One very worthwhile freeware instrument is the MDA Piano, shown in Figure 12.4. An internet search for "MDA Piano" should quickly lead you to a site where you can download a copy. Also, you must check out Delay Lama from Audionerdz.com

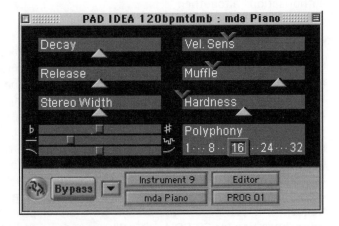

Fig 12.4: MDA piano (freeware)

Anti-piracy protection comes in several forms, the most common systems being the uncopyable master CD-ROM and the challenge-and-response code. Some software is also authorised by means of a master key floppy disk, but as floppy disk drives are now virtually obsolete such systems are rapidly being replaced by something more sensible.

key-disk protection

At the time of writing, a few floppy-disk-key installation systems are still in use, so it's worth describing them here in case you come across one. Users of Macintosh G4s or other Apple models that use external USB floppy drives may need a software patch to enable their drive to authorise their software, while software protected by the Pace copy-protection system requires a patch from the developers' website at www.paceap.com.

Most key-floppy protection systems are based around an uncopyable master floppy disk (how it is made uncopyable is the secret!) from which the software is installed. The key disk includes an invisible authorisation code that is transferred to the computer's hard drive when the software is installed. When the software is de-installed, this code is transferred back to the floppy disk so that it can be used again in another computer. The hidden authorisation file resides on the computer's hard drive, ensuring that the software will work only on that particular computer; copying the installed program to another machine won't work.

If you need to change computers or replace your hard drive, you must de-install all of your copy-protected software first or you may lose your authorisations altogether.

CD copy protection

Using an uncopyable CD-ROM as the master disk feels more secure to me, as with this kind of system there are no authorisation codes to lose and no floppies to corrupt accidentally. Just don't use them as coasters! VST instruments produced by Native Instruments and a number of other companies employ a variation on this system whereby the software is installed from the CD-ROM in the normal way but on random occasions (usually when you start up the program) you're asked to insert the master CD-ROM in order to re-authorise the software. I find this system quite acceptable, provided that I'm not asked to insert the master CD-ROM too frequently. If you have a big system with lots of plug-ins, you can find yourself hunting for CD-ROMs virtually every day!

challenge codes

Another popular form of protection is the so-called *challenge-and-response code system*. With this kind of system, the software itself needs no protection, enabling it to be freely copied and passed around the internet. Once you've installed software utilising this kind of security, however, you may find that it works for a demo period of a few week or that it won't work at all until authorised. Then, when you run the authoriser program, a set of seemingly random words is generated which have to be emailed or faxed to the software manufacturer, along with proof of purchase. In reply, they send you another set of code words which must be typed into your computer to authorise your software. As with the key-floppy system, challenge-and-response software will only run on the computer for which it is authorised.

dongles

The term *dongle* is computerspeak for a hardware key that plugs into one of the ports of your computer. This dongle will contain unreadable microchips and the program for which it was built will be designed so that it won't run unless the presence of the dongle is detected. Emagic went over to USB dongles with the introduction of Version 5 of their sequencing software and also took the step of using the dongle to protect any Emagic plug-ins. Each dongle has a unique serial number and an access code specific to each dongle is issued whenever a new plug-in is purchased. As long as you don't lose the dongle, you can freely move the software between computers and it will still work as long as the dongle is plugged into the computer you're using. However, if you lose the dongle, you lose everything that's authorised by it, so be very careful!

adding new plug-ins

VST plug-ins for both Mac and Windows tend to come with automated installation routines, ensuring that the procedure is fairly straightforward. All of your VST plug-ins will reside in the folder named "VstPlugins" used by your audio software, and if several pieces of software need to access the same folder it is usually possible to create aliases (on the Mac) or shortcuts (on the PC) to the VstPlugins folder from within the applications that need to access it. If your plug-in isn't visible within the VST Plug-In menu (check both mono and stereo plug-ins before panicking!), do a quick search for it on your computer and make sure it's installed in the right place. There may also be additional files containing factory-preset sounds as well as locations to store your own user patches, although the installation process should put these in the correct places, as long as you tell the installer program where the VstPlugins folder is.

If the software you're using is copy-protected, the first time you try to start it up you should see a message telling you how to authorise the software. Note that some programs require you to enter serial numbers before they will operate. These numbers are often found on the software packaging or some equally easy-to-lose place, so it helps to copy the number onto the label side of the installation disk with a felt-tipped marker pen. It's also a good idea to create a Notepad or Read Me file on you computer in which to keep copies of all of your serial numbers and challenge-and-response codes. If you have a dongle attached that you can update, this will also require an authorisation code to be typed into the computer, authorising the plug-in to run only when the dongle is connected to the computer.

Those using dual-processor Macintosh G4 computers with pre-OS X operating systems should note that not all VST plug-ins are able to work in Dual Processor mode and may cause the computer to crash. The solution is either to switch the computer's Dual Processor mode off or to remove temporarily any incompatible plug-ins from the VstPlugins folder. For software that periodically prompts you to reinsert the master CD-ROM, you'll avoid a lot of frustration if you keep all such masters together, near the computer. Currently, the main sequencer software packages aren't available for Mac OS X, but there are great hopes that this new system will improve dual-processor operation efficiently and reduce latency times further when compatible software becomes available.

more power!

Host-powered software instruments are wonderful things and getting more wonderful all the time, but they do require a powerful computer in order to run, especially if you want to run several at one time. Don't be misled by the minimum system requirements quoted on the box – often these are complete nonsense and barely allow the plug-in to run on its own, let alone in the company of several others. Make no mistake, you need something at least half as fast as the most powerful computer you can currently buy if you want to avoid disappointment. Furthermore, you'll need to upgrade to a new computer every couple of years, maximum. This may seem extravagant, but when you consider the cost of doing so against the depreciation of conventional studio hardware, it still looks a very attractive option. While you're at it, make sure that you fit plenty of RAM, ideally between 256Mb and 512Mb more than you think you're going to need, while if you're planning to use a software sampler that uses the host computer's RAM to store sounds, you might want to invest in even more!

If you push your computer to the limit, it's likely to crash, so keep an eye on your sequencer's CPU performance meter and increase the buffer size if playback becomes unreliable. One simple thing that you can do to take a little load off the processor is to zoom out of the song window in your sequencer so that the whole song is visible. This means that your monitor won't have to scroll or redraw and it can make the difference between your computer running smoothly and crashing when you're working close to the edge.

proprietary plug-ins

In addition to supporting VST, Emagic produce their own format of plug-in which looks and works much like its VST counterpart, with the exception that it can be used only within the host application. Some of these plug-ins are later re-engineered into full VST plug-ins, but at the time of writing the full version of the EXS-24 software sampler and the EVP-88 electric piano are available only to Logic users and can't be used within other VST-compatible programs. Furthermore, from Version 5 of Logic Audio onwards, the program comes complete with a suite of built-in virtual instruments as standard. These are loaded and used in a similar way to true VST instruments, and their signal may be routed via true VST effects in subsequent insert slots, but that's where the similarity ends. Figure 12.5 over the page shows Emagic's built-in plug-in instruments.

Steinberg take a slightly different approach with their Cubase software, which comes with a suite of conventional VST plug-ins. These may be used freely within any VST-compatible program but only if Cubase is installed on the machine. If you attempt to copy the plug-ins to a different machine in order to use them without Cubase, they won't work. The VST instruments that come bundled with Cubase are Neon, VB1 and LM9. Neon is a basic polyphonic synth while VB1 is a bass synth with a visual user interface that looks like the body of a guitar. On the latter, instead of adjusting parameters directly, you can change things like the virtual picking position along the strings and the physical position of the guitar pick-up, and on the whole the plug-in sounds halfway between a real bass guitar and a synthesiser. Meanwhile, the LM9 is a scaled-down version of Steinberg's LM4 drum-module plug-in and can be played via nine onscreen drum pads or via MIDI. It can generate a useful range of contemporary electronic-drum sounds, including passable emulations of the old Roland sounds so beloved of dance-music composers. The bundled instruments included by Steinberg and Emagic are fairly simple but still sound good and don't exert too much of a drain on your processor overhead.

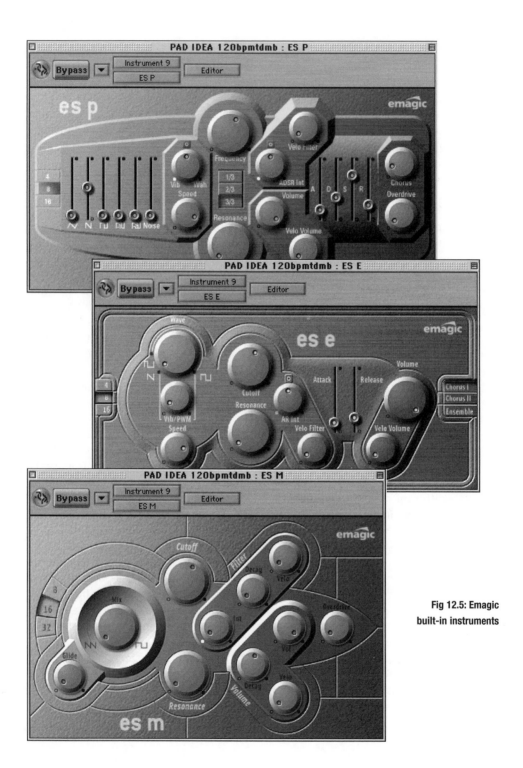

Fig 12.5: Emagic
built-in instruments

using plug-ins

So, now that you know exactly what VST instruments are and what they do, how do you go about using them in your sequencer? For a start, your sequencer needs to have audio capability, and although most software now provides this as standard, you'll need audio hardware or a soundcard with a low-latency driver (probably ASIO). The instruments themselves are played from your MIDI controller keyboard in the usual way.

In Cubase, VST instruments are accessed from within MIDI instrument tracks, while in Logic Audio special "Instrument" channel "Audio Objects" are set up in the Audio Mixer page and then the desired VST instrument is loaded into the uppermost insert point, as shown in Figure 12.6 over the page. Subsequent insert points may then be used to add VST effects in order to process the sound of the instrument. The way in which automation data is stored varies from sequencer to sequencer, but in essence any real-time adjustments that you make to the controls of a VST instrument can be recorded so that they will play back every time you replay the song.

The majority of VST instruments (the commercial ones, at least, as opposed to those distributed via freeware) come with some ready-created preset sounds. If you're new to synthesis, you can learn a lot by adjusting existing presets and then saving your modified versions under new names for use at a later date. When you install your instrument plug-in, check that all of the files relating to these presets are stored where the program documentation indicates or they may prove inaccessible.

conserving CPU power

Despite the powerful nature of current desktop computers, some virtual instruments invoke heavy demands on your available CPU capacity. Many people seem to confuse CPU power with RAM capacity and assume that they can solve speed-related problems by fitting more memory, but while it's true that you'll have problems if you have insufficient RAM with which to run your music software properly, fitting more than you need won't improve the performance of your system. However, there are several techniques and tricks that you can use if you find that you're running low on power.

sample rates

Running your audio interface at high sample rates will reduce the available track count and the number of plug-ins – both effects and instruments – that you can use at one time. Unless you have a good reason for working at

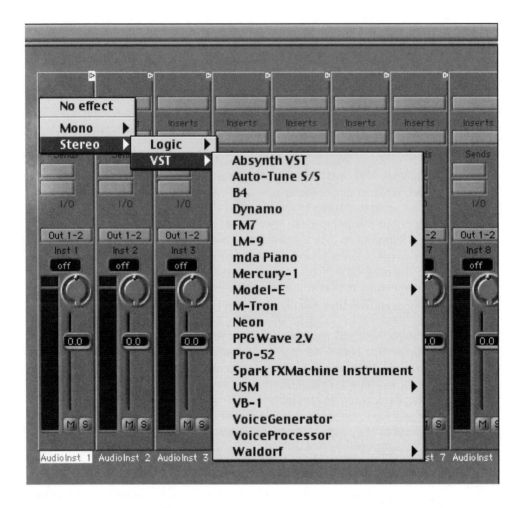

Fig 12.6: Instruments in Logic Audio

higher sample rates, I would suggest sticking to 44.1kHz, as that's the rate that you'll eventually need for CD production, anyway.

Avoid non-essential CPU demands, such as screen redraws. Close unnecessary windows and scale down your Arrange window so that it encompasses the complete song. This will avoid your CPU being hit as the screen redraws after the song cursor has run off the end of the page.

Low latency settings make virtual instruments easier to play but can also cause problems when your system is pushed close to its limit. You need low latency while recording virtual instrument parts so to reduce pressure on your system you should mute any existing virtual-instrument tracks that aren't essential for the performance of your overdub. Keep your system performance meter open to see if simply muting the track produces the saving you need. It also pays not to take the meter too literally – always leave a little free capacity.

guide sounds

Where it isn't possible to get latency down to a playable value, the only option is to use the MIDI data of your existing virtual-instrument parts to play back sounds from a soundcard synth chip or external synth module in order to act as a guide while you're overdubbing your new virtual-instrument part. Once all of your parts have been recorded, you can revert to the original virtual instruments for playback.

Plug-in effects such as reverb use a lot of processing power and so can dramatically reduce the CPU capacity available for your virtual instruments. Sometimes less sophisticated (and less power-hungry) reverb plug-ins sound just as good on instruments as the more sophisticated alternatives, so try out the budget models. You'll also make more economic use of reverb if you configure a single reverb plug-in as a send effect rather than using multiple reverb plug-ins via inserts.

Although they're not cheap, adding a DSP card such as TCWorks' PowerCore or the Universal Audio Unity card will give you high-quality plug-in effects that run largely independent of the host processor. The greater the amount of routine processing that you can move over to these cards, the more CPU power you'll have left for your virtual instruments.

converting to audio

If you use a lot of virtual instruments, you may still find that you run out of power. One simple solution is to take your most power-hungry virtual instrument tracks and record them into a regular audio track. (Your sequencer manual will tell you how to do this.) Once these have been recorded as audio, there will be no load on your CPU as audio tracks impose virtually no burden. Of course, doing this will mean that you lose the ability to add filter effects from your synth after converting to an audio track, but there are plenty of filter plug-in effects that you can press into service if necessary.

Yet another solution is to sample the sounds of more power-hungry instrument plug-ins using your software sampler. These programs demand significantly less CPU overhead than most synths, and using sampling means that a complex rhythmic loop that may have taken half of your CPU power to create can be saved as a single sample, with playback requiring very little processor power. If the loop contains a dynamic control change element, just sample several bars of the loop. You can also apply dynamic filter settings to the loop during playback as you can use the sampler's own filter.

Creating multisamples out of regular synth sounds is a little more time consuming, but if you use a virtual sampler such as Halion or EXS-24 it's pretty straightforward and can be a real power-saving option, especially if there are some sounds that you find yourself using a lot. A benefit of working in this way is that, once a sound has been sampled, it's very easy to change its overall envelope and to apply filter sweeps by using the sampler's controls.

virtual instrument FAQs

Q: There's an audible delay between pressing a key and hearing any sound.

A: The latency is too high for real-time playing. However, with a well-written ASIO driver and a modern computer, you should be able to get the figure down to an acceptable value. Check the audio-driver settings, where you should be able to adjust the latency by adjusting the buffer size. (Consult your sequencer manual and soundcard/interface manual to find out how to do this.) If you select the minimum value, the audio side of the program may become unstable or subject to glitching. Choose the setting that gives you the lowest latency with the most reliable performance. Any setting of under 15ms should be OK for real-time playing.

Q: What if the minimum latency is still too high to be able to play in real time?

A: You can use a hardware sound source – such as your soundcard or a synth module – to provide the sound when you're recording and then switch the track to the desired virtual instrument for playback. Latency is not a problem when playing back or mixing.

Q: I've installed a new VST instrument but it doesn't appear in the VST instrument list within my program.

A: Make sure that the installer program has placed the VST instrument in the "VstPlugins" folder used by the audio program with which you're trying to work. If you have two or more VST programs, you can usually place shortcuts or aliases of the original plug-ins in the VstPlugins folders for each program. Alternatively, create a single VstPlugins folder and then place an alias/shortcut of that in the same folder as each of your VST audio programs. After restarting your computer, the instruments should appear in the menu list of each program.

Q: The VST instrument appears but none of its factory-preset sounds are available.

A: Factory presets are often installed in separate folders which have to be located as specified in the installation instructions of the program you're using. Usually, the installation procedure will do this automatically, but sometimes you may have to move things around manually.

Q: How can I minimise the CPU drain caused by VST instruments?

A: See the section in this chapter starting with "Conserving CPU Power", which provides a useful selection of tips and techniques for maximising CPU resources.

Q: Can I use regular VST effects to process the output from VST instruments?

A: Normally, you can use any VST plug-in after a VST instrument, but because not every audio program designer supports VST properly in every respect, you may find the occasional combination that simply refuses to work.

Q: Will adding more RAM allow me to run more VST instruments at once?

A: If your computer is short on memory, you'll run into trouble, but once you've installed above 256Mb or so of RAM more than you normally need, the only benefit of adding even more is that any sample-based VST instruments (such as samplers) will be able to load more or longer samples. Follow the manufacturer's guidelines concerning how much RAM you need to assign to the host program when running VST instruments.

chapter 13

mixers, monitors and effects

I n any music system where two or more signals have to be blended together to form a single stereo signal, a mixer is required. In a computer-based system, internally generated sounds can be mixed internally using MIDI controller information to set things like level and pan, but if you have a number of soundcards or a combination of soundcards, external synth modules and perhaps even a multitrack hardware recorder running in sync, there's no option but to use a mixer. You should read this section in any event, as most of what applies to a hardware mixer also applies to the virtual mixer within your sequencer.

There's more to a mixer than simply mixing signals together; you can also use it to change the level, pan position and tone-control settings of individual inputs and, with the aid of an external effects-processing box, you can add varying amounts of effects (such as reverb) to the various inputs. In fact, the act of mixing is where all of your efforts are turned into a final artistic event, and for me it's a very creative part of the music-making process.

In principle, a mixing console is pretty straightforward. Mixers comprise several identical "building blocks" known as *channels*, and the purpose of a channel is to change the level of the signal being fed into it, thus enabling the signal to be have equalisation (EQ – just another way of describing tone control) applied to it, and to provide variable feeds to external effect units.

The output of the channel then passes through a pan control onto what's known as a *stereo mix buss*, a sort of two-lane audio highway where the signals coming in from all of the different channels are combined. The output of the channel will also be controlled by a pan (short for *panorama*) control which dictates how much of the signal is fed to the left speaker and how much to the right. This is what's used to position sounds across the stereo soundstage.

mic and line levels

Internally, mixers are designed to work within a particular range of signal levels – if you put in a signal level that's too high, the sound will be distorted, but if the level is too low, the sound will be too quiet and very probably hissy as well. Microphones produce very low-level signals, so these have to be beefed up or amplified right at the start of the mixer channel. On more elaborate mixers, the mic amplifier might also be fitted with *phantom power circuitry*, enabling it to be used with capacitor microphones. This might sound complicated, but all it means is that some types of studio microphone require power in order to operate, and a mixer with a phantom power facility provides them with this. Phantom power is not compatible with non-professional "unbalanced" microphones, so if you don't need phantom power you should make sure it's switched off on your mixer before you plug in any microphones. You can't create a mic pre-amp in software, so if you have a virtual mixer this will need to be fed with the correct level at source. This usually means using an external hardware mixer or microphone pre-amplifier where the actual level of required signal depends on the input sensitivity of the soundcard or interface being used.

channel gain

Because not all microphones produce the same level of output, and because their output levels also depend on their proximity to and the volume of the sound being recorded, microphone amplifiers are invariably equipped with a gain control that determines the amount of amplification applied to the signal. In other words, the setting of the gain control relates to how much bigger the signal will be made. Line-level signals – ie those from electronic keyboards, modules, soundcard audio outputs, tape machines, CD players and so on – don't need to pass through the mic amplifier, so mixer channels also have a line input. Normally, only the channel's line or mic input may be used, not both at once.

The line input on a typical mixer will also be fitted with a gain control because even line-level signals vary (although on most basic mixers a common control is used for both mic- and line-level gain adjustment). Although a virtual mixer may have a line-level control, this comes after A-to-D (Analogue-to-Digital) conversion on the soundcard, so if the input signal is too high and clipping is occurring, you can't fix it by making adjustments in the software. Similarly, if your input signal is too low and you use the gain control in your software mixer to bring it up to level, you run the risk of increasing the background noise to an unacceptable level. As with the mic input, the only solution is to adjust the level at source so that it matches the requirements of the soundcard. The meters in your recording software should make setting levels easy.

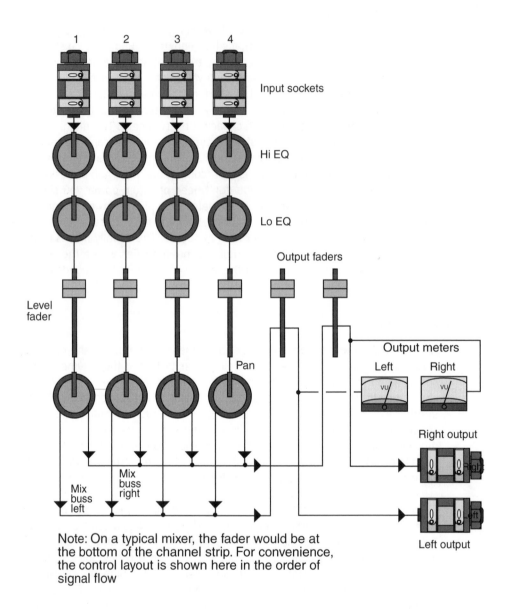

Note: On a typical mixer, the fader would be at the bottom of the channel strip. For convenience, the control layout is shown here in the order of signal flow

Fig 13.1: Stereo mixer with output meters

mixer channels

Figure 13.1 shows a simplified schematic of a four-channel mixer with simple bass and treble equalisation. Separate mic and line gain controls have been shown to aid clarity, but in practice a single shared control is more likely on a mixer of this type. Separate input sockets are shown for both the microphone and line input signals.

After the input-gain stage comes the equalisation section, which can be as simple as the bass/treble (also known as *hi/lo*) arrangement shown here or may have additional controls for the adjusting of mid-range frequencies. Finally, the signal level is controlled by a knob or fader before it passes to the stereo mix buss via the pan control and sometimes an On or Mute switch. Leaving the pan control in the centre routes equal amounts of signal to the left and right busses, making the resulting sound appear to originate from midway between two speakers in a stereo speaker system. Note that all four input channels are identical - a larger mixer would simply have more input channels.

The combined signal on the mix busses passes through further amplification stages performed by *mix amplifiers*, controlled by the master level faders or knobs. These determine the output level of the mixer, allowing it to send the correct signal level to the stereo recorder on which you're recording your finished composition. The master fader may also be used to make controlled fade-outs at the ends of songs. Figure 13.1 shows the controls arranged so as to make the signal flow easy to follow, but in practice the channel fader is usually at the bottom of the strip for convenience of use.

Most mixers have an output level meter, which could take the form of a moving-coil meter with a physical pointer or a row of LEDs (Light Emitting Diodes) arranged in the form of a ladder. A virtual mixer can display either type of meter onscreen, although most mimic the LED-ladder type of display. A stereo mixer of this type is usually described in the form "something into two" - for example, a twelve into two (12:2) mixer has twelve input channels and two outputs, left and right.

auxiliaries

So far, then, you have the tools to change the levels of individual inputs, you can change the tonality using the EQ controls and you can pan the signal from left to right in the mix. However, you'll also need to be able to do things like add effects, and if you have a more sophisticated set-up you may wish to send a mix to the performer's headphones.

pre-fade send

Both effects and the performer's foldback monitoring (headphone mix) can be handled using the auxiliary controls on a mixer, and Figure 13.2 shows how these fit into the channel strip. Here you can see two new controls, aux 1 and aux 2, where aux is short for auxiliary. Aux 1 is simply another level control feeding a mono mix buss that runs across the mixer to the aux 1 master level control and then to the aux 1 output socket. The signal feeding the aux 1 control is picked up from a point in the circuit before the channel fader and so is known as a *pre-fade send*. The implication of this is that the aux 1 signal level doesn't change if the channel fader is adjusted, so any mix set up using the pre-fade aux send will be completely independent of the channel faders.

Using a pre-fade send, the engineer can provide the musician with a monitor mix that is exactly to his or her liking rather than the same mix that's coming over the main monitor speakers. The overall aux 1 mix is under control of the aux 1 master-level control and the aux 1 output would normally feed a headphone amplifier, as you can't plug headphones directly into an aux output. To use an aux send to set up a monitor mix for a computer-based recording system, you need a soundcard or audio interface with at least one spare output to use as an aux output. This would be used to feed a conventional headphone amplifier, as you can't plug headphones directly into the outputs of soundcards, either.

post-fade send

In order to add effects to the mix, you need to use aux 2, the second aux control. This takes its feed after the channel fader (ie post fader), so its level is affected by changes in the channel fader setting. Therefore, when the channel signal level is turned up or down, the amount of signal sent to the external effects unit changes by a corresponding amount. In other words, regardless of the fader setting, the ratio of original sound to added effect remains the same.

By using different settings of the aux 2 control on each channel, it's possible to send different amounts of each channel's signal to the same effects unit. When the output from this effects unit is added to the main stereo mix, this has the advantage that different amounts of the same effect can be added to different sounds in a mix. For example, one reverberation unit might be used to provide a rich reverb for the vocals, less reverb for the drums and little or none for the guitars and bass.

Note: An effects unit used in conjunction with a channel aux send should

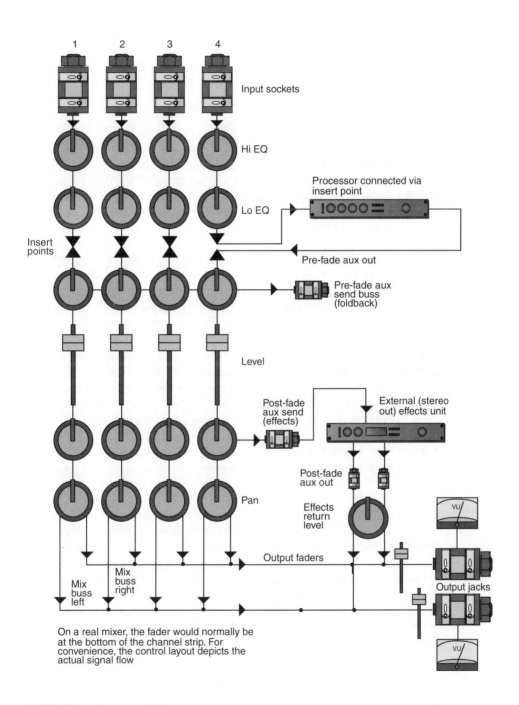

Fig 13.2: Mixer using aux controls

be set up so that it produces only the affected sound and none of the original. This is usually accomplished by means of a mix control or mix parameters accessed from the front-panel controls of your mixer. In either case, the mix should be set to 100% effect, 0% dry.

effects returns

The output of the effects unit may be fed back into the mixer via spare input channels or via dedicated effects-return inputs, also known as *aux returns*. Aux returns are electrically similar to input channels but have more basic facilities. Normally, auxiliary returns are provided as a stereo pair of sockets and feed straight into the main stereo mix, usually via a level control.

A spare input channel (or a pair of input channels panned hard left and right, for stereo use) may be used as an effects return, but in this case you must ensure that the corresponding aux send (in this case aux 2) is turned down on the return channel or the affected signal will feed back, building up to a howl.

To use a hardware effects box with a sequencer's software mixer, you'll need at least one spare output on your soundcard or interface to use as an aux send and two spare inputs to use as a stereo aux return. This is because most effects units can produce a stereo output from a mono input. If you need to use the effects box only while mixing, you could feed it back into the two main inputs of a soundcard that has only a stereo input, as these are unlikely to be needed for anything else during the mixing process.

busses

Busses can be considered as essentially additional outputs for use where you need to feed more than two destinations at once. For example, when tape recorders ruled the Earth, a mixer with 24 output busses was needed if you wanted to send a different signal or mix of signals to each input of a 24-track tape recorder. Like the master stereo outs, each buss has its own output level fader, so while routing switches in the mixer channels, choose the buss to which that channel's signal will be routed. In a software mixer, the busses are generally used to steer specific signals to specific physical outputs on a multi-output soundcard or interface. (For more information on mixers and their uses, check out *basic MIXERS* and *basic MIXING TECHNIQUES*, also available from Sanctuary Publishing.)

monitor speakers

If you're interested in producing high-quality mixes of your compositions, you'll need an accurate pair of monitor speakers or you won't really know how your music sounds. A theoretically perfectly speaker would reproduces the entire audio spectrum with no distortion or coloration, but because of the limitations of both physics and budget there are inevitably compromises that must be made.

So-called near-field monitors have become popular in both professional and home music studios. These are small but nominally accurate loudspeakers that can be used close to the listening position, thus helping to cut out any undesirable effects from the acoustics of the room. With these monitors, the closer you are to the speakers, the greater proportion of direct sound is heard compared with the sound reflected from the room. Furthermore, the nearer you are to a speaker, the less power you need to produce an adequate monitoring level.

Small hi-fi speakers are also often suitable, provided that they are selected for honesty rather than for their ability to flatter the music. And don't expect to get deep bass from small speakers, either. In reality, a very deep bass response is undesirable because, unless the room is acoustically designed to handle it, the results will be unpredictable, leading to inaccurate mixes that don't sound right on other audio systems.

A good two-way loudspeaker system with a bass driver of between five and eight inches in diameter is usually more than adequate for home-studio use, especially when used in the near field. This system may be powered from a hi-fi amplifier, but don't stint on the power or your system might not be able to handle peaks (such as drumbeats) cleanly. Around 50W per channel should be considered a realistic minimum, even if you tend to monitor at moderate levels. Use proper heavy-duty speaker cable, too, not bell wire, although don't be conned into buying anything too esoteric – it won't make any significant difference.

where to mix?

Domestic living rooms and bedrooms tend to absorb quite a lot of sound because of the amount of carpeting, curtains and soft furnishings that they contain, but because we're used to listening to music under these conditions a studio with a similar acoustic characteristic makes a perfectly workable alternative to a purpose-built studio. However, because no monitoring systems or rooms sound exactly alike, it's important to compare your own mixes with commercial music played back over the same system in the same room. Bedrooms or living rooms with carpets and soft furnishings are perfectly adequate for mixing music demos and even some commercial projects. If your room seems too lively or reverberant, it often helps to hang rugs or heavy curtains on the rear wall and on either side of the mixing position.

speaker positions

Speakers should be arranged so that they form two points of an equilateral triangle, with the listener at the third point. They should be angled inwards so that they point directly at the head of the listener and they should be at around head height. Consult the instructions that come with the speakers to find out whether they work best close to a wall or a little further away, and if at all possible you should avoid putting speakers in or close to corners, as this has an unpredictable effect on the sound of the bass end. You may seem to get more bass by doing this, but in reality you'll probably EQ your mix to compensate for it and then, when you play your songs back on anybody else's system, they'll sound bass-light. Figure 13.3 shows how the monitor speakers should be positioned in relation to the listener.

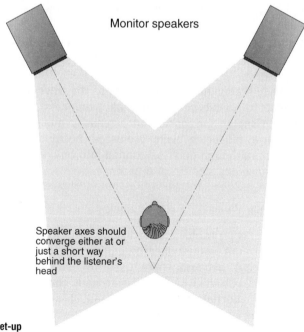

Monitor speakers

Speaker axes should converge either at or just a short way behind the listener's head

Fig 13.3: Monitor speaker set-up

using effects

Studio effects that used to be hugely expensive are now available both as inexpensive hardware boxes and as software plug-ins, such as VST, that can be used within your sequencer. There are other books in this series dedicated to explaining effects in great depth (see for instance *basic EFFECTS & PROCESSORS* or *Creative Recording 1 - Effects & Processors*, also available from Sanctuary Publishing), but a brief overview is warranted here, not only because of the importance of effects in modern music production but also because MIDI can be used to remotely control and automate the parameters of both hardware and plug-in effects.

Whereas conventional instruments are usually played in real acoustic spaces to give them character, electronic instruments, or indeed "acoustic" sounds recorded in an acoustically dead studio, have to rely on electronic effects to give them interest and realism. In today's MIDI studio, many instruments, modules and soundcards come equipped with their own effects - although, if these are inadequate in any way, external effects may also be connected via a hardware or virtual mixer. Wherever your effects come from, the basic principle is the same, and the purpose of this section is to describe the more common effects and their applications. If you don't want to get involved with these just yet, simply use the default settings on your instrument or soundcard. Most default settings tend to be slightly heavy on the effects, but they are fine for demo work or for just getting to know your system.

Earlier in the book, I explained some of the main types of effects used in modern music production, but I'm now going to expand on the more common ones a little so that you'll know when the use of these effects is appropriate.

reverberation

Western music is invariably performed indoors, where a degree of room reverberation is part of the sound. Conversely, most pop music is recorded in a relatively small, dry-sounding studio so artificial reverberation has to be added in order to create a sense of space and reality.

Reverberation is created naturally when a sound is reflected and re-reflected from the surfaces within a room, hall or other large structure. Clap your hands in a large hall or church and you'll hear reverberation. Digital reverberation units simulate this natural phenomenon by creating thousands of random echoes every second, and most provide a choice of settings, from imitating small rooms to mimicking the effect produced by great echoing caverns. Although long reverb times are initially impressive, most musical applications require a relatively short reverb time of between one and a half and four seconds. A popular reverb setting is the *plate* (a patch designed to simulate the mechanical plates that were used in studios before digital reverb was developed). The plate setting on a reverb unit has a bright, diffuse sound that works well on virtually anything, from drums to vocals.

Electronic reverb devices produce a stereo output (even though the sound they're treating may be mono), which is how they create the illusion of spaciousness. If you want a natural-sounding result, the reverb unit's outputs should be panned hard left and right, regardless of whereabouts in the mix the original dry signal is panned. If the effects are plugged into the stereo returns of a mixer, this will happen automatically, and if the effects are internal to a soundcard or module the added effects will also be heard in stereo.

Note that, because of the complexity of simulating the huge number of reflections that comprise natural reverb, good-quality reverb plug-ins tend to be quite processor hungry.

On an artistic level, busy music works best with shorter reverb settings while slower, less complicated music can benefit from longer settings. It also helps to avoid putting much reverb, if any, on bass sounds, as this can make your mix sound muddy. Listen to the commercial records in your collection and try to spot how reverb has been used on these. You'll probably be surprised at how little is needed in order to achieve the required result. Use your best reverb units or plug-ins on vocals and percussion as these are the two areas in which reverb quality shows up the most.

echo

Echo was used extensively on both guitars and vocals in the '60s and '70s, although at the time it was created via a tape-loop system rather than via digital electronics, as it is today. Unlike reverb, echo (sometimes called *delay*) produces distinct, evenly spaced repeats, and if you can set the delay time to a multiple of the tempo of the song some very interesting rhythmic effects can be created. Try echo on vocals, guitars and keyboard sounds. A tape-delay emulation plug-in causes successive delays to become less bright, similar to the effect produced by a tape-loop echo device, and often this sounds more natural than a delay effect where each repeat is perfectly clear.

chorus and flanging

Chorus is based on a short delay combined with pitch modulation, creating the effect of two or more instruments playing the same part. In effect, the original part is accompanied by a slightly delayed part that varies slightly in pitch, thus creating the ensemble illusion. Chorus is most effective on keyboard pad parts, string pads and some types of electric-guitar sound, particularly clean electric guitar when used in combination with echo or delay.

Flanging is also a modulated delay effect, but on flangers the delay time is very short and feedback is used to create a much stronger effect, not unlike the phasing produced by old tape. Both of these treatments work well on synth-pad sounds such as strings and are best used in stereo, creating a sense of movement as well as width. Because flanging is quite a dramatic effect, it is best used sparingly.

pitch shifters

Pitch shifters are to be found in almost all external multi-effects units, although they aren't often included in soundcards. When you're working purely with MIDI sounds, of course, you can change pitch simply by transposing a part.

As the name implies, pitch shifters can change the pitch of an original audio signal, usually by up to an octave in either direction. Small pitch shifts are useful for creating detuning or doubling effects (a nice alterative to chorus) while larger shifts can be used to create octaves or parallel harmonies. In my experience, pitch shifting seldom sounds natural when used for more than very small pitch shifts, so I like to use it as an alternative to chorus for doubling or fattening sounds. Try adding the untreated sound to two pitch-shifted versions – one seven cents sharp and the other seven cents flat – to produce a rich, layered sound.

rotary speakers

Although designed for the electric organ, rotary speakers have been used for all kinds of processing, from guitars to vocals. Back in their psychedelic years, The Beatles often passed vocals through a rotary cabinet and then miked it up in order to create "trippy" vocals sounds. Plug-in rotary-speaker emulators make this type of processing very easy and most can be switched between their two speeds using a MIDI controller, such as the pitch-bend wheel. This provides a simple means of automating speed changes within a MIDI sequence.

the virtual mixing environment

MIDI-plus-audio sequencers include a mixer section that is more or less a representation of the hardware mixer that would be required to do the same job, although without the mic pre-amps or input-level trim controls. Most MIDI-plus-audio sequencers offer more tracks of recording than the hardware can provide physical outputs for, which means that some way of mixing the tracks inside the computer is essential. This is why all MIDI-plus-audio sequencers include a virtual audio-mixer section. At its simplest, the mixer will combine the audio outputs from the different tracks and mix them down to a stereo pair, although if the hardware has multiple outputs, some means of routing channels or submixes of these channels to the various outputs (usually configured as busses) will also be included.

Depending on the way in which your particular sequencer is designed, you might find that some channels handle playback from the audio tracks of your sequencer, some control the levels and pan of internal MIDI sound sources such as virtual instrument plug-ins and others control the levels of "live" inputs fed in via the inputs of your audio interface. Also, some sequencers allow plug-in effects to be added to live inputs while others don't. When a channel is switched to Record, it's normal to be able to use it to set a monitoring level for the signal being recorded. The fader doesn't actually affect the level of the signal being recorded, as this adjustment needs to be made at source.

As with a hardware mixer, the user has control over level and pan and basic EQ, although to conserve resources more sophisticated EQ is usually available as plug-ins, to be deployed only when needed. The other big difference between a virtual mixer and a hardware mixer is that, with some virtual mixers, you can remove any channels that aren't being used from the display to make better use of the available screen space.

The mixer section of a sequencer is usually where third-party plug-in effects are configured, and it's now pretty standard for mix automation to be included, too. Mixes may be controlled by sending in MIDI controller information from external hardware recorders or simply by recording the movements of onscreen faders. The automation data is represented as regular MIDI data, but because everything is handled internally within the computer no MIDI interface is needed, unless an external hardware control surface is being used. There may also be support for surround-sound mixing and monitoring, although this is somewhat beyond the scope of this book.

the virtual mixer layout

The balance of the audio tracks recorded in your sequencer is adjusted using the onscreen virtual mixer, most examples of which follow a straightforward "all-input" format where all of the channels, busses and outputs are arranged side by side, in a row.

Most software designers try to make their mixers look as much like conventional mixers as possible, right down to level faders that can be dragged up or down using the computer mouse. Rotary controls can usually be adjusted by clicking on them with the mouse and then moving the mouse left/right, up/down or around in circles – it all depends on which method the software designer chose to use. A separate virtual mixer channel is used for each mono and stereo audio track on the sequencer and, just as with a hardware mixer, the channel signals may be routed directly to the main stereo outputs or via a group. If the audio interface has several audio outputs, these are likely to correspond with the groups in the virtual mixer. MIDI tracks may have a separate mixer from the audio tracks or they may be combined. Hardware MIDI instruments, including those supplied via soundcard hardware, can't be processed via plug-in effects designed for audio unless those parts are first recorded into the system as regular audio tracks, and this is done by feeding them back into the audio inputs of the soundcard or interface. Similarly, mixer EQ can't be applied to MIDI parts for the same reason – MIDI is control data, not audio. However, plug-ins can be used to process the outputs from plug-in software instruments as these generate audio just like regular audio tracks.

effects and processors

The rules regarding effects and processors are the same as for hardware mixers, although it pays not to get the two confused. Gates, expanders, compressors, limiters, equalisers, enhancers and distortion devices are all processors while reverberators, digital delay lines, chorus units, flangers and pitch shifters are effects. Effects usually have a mix facility, enabling the user to blend the processed and unprocessed sound. An effect may be used either in conjunction with the auxiliary-send circuit (in which case mixing is performed by the mixer) or via an insert point (in which case the unit's own mix control is used) while a processor is normally used only via an insert point (channel, group or master). Plug-in effects tend to come in both mono and stereo versions, so if you're processing a stereo audio track, the stereo version of the plug-in will be visible in the list of available plug-ins. In some instances, there is the option to use a mono-in/stereo-out effect, such as reverb, within a stereo audio track.

patching virtual effects

VST plug-ins are used inside the sequencer's virtual audio-mixer section, and there are three main ways in which these plug-ins can be used. Each channel on a VST (or comparable plug-in format) -compatible virtual mixer typically has one or more insert points into which an effect can be placed, with the signal flowing through the topmost plug-in first when more than one plug-in is loaded. Normally, these plug-ins are chosen from a pull-down menu and activating an effect or processor in a channel-insert point means that everything fed through that channel passes through the plug-in.

If the same effect or process is required elsewhere, you can open another copy of the same plug-in and place it in the insert point of a different channel, although this will use more CPU power. (Note that, for effects used in insert points, the dry/effect balance is set using the plug-in's own mix control.)

Fig 13.4: Plug-ins used in a subgroup

236

A more economic way of using a processing plug-in, such as compression, is to place it in the insert point of a group and then route any channels that need processing to that group/buss. In conventional mixing terms, this is the same as creating a subgroup, and the signal would normally be in stereo to preserve the pan positions of the channels being mixed. The output of the group/buss is then routed to the stereo mix, as shown in Figure 13.4. This means that you have to use only one instance of the plug-in (a stereo version if you're processing a stereo submix) while everything fed via that group will be treated by it. (Note that, in the case of compression, compressing a mix of signals, such as layered vocals, isn't quite the same thing as compressing the individual vocal parts first and then layering them. However, provided that there are no excessive level changes or other level-related problems, it normally works quite well.) You could also use this routing trick to feed several audio tracks through the same effects plug-in, such as reverb, but all would be subjected to the same amount of reverb, which might not be what you had in mind. In this case, it's better to use the post-fade aux sends, just as you would on a hardware console, but remember that this applies only to effects and not to processors.

The way in which aux sends are set up will vary a little depending on which sequencer software you're using, but despite some differences in terminology most work in essentially the same way. You should, however, consult your sequencer manual to find out how to arrange aux-send effects in your choice of sequencing software. Once they have been configured correctly, the individual aux-send control on each channel sets the effect level for that channel. When you're using aux sends, the mix control on the plug-in should be set to maximum so that it produces all effect and no dry signal. In this way, the channel aux controls can be used to regulate the overall amount of effect added to each channel. Figure 13.5 over the page shows the aux-routing systems for both Logic Audio and Cubase VST.

MIDI mix automation

Returning to the core theme of this book, the settings of all of the controls on your virtual mixer can be automated via MIDI, offering you more control than hardware studio mixers costing the price of a large house offered little more than a decade ago! Not only can you automate mix levels on a virtual mixer but you can also automate the rotary controls to adjust things like EQ, pan and aux-send level during the course of a mix. These control changes are recorded in the same way as any other MIDI performance data that includes controller information so that, when your sequence is played back, all of the dynamic changes that you made are reproduced exactly as you made them.

Fig 13.5: Plug-ins and aux sends

Far from being a luxury, however, mix automation is pretty much essential on a computer sequencer, as there's no way to adjust more than one control at once if you're using a mouse. If you want to use hardware knobs or faders to control the mixer's channel levels and other criteria, there are numerous hardware boxes on the market that can do this via MIDI, but most users seem to get by using just the mouse and keyboard.

getting automated

If you haven't used mix automation before, it works like this: The knobs or faders on your virtual mixer generate MIDI data when moved, and when you're recording automation moves (ie when the mixer is in Write mode) this data is stored by the sequencer against it own internal time clock. You can put one or more tracks into Write mode at one time and then move the controls whenever you want to make a change. Also, you can repeat this process as many times as you like until automation has been added to all of the tracks that need it. Also, as with other MIDI information, you can delete or edit mix data, if necessary.

As it's unlikely that you'll get the mix right the first time, there's always an option on virtual mixers that will allow you to rewrite sections of a mix. There may also be an Update mode that adds your new fader movements to your earlier ones rather than replacing them. This is very useful when your original automation just needs a little lifting or dropping in level in some places. The usual way to use automation is first to set a nominal static mix that sounds roughly correct, complete with pan positions for the various sound sources. (Convention has it that bass sounds and lead vocals are panned to the centre.) You can fine-tune this static mix a track at a time by automating the levels of instruments so that they come up during solos and so on. You can then go on to automate effects and EQ if you feel that your mix needs it.

It's also common to have a graphic display of the mix-automation data comprising a series of points joined by lines or curves. You can edit the mix automation graphically or even use this mode to "draw in" entire automation parts by adding new points or by dragging existing points to new positions, a highly convenient way of fine-tuning automation data. Similar graphics are used to display and edit other control information, such as pan position. Figure 13.6 shows the graphic-automation facilities in Logic Audio.

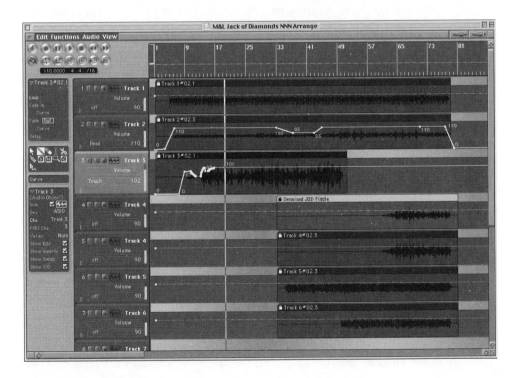

Fig 13.6: Graphical mix editing in Logic Audio

plug-in automation

MIDI automation also extends to plug-ins, both effects and processors and virtual instruments. The degree to which your plug-ins can be automated depends on the type of plug-in supported by your software, but VST and comparable-format plug-ins can have virtually every adjustable parameter automated in a similar way to the regular mixer parameters. For example, if you want the delay time of an echo plug-in to change between verse and chorus, just record the control movements and it's done. Sequencing software such as Logic Audio that comes with its own effects and virtual instruments tends to access these for automation purposes in exactly the same way as VST and similar plug-ins, and the same is true of virtual instruments, so if you want to change a synthesiser parameter, such as filter resonance, as a track progresses, you can again just record the control movements.

A useful tip for composers of dance music is to create rhythmic templates of MIDI control data using the graphic automation-editing facilities of your sequencer and then save these in a library for future use. For example, you could set up a rhythmic filter or gating effect related to the tempo of the song and then paste this into any song. Even if the tempo of the song is different, controller information imported in this way will still stay in time. As with other MIDI data, there's usually an easy way of looping or copying sections of automation data so that you can affect several bars of music by using just one bar of automation data.

MIDI control hardware

A common complaint about computer-based studio systems is that the keyboard and mouse don't provide the same degree of tactical control as the traditional studio's knobs and faders. With knobs and faders, several parameters can be changed simultaneously, whereas a mouse can access only one thing at a time. The solution to this problem is to use a MIDI control surface that will translate the action of physical knobs and faders into MIDI messages, enabling you to control the sequencer's virtual knobs and faders that you see on screen.

There are several different types of controller available, the simplest being the familiar MIDI fader box. A typical model might offer eight or 16 faders plus a number of knobs, all sending MIDI controller data when operated. These simple controllers use standard pots and faders, making them relatively inexpensive, and most allow you to define which type of MIDI message is sent by each fader. For example, if you want to control the levels of the channel faders on a typical sequencer mixer, you'd probably need to set each fader to a different MIDI channel and have it send MIDI controller 7 data over the range 0-127. Similarly, you might want to set the knobs to send MIDI pan data (controller 10).

So far, so good. However, most users require more flexibility so that they can also use the controls to adjust aux sends, EQ or even plug-in parameters. To make this work, the controller needs to be programmable (in much the same way as a synthesiser), where patch 1 might configure the faders to control volume, patch 2 might assign them to aux send 1, patch 3 might assign them to aux send 3 and so on. A display plus a number of programming buttons must be added to allow this, while the addition of a data wheel aids programming.

Before you can start work, you'll need to set up the fader and knob assignments for each bank, and although this isn't a difficult job, it is time consuming. Fortunately, some controllers come with ready-made templates to control common sequencers or to edit the more popular synthesisers, and the inclusion of an automatic MIDI Learn mode is also quite common. The usual arrangement is that, once a fader has been put into Learn mode, waggling any onscreen knob or fader will automatically assign the selected fader to operate that particular parameter. A MIDI In as well as a MIDI Out is required for this, as controllers have to be able to receive MIDI data from the sequencer's MIDI Out so that they know what the stored parameter values are at any time. The MIDI set-up for a simple hardware controller is shown in Figure 13.7a and involves connecting the controller's MIDI Out to a MIDI In port on the sequencer and a sequencer MIDI Out to the controller's MIDI In. Here, a multiport MIDI interface is needed.

Because many users have only a single MIDI port at their disposal, it's not uncommon to find MIDI controllers offering some kind of MIDI merge capability so that the controller keyboard and fader-control data are merged before being sent to the sequencer, as shown in Figure 13.7b. Of course, a standard MIDI merge box can be used on occasions where this facility is not provided.

compromises

Because the faders on a unit of this type don't move unless you move them yourself, when you start to use mix level automation or you switch to a different bank to select a new fader function the faders are likely to be in physical positions that don't match the current value of the parameter to which they are assigned. Several systems are used to get around this limitation, the most common being that the fader takes control of the assigned parameter only once it has been moved through the position that corresponds to the current parameter value. This prevents the sudden jump in controller value that occurs when the other system is used - ie where the data changes to reflect the fader

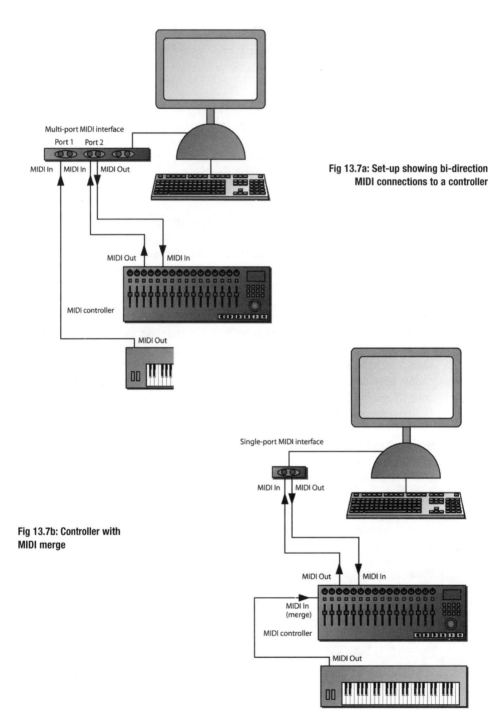

Multi-port MIDI interface
Port 1   Port 2
MIDI In   MIDI In   MIDI Out

Fig 13.7a: Set-up showing bi-direction
MIDI connections to a controller

MIDI Out   MIDI In

MIDI controller

MIDI Out

Single-port MIDI interface

MIDI In   MIDI Out

Fig 13.7b: Controller with
MIDI merge

MIDI Out   MIDI In

MIDI In
(merge)

MIDI controller

MIDI Out

position as soon as the fader is moved. Status LEDs may also be used to show which way the fader needs to be moved in order to approach the stored value. Even so, I can say that, having used such a system for a while, it's really hard work if you constantly need to keep switching from one function to another.

In conclusion, I feel that fader systems with regular manual controls are most useful when they're spending most of their time doing one job, such as controlling levels and pan positions. If you need the ability to switch functions frequently, the fact that you have to realign the faders manually with their new parameter values each time negates most of their benefits. The real solution is to use an interface with motorised, moving faders.

digital mixers

Moving-fader digital mixers can make useful MIDI controllers, but they may not give you the same ability to define the MIDI messages sent by the faders as dedicated hardware controllers. If your mixer can't be reprogrammed to send different messages, you're left with the task of transforming the data as it enters your sequencer. In Logic Audio, this would be done using the Environment parameter, whereas in Cubase you'd use Mixer Maps. Although you can set this up yourself, you'll probably find ready-made solutions for the more common digital mixers and sequencers available for download on some of the software-support websites or newsgroups.

On moving-fader digital mixers, the faders can be made to follow the sequencer data so that their physical positions follow any changes made to their onscreen values. As before, this requires both MIDI In and Out connections to be made between sequencer and mixer, and as mixers aren't designed specifically as MIDI controllers they may not offer a MIDI merge facility. The solution is to use either a multiport MIDI interface or a separate MIDI merge box.

dedicated controllers

Of course, it's also possible (although rather expensive) to use a dedicated moving-fader controller designed specifically to work with the sequencing software you're using, and Emagic's Logic Control and Steinberg's Houston are examples of such dedicated controllers. Using these, you can switch functions quickly and the faders will immediately jump to their new positions. Other benefits may include tape-recorder-style transport controls plus Mute and Solo buttons, which make using the controller much more like working with a hardware mixer. In the case of Logic Control, there are also track-arming buttons and the ability to access and edit plug-ins. The combination of this type of control surface and a fast computer makes the whole recording experience more like working in a traditional hardware studio, and yet it still retains the flexibility of the computer approach.

Ultimately, there are now so many different ways of accomplishing the same task that no single way can be described as being best, which is why there's room in the marketplace for all of the different types (and prices) of hardware controller that are available today. Only you can decide what's best for you.

and finally…

The PC-based MIDI-plus-audio studio has the advantages of being inexpensive, compact and (once set up) convenient. With the addition of a mixer, a monitoring system and possibly some outboard signal-processing equipment, you have the basis of a serious desktop music recording system. Also, as soundcards continue to become more powerful and better specified, you can upgrade your system a piece at a time without having to sell up and start from scratch, and you can add new plug-ins as they are developed.

Undoubtedly, the more traditional MIDI studio comprising racks of modules, samplers and drum machines will be with us for very many years to come, but as the capabilities of PC-based systems continue to increase, so the boundaries are bound to become blurred. By choosing your soundcards carefully and by incorporating a small mixer plus a modest amount of external signal processing, you can build a complete desktop studio for less than you might once have paid for a stereo sampler.

Although the audio capabilities of sequencers continues to grow in power with every generation of computer hardware, MIDI is still a hugely powerful tool and one that I think will be with us for a very long time yet. Not only does it provide us with a means of recording and editing the control data that drives our synthesisers and samplers but it also provides an extremely convenient automation protocol. Some people criticise MIDI for being slow – after all, it *is* based on a relatively slow serial-interface technology that's been with us for decades – but the need to replace it with something faster recedes as software instruments take over from their hardware ancestors. This is because, although virtual instruments follow the rules of MIDI, the data transmission within the computer isn't limited by the same constraints as external MIDI and so can be made as fast and as accurate as we're ever likely to need. So, rather than seeing MIDI take a back seat in relation to traditional audio, now that we have access to fast and cheap computers, it has instead expanded its role to encompass hardware control and the automation of software-mixer, effect, processor and instrument parameters that could never have been achieved by using conventional hardware solutions.

glossary

additive synthesis

Type of synthesis where simpler waveforms (usually sine waves) are added together in order to recreate the harmonic structure of the original sound.

ADSR

Envelope generator with Attack, Sustain, Decay and Release parameters. This is a simple type of envelope generator and was first used on early analogue synthesisers. This form of envelope generator continues to be popular on modern instruments. (See the entry for "Decay" for further details.)

active sensing

System used to verify that a MIDI connection is working which involves one device sending frequent short messages to the receiving device in order to reassure it that all is well. If these active-sensing messages stop for any reason, the receiving device will recognise a fault and switch off all notes. Few modern MIDI devices support active sensing.

aftertouch

Means of generating a control signal based on the degree of pressure that is applied to the keys of a MIDI keyboard. Most instruments that support this do not have independent pressure sensing for all keys but instead detect the overall pressure by means of a sensing strip that runs beneath the keys. Aftertouch may be used to control such functions as vibrato depth, filter brightness, loudness and so on.

analogue

Circuitry that uses a continually changing voltage or current to represent a signal. The origin of the term lies in the fact that the electrical signal can be thought of as being analogous to the original signal.

ASIO

Audio Streaming Input/Output, a low-latency audio-driver protocol developed by Steinberg.

attenuate

To reduce in level.

audio frequency

Signals in the human audio range, nominally 20Hz-20kHz.

balanced

Term used to describe a wiring system that uses two out-of-phase conductors and a common screen to reduce the effect of interference. In order for the process of balancing to be effective, both the sending and receiving device must have balanced output and input stages, respectively.

bandpass filter

Filter that removes or attenuates frequencies above and below the frequency at which it is set while emphasising those falling within the band. Bandpass filers are often used in synthesisers as tone-shaping elements.

binary

Numbering system comprising ones and zeros.

bit

Abbreviation of binary digit, a single unit of digital data.

byte

Unit of digital data comprising eight bits.

CV

Abbreviation of Control Voltage, used to control the pitch of an oscillator or the frequency of a filter in an analogue synthesiser. Most analogue synthesisers follow a one-volt-per-octave convention, although there are exceptions to this. In order to use a pre-MIDI analogue synthesiser under MIDI control, a MIDI-to-CV converter is required.

channel

In the context of MIDI, the term *channel* refers to one of 16 possible data channels over which MIDI data may be sent. The organisation of data by channels means that up to 16 different MIDI instruments or parts may be addressed over a single cable. In the context of mixing consoles, a channel is a single strip of controls relating to one input.

chase

Term used to describe the process by which a slave device attempts to synchronise itself with a master device. In the context of a MIDI sequence, the term *chase* may also involve chasing events (ie looking back to earlier positions in a song to see if there are any Program Change messages or other events that need to be acted upon).

cut-off frequency

Frequency above or below which attenuation begins in a filter circuit.

cycle

One complete vibration of a sound source or its electrical equivalent. One cycle per second is expressed as 1Hz (hertz).

decay

Term used to describe the progressive reduction in amplitude of a sound or electrical signal over time. In the context of an ADSR envelope shaper, the Decay phase starts as soon as the Attack phase has reached its maximum level. In the Decay phase, the signal level drops until it reaches the Sustain level set by the user. The signal then remains at this level until the key is released, at which point the Release phase is entered.

digital

Electronic system that represents data and signals in the form of codes comprising ones and zeros.

DMA

Abbreviation of Direct Memory Access, part of a computer operating system that allows peripheral devices to communicate directly with the computer memory without going via the CPU (Central Processing Unit).

driver

Piece of software that acts as a link between the host software and a connected piece of hardware, such as a soundcard.

DSP

Abbreviation of Digital Signal Processor, a powerful microchip used to process digital signals.

envelope

Term used to describe the way in which the level of a sound or signal varies over time.

envelope generator

Circuit capable of generating a control signal that represents the envelope of the sound being recreated. This may then be used to control the level of an oscillator or other sound source, although envelopes may also be used to control filter or modulation settings. The most common example of an envelope generator is the ADSR generator.

event

In MIDI terms, an event is a single unit of MIDI data, such as a note being turned on or off, a piece of controller information or a Program Change message.

file

Meaningful list of data stored in digital form. An SMF (Standard MIDI File) is a specific type of file designed to allow sequence information to be interchanged between different types of sequencer.

filter

Type of powerful tone-shaping network used in synthesisers to create tonal sweeps and wah-wah effects. The term may also be applied to some MIDI sequencers that have the provision to exclude or filter out certain types of MIDI data - for example, aftertouch information.

FireWire

Popular name given to the IEEE 1394 protocol used for high-speed data transfer between computers or between computers and peripherals, such as external hard drives, audio interfaces and video cameras. In situations where multiple channels of audio need to be transferred at once, FireWire is a good option, especially where the computer being used has no spare PCI slots to accommodate more conventional audio interfaces or soundcards.

gate

Electrical signal generated whenever a key is depressed on an electronic keyboard. This is used to trigger envelope generators and other events that need to be synchronised to the action of keys.

General MIDI

Addition to the basic MIDI specification designed to ensure a minimum level of compatibility when playing back GM-format song files. The specification covers type and program number of sounds, minimum levels of polyphony and multitimbrality, response to controller information and so on.

GM Reset

Universal sysex command that activates the General MIDI mode on a GM instrument. The same command also sets all controllers to their default values and switches off any notes still playing by means of an All Notes Off message.

Groove Control

Sample-library file format that is similar to ReCycle (which uses REX files) where drum rhythms are split into "slices" that can then be retriggered at a different tempo to that originally recorded without resulting in a pitch change. A MIDI file accompanies each Groove Control sample set so as to trigger the slices at the correct time.

GS

Roland's own extension to the General MIDI protocol.

high-pass filter

Filter that attenuates frequencies below its cut-off frequency.

host powered

Term used to describe software that runs on a computer's own CPU rather than on plug-in DSP cards.

IRQ

Abbreviation of Interrupt Request, part of the operating system of a computer that allows a connected device to request attention from the processor in order to transfer data to it or from it.

latency

Delay that occurs between a MIDI keyboard being played and the sound of a VST instrument appearing at the output of the soundcard or interface. Latency can be minimised by using a fast computer and efficient audio drivers (such as ASIO or EASI) and by setting the minimum playback buffer size that will allow the system to work reliably.

LSB

Abbreviation of Least Significant Byte. If a piece of data has to be conveyed as two bytes, one byte represents high-value numbers and the other low-value numbers, much in the same way as tens and units function in the decimal system. The high value, or most significant part of the message, is called the MSB (Most Significant Byte).

Local On/Off

Function that allows the keyboard and sound-generating sections of a keyboard synthesiser to be used independently of each other.

low-frequency oscillator

Oscillator used as a modulation source, usually below 20Hz. The most common LFO waveshape is the sine wave, although many LFOs provide a choice of sine, square, triangular and sawtooth waveforms.

low-pass filter

Filter that attenuates frequencies above its cut-off frequency.

MIDI

Abbreviation of Musical Instrument Digital Interface.

MIDI controller

Term used to describe the physical interface by means of which a musician plays a MIDI synthesiser or other sound generator. Examples of controllers include keyboards, drum pads and wind synths.

standard MIDI file

Standard file format for storing song data recorded on a MIDI sequencer in such a way as to allow them to be read by other makes or models of MIDI sequencer.

MIDI implementation chart

Chart usually found in MIDI product manuals that provides information concerning the MIDI features that are supported by the device in question. Supported features are marked with an "O" while unsupported feature are marked with an "X". Additional information may also be provided, such as the exact form of Bank Change messages.

MIDI merge

Function of a device or sequencer that enables two or more streams of MIDI data to be combined.

MIDI module

Sound-generating device with no integral keyboard.

multitimbral module

MIDI sound source capable of producing several different sounds at the same time and controlled on different MIDI channels.

MIDI modes

MIDI information can be interpreted by the receiving MIDI instrument in a number of ways, the most common being polyphonically on a single MIDI channel (ie in Poly/Omni Off mode). Omni mode enables a MIDI Instrument to play all incoming data on all channels.

MIDI note number

Every key on a MIDI keyboard is designated its own note number, ranging from 0-127, with 60 representing middle C. Some systems use C3 as middle C while others use C4.

MIDI Note On

MIDI message sent when a note is played (ie a key is pressed).

MIDI Note Off

MIDI message sent when a key is released.

MIDI Out

MIDI connector used to send data from a master device to the MIDI In of a connected slave device.

MIDI port

MIDI connection of a MIDI-compatible device. A multiport, in the context of a MIDI interface, is a device with multiple MIDI output sockets, each capable of carrying data relating to a different set of 16 MIDI channels. Multiports are the only means of exceeding the limitations imposed by the 16-channel MIDI specification.

MIDI splitter

Alternative term for a MIDI thru box.

MIDI thru box

Device that splits the MIDI Out signal of a master instrument or sequencer to avoid the need to daisy-chain equipment. Powered circuitry is used to "buffer" the outputs in order to prevent problems that may arise from many pieces of equipment being driven from a single MIDI output.

MIDI In

Socket used to receive information from a master controller or from the MIDI Thru socket of a slave unit.

MIDI Out

Socket on a master controller or sequencer used to send MIDI information to the slave units.

MIDI sync

Term used to describe the synchronisation systems available to MIDI users: MIDI Clock and MIDI Time Code.

MIDI Thru

Socket on a slave unit used to feed the MIDI In socket of the next unit in line.

non-registered parameter number

Addition to the basic MIDI specification that allows controllers 98 and 99 to be used to control non-standard parameters relating to particular models of synthesiser. This is an alternative to using sysex (system-exclusive) data to achieve the same ends. Note, however, that NRPNs tend to be used mainly by instruments manufactured by Yamaha and Roland.

OMS

Abbreviation of Opcode's Open MIDI System software that acts as an intermediary between many types of Macintosh-based audio software and multiport hardware MIDI interfaces. OMS also supports USB MIDI interfaces.

oscillator

Circuit designed to generate a periodic electrical waveform.

patch

Alternative term for *program*, referring to a single programmed sound within a synthesiser that can be called up via a MIDI Program Change command. MIDI effects units and samplers also have patches.

pitch bend

Special control message designed to produce a change in pitch in response to the movement of a pitch-bend wheel or lever. Pitch-bend data can be recorded and edited just like any other MIDI controller data, even though it isn't part of the controller message group.

plug-in

Piece of software designed to add capabilities and features to the host application.

polyphony

Term used to describe the ability of an instrument to play two or more notes simultaneously. An instrument that can play only one note at a time is described as monophonic.

portamento

Gliding effect that allows a sound to change in pitch at a gradual rate rather than abruptly when a new key is pressed or MIDI note data is sent.

pressure

Alternative term for *aftertouch*.

pulse wave

Similar to a square wave but asymmetrical. Pulse waves sound brighter and thinner than square waves, making them useful in the synthesis of reed instruments. The timbre changes according to the mark/space ratio of the waveform.

pulse-width modulation

Means of modulating the duty cycle (mark/space ratio) of a pulse wave. This changes the timbre of the basic tone. LFO modulation of pulse width can be used to produce a pseudo-chorus effect.

Q

Measure of the resonant properties of a filter. The higher the Q, the more resonant the filter and the narrower the range of frequencies that are allowed to pass.

quantise

Term used to describe the facility present on many sequencers that allows notes recorded in a MIDI sequencer to be moved so that they line up to user-defined subdivisions of a bar of music - for example, 16th notes. The facility may be used to correct timing errors, although over-quantisation can remove the human feel from a performance.

RAM

Abbreviation for Random Access Memory, a type of memory used by computers for the temporary storage of programs and data. All data stored in RAM is lost when the power is turned off, and for this reason all work needs to be saved to disk if it is not to be lost.

ReWire

System designed to connect separate audio applications, enabling them to be used together. ReWire was invented by Propellerhead and can support up to 64 channels of audio.

REX file

Sample-file format supporting rhythmic loops created in Propellerhead's ReCycle software.

ROM

Abbreviation of Read-Only Memory. This is a permanent or non-volatile type of memory containing data that can't be changed. Operating systems are often stored on ROM, as this means that the memory remains intact when the power is removed.

release

Rate at which a signal amplitude decays once a key has been released.

resonance

Characteristic of a filter that allows it to pass a narrow range of frequencies. (See "Q".)

sample and hold

Term that usually refers to a feature in some devices whereby random values are generated at regular intervals and then used to control another function, such as pitch or filter frequency. Sample-and-hold circuits were also used in old analogue synthesisers to "remember" the note played after a key had been released.

SCSI

Abbreviation of Small Computer System Interface (pronounced "skuzzi"), describing an interfacing system for connecting up hard drives, scanners, CD-ROM drives and similar peripherals with a computer. Each SCSI device has its own ID number and no two SCSI devices in the same chain may be set to the same number. The last SCSI device in the chain should be terminated, either via an internal terminator (where provided) or via a plug-in terminator fitted to a free SCSI socket.

sequencer

Device for recording and replaying MIDI data, usually in a multitrack format, allowing complex compositions to be built up a part at a time. Most modern sequencers allow the user to record and edit audio.

sine wave

Waveform of a pure tone with no harmonics.

slave

MIDI device under the control of a master device, such as a sequencer or master keyboard.

square wave

Symmetrical, rectangular waveform. Square waves contain a series of odd harmonics.

sawtooth wave

Waveform that resembles the teeth of a saw, containing only even harmonics.

streaming

Process of delivering audio in real time from a hard drive. In the context of sampling, this permits the use of samples that are larger than a computer's RAM capacity.

subtractive synthesis

Process of creating a new sound by filtering and shaping a raw, harmonically complex waveform.

timbre

The tonal "colour" of a sound.

tremolo

Modulation of the amplitude of a sound carried out by an LFO (Low-Frequency Oscillator).

triangle wave

Symmetrical, triangular wave containing only odd harmonics but with a lower harmonic content than the square wave.

unbalanced

Term used to describe a two-wire electrical signal connection on which the inner or hot (positive) conductor is usually currounded by the cold (negative) conductor, thus forming a screen against interference.

USB

Abbreviation of Universal Serial Buss, a standard interface designed to allow peripherals such as scanners, cameras, audio interfaces and MIDI interfaces to connect to both Mac and PC computers. USB is also commonly used to connect security keys for the prevention of software piracy. While USB is fast enough for most applications, it is a little slow for anything more than two to four channels of audio and so should be used to connect an audio interface only when there is no alternative.

velocity

Term used to describe the rate at which a key is depressed. MIDI velocity information may be used to control loudness (to simulate the response of instruments such as pianos) or other parameters on later synthesisers.

voice

Term used to indicate the capacity of a synthesiser to play a single musical note. An instrument capable of playing 16 simultaneous notes is said to be a 16-voice instrument.

vibrato

Pitch modulation performed by an LFO to modulate a VCO (Voltage-Controlled Oscillator).

virtual instrument

Any instrument that runs entirely within the software domain rather than in hardware form.

VST

Abbreviation of Virtual Studio Technology, a Steinberg-instigated standard that allows VST plug-in effects, processors and instruments to be used within their Cubase range of sequencers and within any other VST-compatible audio software.

VST instrument

Virtual instrument provided as a VST plug-in.

waveform

Graphic representation of the way in which a sound wave or electrical wave changes over time.

XG

Yamaha's alternative to Roland's GS system for enhancing the General MIDI protocol in order to provide additional banks of patches and further editing facilities.